SOCIAL INNOVATION

SOCIAL INNOVATION

How Societies Find the Power to Change

Geoff Mulgan

P

First published in Great Britain in 2019 by

Policy Press
University of Bristol
1-9 Old Park Hill
Bristol
BS2 8BB
UK
t: +44 (0)117 954 5940
pp-info@bristol.ac.uk
www.policypress.co.uk

North America office:
Policy Press
c/o The University of Chicago Press
1427 East 60th Street
Chicago, IL 60637, USA
t: +1 773 702 7700
f: +1 773 702 9756
sales@press.uchicago.edu
www.press.uchicago.edu

© Policy Press 2019

British Library Cataloguing in Publication Data
A catalogue record for this book is available from the British Library.

Library of Congress Cataloging-in-Publication Data
A catalog record for this book has been requested.

ISBN 978-1-4473-5379-9 paperback
ISBN 978-1-4473-5381-2 ePub
ISBN 978-1-4473-5380-5 ePdf

Cover design and cover image credit: Liron Gilenberg
Printed and bound in Great Britain by TJ International,
Padstow
Policy Press uses environmentally responsible print
partners

MIX
Paper from
responsible sources
FSC® C013056
www.fsc.org

Contents

List of abbreviations

AI	artificial intelligence
API	application programming interface
DALY	disability-adjusted life year
DSI	digital social innovation
GDP	gross domestic product
MOOC	massive open online course
NCDI	National Community Development Initiative
NGO	non-governmental organisation
OECD	Organisation for Economic Co-operation and Development
QALY	quality-adjusted life year
R&D	research and development
RCT	randomised controlled trial
TA	technology assessment

About the author

Geoff Mulgan is Chief Executive of Nesta, the UK's innovation foundation. He has previously been Director of the government's Strategy Unit and Head of Policy in the Prime Minister's office, Chief Executive of the Young Foundation, Director of the think-tank Demos, Chief Adviser to Gordon Brown MP and a reporter on BBC TV and radio. He is a senior visiting scholar at Harvard University and advises governments around the world. He is the author of many books, including *Good and Bad Power* (Penguin) and *Big Mind* (Princeton University Press).

Acknowledgements

Many hundreds of people have been active collaborators with me in social innovation over the years. There's not space to name them all, but here are a few to whom I owe a debt for many of the observations contained in this book.

Some are no longer with us, including my very dear friends Robin Murray, Diogo Vasconcelos and Michael Young. Others are still very active in what remains a highly social field, including Louise Pulford, Martin Stewart Weeks, Rushanara Ali, Mark Moore, Chris Sigaloff, Joeri van Steenhoven, Brenton Caffin, Carolyn Curtis, Tim Draimin, Stephen Huddart, Kriss Deiglmeier, Jaff Shen, Ada Wong, Roberto Mangabeira Unger, Charlie Leadbeater, Jon Huggett, Simon Tucker, Alison Hewitt, Kippy Joseph, Frances Westley, Sonal Shah, Stephen Goldsmith, Christian Bason, Sunkyung Han, Allyson Hewitt, Won Soon Park, Lawrence Lien, Julie Simon, Sonia Navarro, Yvonne Roberts, Aditya Devsood, Yu Ke Ping, Tom Bentley, Anil Gupta, Sunit Shresta, Marthe Zirngiebl, Tonya Surman, Agnes Hubert, Madeleine Gabriel, Natalia Currea, Femi Longe and Laura Villa.

I also want to thank another group who commissioned pieces which were precursors of some of the ones contained here, including: Alex Nicholls, Rowena Young, Jurgen Howaldt and Alex Murdock. None of them bears any responsibility for any errors of fact or judgement in the book. But I'm grateful to all of the people listed here not just for their ideas and insights but also for being part of a movement that I have found always stimulating and full of joy and life, even as it's had to face dark problems.

Last but not least I would like to thank the various publishers who have published my writings on social innovation over the years, including Princeton University Press, Oxford University Press and Palgrave Macmillan.

Introduction: The great imbalances

The world entered the first decades of the 21st century out of balance. The flood of new knowledge and new technology that had so shaped the 20th century showed no signs of letting up. Most objective data showed a world enjoying unprecedented progress – in average levels of income, health and education, the spread of democracy and reductions in absolute poverty.

But on many fronts acute social imbalances and problems – from inequality to mental illness to feelings of lost dignity – undermined much sense of satisfaction. These pointed to a widening gulf between cumulative progress in science and technology and modest, if any, progress in social organisation. The world seemed to have taken an anti-social turn: devaluing social matters, social value and social concerns. The progressive story of cumulative advance, rights building on rights, was stuttering to a halt; life chances were being spread more narrowly; income was stagnant for large minorities; the economy more often seemed to be a threat to society rather than a support; and in some countries there were signs of an epidemic of social isolation.

Since the Second World War economics had supplanted other social sciences as the primary source of insight and its blind spots were reflected in the failings of the new order: not acknowledging social and environmental costs; knowing the price of everything and the value of nothing; and underestimating the importance of the social environments that make economies work. In innovation policy all efforts focused on hardware. And the dominant disciplines had little to say as powerful new social media permeated social life, often weakening social ties rather than strengthening them.

These various pathologies are now prompting a return of attention to the social, the detailed relationships of societies, the

1

knowledge needed to understand them and the actions needed to put them right.

To take just one example of many. The *World Happiness Report* in 2019[1] concluded that relationships explained more of the differences in wellbeing between nations than anything else. People's answers to the question 'If you were in trouble, do you have relatives or friends you can count on to help you whenever you need them, or not?' explained 34% of the wellbeing score, more than income (26%) or healthy life expectancy (21%). Yet most policy thinking and scientific research and development (R&D) ignored this simple point and the obvious truth that humans are deeply social creatures and deeply dependent on each other.

These chapters aim to describe a better response. They explore the ideas of social innovation and how, in both their minimalist and maximalist versions, they provide answers to the problems of the early 21st century. Social innovation opens up a different kind of conversation: about what's really valuable; about what matters; and about how imagination can be harnessed to make lives better. It promises a high-energy response to challenges – active, imaginative and restless – and an alternative to fatalism and retreat.

I argue that there can be no coherent progressive approach to political and social change without these ideas, and without their specific promise of spreading agency or the capacity to imagine, design and create the future. They are nothing less than ways that people and societies can take back control of their own destiny – the alternative to submission, authoritarianism and defeat. The converse is that top-down programmes and missions that fail to draw on the collective intelligence of their societies risk being seen as illegitimate, however well intentioned they are.

Part I sets out the main ideas of social innovation – the deliberate invention of new solutions to meet social needs – a field that has rapidly come of age since the turn of the century. I analyse how societies learn to experiment and innovate and show some of the tensions that arise. I also provide a broader overview of why the imbalances between innovation in the military and business, on the one hand, and society, on the other, have been so damaging.

Part II turns to the present and the context for social innovation in the second and third decades of the century. I look at the failure of the promise that globalisation, technological progress and liberalisation would benefit the lives of the majority; at the causes of the backlash; and at how new syntheses can address the causes of distrust and disillusion. Some social innovation is micro in nature. But it also has to connect to the macro questions of structure. So I turn to some of the big questions of political economy and social design, including how welfare states can be reshaped (and how, at a global level, this is an age of great fertility and expansion of welfare, even if it often looks very different from the vantage point of the rich countries of the North). I also examine the practical questions of social innovation: how to orchestrate coordination across multiple organisations; how to think about the production systems that give us such things as childcare or a better environment, human rights or training programmes.

Part III turns to sources and theory, with an overview of the theoretical dimensions of social innovation, and how it could become more prominent and relevant, part of common sense in the way that economics succeeded in doing in the second half of the 20th century. I describe how social sciences may be transformed in the near future by new generations of machine intelligence, and by engagement with citizens who become generators of their own knowledge. I show how social science can become more embedded and engaged, with practice and theory more tightly looped together. I highlight the contemporary relevance of prominent thinkers whose work should be part of the common sense of anyone interested in social innovation – from Mary Douglas, whose work does so much to illuminate how social change happens, to Charles Tilly, whose work provides invaluable insights into conflict. I look at how to revive traditions of observation and engagement. There are also essays on fundamental questions that dominate contemporary politics and social innovation on the ground – why do people feel they belong, or not, whether they are migrants or families that have lived for many generations in the same city or region?

Part IV turns to questions of good and bad, and value: innovations are useful only if they result in value. So, I analyse how societies value the things that really matter to them and how their measures have changed, and I examine how they direct scarce brainpower to innovations that will be socially beneficial rather than damaging.

Part V is on how to think about the future. The future is by definition unknowable, yet also vital to explore and understand. The premise is that citizens can be shapers and makers of their own future, not just passive observers: but this requires capabilities, resources and work. Here I pull some of the threads together, showing how social innovation in its more ambitious forms aims to involve people in the conscious creation of their own future.

Finally, Part VI brings together short pieces on the dilemmas of the field in a more personal and opinionated way. These include pieces on why the recent experience of do-it-yourself (DIY) makes me confident that we currently tap only a small fraction of potential social creativity and another suggesting a 'representational theory' of social innovation. Some readers may prefer to start here, at the end, before turning to the longer chapters.

The book deliberately avoids offering a single explanation for social innovation, which I see as a healthily protean activity, constantly mutating and evolving in both its means and its ends. Instead the book aims to provide a composite picture, a mosaic of ways of seeing and acting that I hope the reader can reconstruct into the forms most useful to them.

Karl Marx wrote of capital as representing dead labour that fed off the living, like a vampire. A common theme of the book is the challenge of dealing with zombie orthodoxies. Social structures survive long after they have ceased to be appropriate or useful. So how do we find the courage to leave behind ideas, habits and power structures that once made sense but no longer serve human and planetary interests? How can we speed up the cultivation of alternatives: a higher-energy society better able to understand its needs and act on them?

Social innovation is not a complete answer. In its multiple forms it's a complement, not an alternative, to a well-functioning state and a well-functioning economy. But any answers which don't have a significant place for social innovation now look seriously incomplete.

Part I
Making sense of social innovation

1

What is social innovation and how is it done?

Every truth passes through three stages. First, it is ridiculed. Second, it is violently opposed. Finally, it is taken to be self-evident.[1]

Introduction

The first two decades of the 21st century brought burgeoning interest in social innovation – its nature, needs, possibilities and dilemmas.[2] There were new policies; funds; research studies; accelerators; emerging fields around design, the maker movement, open data and the sharing economy, climate transition and social justice; and action involving many hundreds of thousands of people, from Canada to China, Sweden to South Africa, with benefits reaching billions.

This effervescence marked a shift in perception of both ends and means. It grew out of a recognition that too much innovation was being directed to the wrong ends – to warfare and killing; to the needs of the rich; or to trivial or harmful purposes. Too many of the world's most creative brains were working on the wrong tasks, while the world's most urgent needs were left underserved.

Just as important was a shift in thinking about means: a recognition that innovation had become too focused on hardware and things, and that it was far too much an elite preoccupation, for the well-educated and well-connected in big cities, with far too little role for the rest in making and shaping. So, attention turned to how to make innovation more inclusive; how to tap into household innovators; civil society; and the creativity of communities.

In both respects social innovation fed off a widespread desire of people to take more control of their lives and their futures and a dissatisfaction with existing institutions. As I show later in this book, this is a story in progress, and still in its early stages. But it has allowed us to see the past, the present and the future in a quite different light.

The heritage of social innovation

Much of what we take for granted in social life began as radical innovation, the work of dreamers not content just to dream. A century ago few believed that ordinary people could be trusted to drive cars at high speed; the idea of a national health service freely available to all was seen as absurdly utopian; the concept of a 'kindergarten' was still considered revolutionary; and in 1900 only one country had given women the vote. The idea that we might regularly separate our waste for recycling or measure our carbon footprint would have seemed incredible. Yet these and many other social innovations have progressed from the margins to the mainstream and become part of daily life.

During some periods in recent history civil society provided most of the impetus for social innovation. The great wave of industrialisation and urbanisation in the 19th century was accompanied by an extraordinary upsurge of social enterprise and innovation, including mutual self-help, microcredit, building societies, cooperatives, trade unions, reading clubs and philanthropic business leaders creating model towns and model schools. In 19th- and early 20th-century Britain, for example, civil society pioneered the most influential new models of childcare (Barnardo's), housing (Peabody), community development (the Edwardian settlements) and social care (Rowntree).

At other times governments have taken the lead in social innovation, for example in the years after 1945 when democratic governments built welfare states, schooling systems and institutions as various as credit banks for farmers and networks of adult education colleges (this was a period when many came to see civic and charitable organisations as too parochial, paternalist and inefficient to meet social needs on any scale).

In both of these periods social innovation brought new power relationships – with new rights, movements and parties to empower the victims of oppression and injustice – as well as new knowledge and solutions.

A longer historical perspective also helps us to see how social change goes through occasional surges as well as long periods of stasis. Social movements can grow quietly over decades, and then suddenly hit the streets, fuelled by crises or conflicts, and transform everyday common sense in irreversible ways. The #MeToo movement against sexual harassment, veganism, and disability rights, have all at times had this giddy feel that revolutions share, confirming that there are decades when nothing happens; and there are weeks when decades happen.[3]

How, then, is the heat and passion turned into the cool of new institutions and laws? How do the new ideas become habits, so obvious that they become almost invisible? The social innovation movement in its many forms has shown that there are many ways to achieve change, and this shift from hot to cool, without the need to wait for convulsive revolutions. It straddles the warm and the cool, the world of stories, feelings, anger, frustration, lived experience and hope, on the one hand, and the world of budgets, programmes, evidence and data, on the other.

As such, its constant dilemma is scale: how to retain the warmth and intimacy of the small and the local while also facing up to the vast scale of social needs. A thousand points of light are wonderful in themselves, but less wonderful if that's all they are.

Luckily, there are thousands of recent examples of successful social innovations that achieved real scale. They include neighbourhood nurseries and neighbourhood wardens; Wikipedia and the Open University; complementary medicine, holistic health and hospices; microcredit and consumer cooperatives; charity shops, veganism and the fair trade movement; zero-carbon housing schemes and community wind farms; restorative justice and community courts; online self-help health groups and crowdfunding; as well as ideas like the API (application programming interface) and the carbon credit.

As I show later, the ways they have grown are often very different from the patterns found in business or public administration. Growth has generally come from replication, spread and copying, fuelled by enthusiasm, rather than from the linear scaling of manufacturing or software, or the direct assertion of scale that state machineries are designed for. But the funding available for social innovation is dwarfed by funding for commercial and military innovation. As a result most social creativity goes to waste.

In what follows I describe some of the stages through which innovations grow, and how ideas can be helped to thrive.

First, though, a comment on words and definitions. There are many definitions of the word 'innovation' and even more of the word 'social', and not surprisingly there are competing accounts of how they should be linked together. My preference is for a simple definition which describes social innovations as 'innovations that are social both in their ends and their means'. They are social in their ends because they are motivated by the goal of meeting a social need. They are social in their means because they leave behind a stronger social capacity to act, and are usually, though not exclusively, spread through organisations whose primary purposes are social. There are many borderline cases, for example models of distance learning that were pioneered in social organisations but then adopted by businesses, or for-profit businesses innovating new approaches to helping disabled people into work. The term does not describe a single phenomenon but many, loosely related ones.

A good example of a socially innovative *activity* in this sense is the spread of cognitive behavioural therapy, proposed in the 1960s by Aaron Beck, tested empirically in the 1970s and then spread through professional and policy networks in the subsequent decades. A good example of a socially innovative *organisation* is BRAC, the huge non-governmental organisation (NGO) based in Bangladesh that has pioneered microcredit, schooling and universities. A good example of a socially innovative *ecosystem* is Ushahidi, which, from its base in East Africa, has initiated lots of imaginative uses of technology to strengthen democracy or cope with disasters. A good example of a socially innovative *product* is Fairphone, a mobile phone founded on ethically strong supply chains. Each, in different ways, is socially innovative in both its ends and its means.

Who does social innovation?

Most discussion of social innovation adopts one of two lenses for understanding how change happens. In the first, social change is portrayed as having been driven by a very small number of heroic, energetic and impatient individuals. History is told as the story of how they remade the world, persuading and cajoling the lazy and timid majority into change. Robert Owen, Octavia Hill (inventor of many ideas in heritage protection and community housing) and Michael Young are three examples drawn from British history who combined an ability to communicate complex ideas in compelling ways with a practical ability to make things happen. Young, who was once described by Harvard's Daniel Bell as the world's most successful entrepreneur of social enterprises, helped to create dozens of new institutions, including the Open University and its parallels around the world; the Consumers' Association and *Which?* magazine; the School for Social Entrepreneurs; and what became the Economic and Social Research Council. He pioneered new social models, such as phone-based health diagnosis, extended schooling and patient-led healthcare.[4]

There are countless other examples of similar social innovators from around the world – and the leaders of social innovation have included politicians, bureaucrats, intellectuals and business people as well as NGO activists. Some are widely celebrated, like Muhammad Yunnus, the founder of Grameen; and the Kenyan Nobel Prize winner Wangari Maathai; Saul Alinsky, the evangelist of community organising in the US; and Anil Gupta, champion of grassroots innovation in contemporary India.[5] These individual stories are always inspiring, energising and impressive. They show just how much persistent, dedicated people can achieve against the odds; and they serve as reminders of the courage and personal sacrifice that always accompany radical social change.

There is, however, a very different lens through which to understand the question of who drives social innovation. Seen through this lens, individuals are the carriers of ideas rather than originators. If we ask which innovations had the most impact over the last half-century the role of individuals quickly fades into the background. The far-reaching movements of change, such as feminism, LGBTQ rights or environmentalism, involved millions of people and had dozens of intellectual and organisational leaders, many of whom had the humility to realise that they were often as much following changes in public consciousness as they were standing above them. Like individual change-makers, these movements have their roots in ideas growing out of discontent. But their histories look very different. Environmentalism, for example, grew from many different sources. There were precursors in the 19th century, including movements for protecting forests and landscapes; scientifically inspired movements to protect biodiversity; more politicised movements to counter the pollution of big companies or gain redress for their victims; movements of direct action like Greenpeace (which itself drew on much older Quaker traditions); and the various Green parties around the world which have always been suspicious of individual leaders.

Environmentalism has spawned a huge range of social innovations, from urban recycling to community-owned wind farms. Today environmentalism is as much part of big business culture (led by pioneering companies such as Unilever) as it is part of the alternative business culture of organic food and household composting, municipal government (for example, the many dozens of US mayors who committed themselves to the Kyoto Protocol in the early 2000s, and the Paris Agreement after 2016) and civil society (through mass campaigns like Friends of the Earth and Extinction Rebellion). Along with feminism or the movement for disability rights, environmentalists have generally been suspicious of overly individualistic pictures of change. In their view the idea that progress comes from the wisdom of a few exceptional individuals is an anachronism, a throwback to pre-democratic times.

Both of these accounts of social innovation – the one focused on individuals, the other focused on broader movements – bring with them useful insights. Both call attention to the cultural base for social innovation – the combination of exclusion, resentment, passion and commitment that make social change possible. Both confirm that social innovations also spread in an 'S curve', with an early phase of slow growth among a small group of committed supporters, then a phase of rapid take-off and then a slowing down as saturation and maturity are achieved. Both accounts also rightly emphasise the importance of ideas – visions of how things could be different and better. Every successful social innovator or movement has succeeded because it has planted the seeds of an idea in many minds. In the long run, ideas are more powerful than individuals or institutions; indeed, as John Maynard Keynes noted, 'the world is ruled by little else'.[6]

But neither story is adequate to explain the complexities of social change. Change rarely happens without some brave people willing to take risks and make a stand. Leadership matters even in the most egalitarian and democratic of movements. But equally it is the nature of social change that it depends on many people being persuaded to abandon old habits, as well as favourable structural conditions. Even the great religious prophets spawned great religions only because they were followed by great organisers and evangelists and military conquerors who were able to focus their energies and create great organisations.[7] Even the most impressive ideas spread only when the right conditions are in place – well-enough organised potential beneficiaries with access to power and money who can counter the many interests that may lose out.

The anti-slavery movement of the late 18th and early 19th centuries is a good example. It pioneered many of the tools of modern campaigning. It had a visual identity (Josiah Wedgwood's image of an African slave on his knees with his manacled hands outstretched); a slogan ('Am I not a man and a brother?'); and multi-tiered campaigning, from the streets and business to Parliament. It was also both a broad-based movement (notably led by the Quakers) and one pushed along by some very visible leaders (like William Wilberforce).

Can social innovation solve social problems?

The promise of social innovation is that it can solve or at least ameliorate the social problems that matter: underemployment, community conflict, loneliness, exclusion of all kinds. That promise can overreach itself. Some social entrepreneurs have been particularly prone to grandiose claims that their ideas will solve the problems of welfare or poverty. They never do, and it is easy to mock the more extreme variants of 'solutionism' which talk of societies as if they are machines, just waiting for a smart technical fix.

But social problems are sometimes resolved, and sometimes this happens in dramatic ways. China's alleviation of poverty over the last four decades; dramatic reductions in homelessness in many cities; Bangladesh's steady advances in development; improvements in public health or schooling. These and many others give the lie to the casual fatalism which presumes that improvement is impossible.

In all these cases, however, the story of success involved many actors and many complementary actions, with new methods, policies and innovations creating a reinforcing spiral of effects. There was very rarely a single cause or a single hero, and it is as wrong to assume that a single top-down policy will solve a problem as it is to believe that a single entrepreneurial action will do so.

Social innovation is always a crucial part of these stories because there is always improvisation and adaptation, trial and error. But the language can overshoot too, presenting a world full of problems just waiting for clever solutions to come along. Bill Clinton's much-quoted comment that 'nearly every problem has been solved by someone, somewhere',[8] has more than a grain of truth, but didn't help when it was taken to mean that existing solutions just needed to be scaled up and all would be well. Social innovations can contribute to solving social problems – but always as parts of larger patterns of change, and always with a mutual interdependence of the 'bees' and the 'trees': the bees being the innovative entrepreneurs, often full of energy and ideas but lacking power and money, and the trees being big institutions – governments, businesses, NGOs – which command resources but often lack creativity.

The rest of this chapter describes some of the stages of social innovation, which can be roughly mapped against the 'innovation spiral' as ideas make the journey from an understanding of challenges and opportunities, through the generation of ideas to testing and implementation, scaling and, ultimately, the transformation of whole systems.[9] As Martin Luther King put it, 'the line of progress is never straight. For a period a movement may follow a straight line and then it encounters obstacles and the path bends. It is like curving around a mountain when you are approaching a city.'[10] Social innovations, too, rarely evolve in neat or predictable ways.

This picture of the 'innovation spiral' provides a useful summary of the stages that many innovations pass through – from prompts that come from problems or opportunities, through the generation of ideas, testing, development, implementation, growth to scale and ultimately the transformation of whole systems.

Generating ideas by understanding needs and identifying potential solutions

One starting point for innovation is a need that isn't being met and some idea of how it could be. Sometimes needs are

Figure 1.1: The innovation spiral

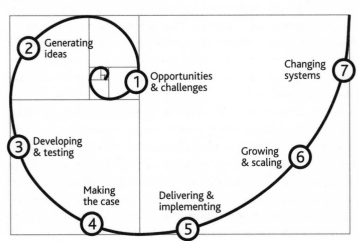

Source: Author's own, adapted from https://www.nesta.org.uk/feature/innovation-methods/

glaringly obvious – like hunger, homelessness or disease. But sometimes needs are less obvious, or are not recognised – like the need for protection from domestic violence, or the epidemic of loneliness – and it takes campaigners and movements to name and describe these.

The Victorian historian Lord Macaulay wrote that 'there is constant improvement precisely because there is constant discontent'.[11] Needs come to the fore in many ways – through angry individuals and groups, campaigns, political movements, as well as through careful observation. They may come from informal social movements (like health self-help groups[12]); religious movements; existing voluntary organisations; individual social entrepreneurs; rising citizen expectations and aspirations (such as patient attitudes towards health professionals resulting in patient choice); or demographic change (such as new co-housing models for the elderly in the Netherlands).

Some of the best innovators spot needs which aren't being adequately met by the market or the state. Their own lives may propel them into action, making them determined to share their story and solve the problem that has harmed them or those they love.

Others are good at talking and listening, digging below the surface to understand people's needs and dislocations, dissatisfactions and blockages (Michael Young got many of his best ideas from random conversations on street corners, on buses and even in cemeteries). Empathy is the starting point, and ethnography is usually a more relevant formal tool than statistical analysis.

Some of the most effective methods for cultivating social innovation start from the presumption that people are competent interpreters of their own lives and competent solvers of their own problems. Anyone seeking to find an answer to the management of chronic diseases or alienation among teenagers would do well to find how people are handling their problems themselves. Another method is to find the people who are solving their problems against the odds – the ex-prisoners who do not re-offend or the 18-year-old without any qualifications who nevertheless finds a job. Looking for the 'positive deviants' – the approaches that work when most others are failing – gives insights into what might be possible, and usually at much lower cost than top-down solutions.

Needs then have to be tied to new possibilities. New possibilities may be technological – for example, using the smartphone to support front-line workers, using virtual reality to enhance education or using artificial intelligence to guide family law. The internet in all its forms made possible a host of new business models that have had enormous impact in the social field, as in business.

Some of these possibilities are surprising: like the Dutch city of Tilburg, which in 2017 allowed old people to download an app that let them control traffic lights to give them longer to cross the road; or Lima in Peru, which attached GoPro cameras to vultures to monitor illegal waste disposal; or Stockholm, which allowed biohackers to use their implants to buy tickets to ride on the public subway system.

Other possibilities may derive from new organisational forms, like community interest companies in the UK, or B-Corps, that help for-profit firms to commit to social purposes, or the special-purpose vehicles increasingly used in global development. Or possibilities may derive from new knowledge – for example, newly acquired understanding of the importance of early years development in shaping future life chances. Innovators generally have a wide peripheral vision – and are good at spotting how apparently unrelated methods and ideas can be used.

Few ideas emerge fully formed. Instead, innovators often try things out, and then quickly adjust them in the light of experience. Tinkering seems to play a vital role in all kinds of innovation, involving trial and error, hunches and experiments that only in retrospect look rational and planned.

New social ideas are also rarely inherently new in themselves. More often they combine ideas that had previously been separate, and sometimes straddle previously distinct fields – what I've called 'connected difference'. Examples of creative combinations include diagnostic health lines (which combined the telephone, nurses and diagnostic software); the scheme in Surabaya in Indonesia which allowed people to pay for bus rides by bringing plastic for recycling, making mobility more affordable and reducing the plastic problem; magazines sold by homeless people; the linking of gay rights to marriage; applying the idea of rights to animals; or the use of swipe cards to make possible large-scale bicycle hiring schemes, located in stations or next to bus shelters. Many of the most important ideas straddle the boundaries between sectors and disciplines (about 50% of public sector innovation is now reckoned to cross organisational boundaries, for example). And some of the most powerful ones are recycled: the Green New Deal in the US is a good example, drawing on decades of programmes using similar labels in other countries.

Some organisations use formal creativity methods to generate possibilities, including the ones devised by Edward de Bono,[13] all of which aim to free groups to think more imaginatively and to spot new patterns. Some of these methods force creativity – for example, getting developers and designers to engage with the toughest customers, or those facing the most serious problems, to force more lateral solutions. Creativity can be stimulated by other people's ideas, which are increasingly being collected and banked.[14]

A high proportion of creativity can be described, and encouraged, through a small number of moves: social innovation is particularly fuelled by the use of inversion, turning an established idea on its head: for example, peasants become bankers as in the Grameen Bank, or patients becoming doctors. Others which are more common in other fields include extension (taking an existing idea and extending it to a new field, like the idea of rights extended to disability); grafting (planting an idea from one field into a new setting); addition or subtraction; creative extremism (pushing ideas and methods to their furthest boundaries); or use of random inputs (for example, taking a word at random from dictionaries as a prompt for creative thinking).[15] Using frameworks like this, any group can quickly generate many new options. The great majority can be quickly discarded, but some may turn out to be very valuable.

Most creative ideas are in some sense combinations, sometimes surprising ones. I like the idea described by Thomas Schelling in his classic paper on negotiation: the rehabilitation clinic for rich cocaine users who are given the chance to write an incriminating letter which will be sent only if the patient fails a random test

Figure 1.2: How to create ideas

∧	**Inversion**	Turn common practice upside down
∫	**Integration**	Integrate the offer with other offers
x	**Extension**	Extend the offer
∂	**Differentiation**	Segment the offer
+	**Addition**	Add a new element
−	**Subtraction**	Take something away
t	**Translation**	Translate a practice associated with another field
g	**Grafting**	Graft on an element of practice from another field
∞	**Exaggeration**	Push something to its most extreme expression

showing they've used cocaine. This model of 'self-blackmail' is a classic kind of innovation, combining a series of established methods but in a novel way.[16] Another example is the 'shared lives' model which extends the idea of foster parenting to adults. A family is paid to provide a home for adults with learning disabilities or the frail elderly, as an alternative to traditional residential care. Another example of an inversion is the idea of negawatts and negakilometres: laws and regulations to incentivise reduced use of energy or transport as a desirable goal, rather than the opposite.

In some cases, ideas can be bought, or rewarded, on the open market. Britain's Parliament pioneered this approach with the Longitude Prize in the 18th century, offering a cash reward to anyone from any background who could design a device to measure longitude at sea. Gandhi used a challenge prize in the late 1920s to reward designers – from anywhere – who could design a precisely specified cheap cloth loom. Today the same approach is used by the company Innocentive, which offers cash rewards on the web for innovators who have workable solutions to problems, and Nesta's Challenge Prize Centre does the same – mobilising creative solutions from anyone anywhere on topics ranging from data for farming in South Asia to alternatives to wheelchairs.

There are also now many innovation labs, some linked to universities, some linked to companies and some focused on particular problems.[17] One key to success is to ensure that there is as wide a range of choices to draw on as possible. As Linus Pauling (who won the Nobel Prize in Chemistry and the Nobel Peace Prize) observed, 'If you want to have good ideas you must have many ideas. Most of them will be wrong, and what you have to learn is which ones to throw away.'[18] Thomas Watson, founder of IBM, made a similar point: 'If you want to succeed faster, double your failure rate.'[19]

All societies throw up many possible social innovations. Some never get beyond a conversation in a kitchen or a bar. Many briefly take organisational form but then fade as enthusiasm dims or it becomes obvious that the idea isn't so good after all. To grow, they have to tap into resources – time, money, commitment and passion. Most don't. The definition of a crank is someone who believes they know the solution to the world's problems, talks of nothing else, but fails to persuade anyone else to go along with them.

Developing, prototyping and piloting ideas

The second phase of any innovation process involves taking a promising idea and testing it out in practice. Few plans survive their first encounter with reality, but it is through action that they evolve and improve. Social innovations may be helped by formal market research or desk analysis, but progress is often achieved more quickly through turning the idea into a prototype or pilot and then galvanising enthusiasm.

Social innovations are often implemented early. Because those involved are usually highly motivated, they are too impatient to wait for governments or professions. The experience of trying to make them work then speeds up their evolution, and the power of example then turns out to be as persuasive as written argument or advocacy. Michael Young usually moved very quickly to set up an embryonic organisation rather than waiting for detailed business plans and analyses. The Language Line organisation, for example, began as two people with telephones and a tiny contract with the neighbouring police station.

A virtue of quick prototyping is that innovations often require several goes before they work. The first outings are invariably flawed. The UK National Health Service (NHS) took 40 years to move from impossible dream to reality; the radio took a decade to find its form (its early pioneers wrongly assumed that members of the public would purchase airtime to send messages to their friends and families, as with the telephone); what became Wikipedia was a failure in its first outing, just as Google almost collapsed before it hit on search-based advertising as its main source of revenue.

In business there has long been talk of the 'chasm' that innovations have to cross as they pass from being promising pilot ideas to becoming mainstream products or services. There are likely to be long phases when revenues are negative, and when investors have to hold their nerve. Exactly the same challenge faces any social innovation. Several methods have been designed to speed up this period, including faster prototyping, intensive handholding by venture capital companies and the use of rigorous milestones against which funds are released – but there is no avoiding a period of uncertainty while success is uncertain (and, as Rosabeth Moss Kanter memorably put it, every success looks like a failure in the middle).[20]

There is now a much richer range of methods available for prototyping, piloting and testing new ideas either in real environments or in protected conditions, halfway between the real world and the laboratory. The relatively free money of foundations and philanthropists can be decisive in helping ideas through this phase. Governments have also become more sophisticated in their use of evidence and knowledge,[21] with a proliferation of pilots, pathfinders and experiments. Incubators, which have long been widespread in business, have started to take off in the public sector and among NGOs, though practice and understanding remain very patchy. In business, devices like 3D printers have made it easier to turn ideas quickly into prototypes;

in the social field parallel methods are being developed to crystallise promising ideas so that they can be quickly tested.

Some ideas that seem good on paper fall at this stage. Michael Young, for example, launched a DIY garage, convinced that most motorists would prefer to invest some of their time in fixing cars in exchange for lower costs. They didn't.[22] But even failed ideas often point the way to related ideas that will succeed. As Samuel Beckett put it: 'Try again. Fail again. Fail better.'[23]

Assessing ideas, then scaling up and diffusing the good ones

The third stage of the social innovation process comes when an idea is proving itself in practice and can then be grown, potentially through organic growth, replication, adaptation or franchising. Taking a good idea to scale requires skilful strategy and coherent vision, combined with the ability to marshal resources and support and identify the key points of leverage, the weak chinks in opponents' walls. 'Bees' need to find supportive 'trees' with the machineries to make things happen on a big scale. That in turn may demand formal methods to persuade potential backers, including investment appraisals and impact assessments.

Communication is essential at this stage – social innovators need to capture the imagination of a community of supporters through the combination of contagious courage and pragmatic persistence. Good names, along with brands, identities and stories, play a critical role. Some social innovations then spread through the organic growth of the organisations that conceived them – like the Samaritans volunteer service providing confidential, emotional support. Some have grown through federations – including many NGOs like Age Concern or the Citizens Advice Bureau. Governments have often played the critical role in scaling up social innovations and have unique capacities to do this by passing laws (many social movements have achieved their greatest impact by persuading parliaments to pass new laws, for example giving women the vote, or legalising gay marriage); by committing spending (for example, to extended schools); and by conferring authority on public agencies (for example, to grow the role of health visitors). Business grows ideas through a well-established range of methods, some of which are becoming more commonly used in the social sector, including the organic growth of an originating organisation; franchising and licensing; and takeover of similar but less effective organisations.

This growth phase is potentially becoming much faster. With the help of the web, innovations can spread very quickly, and indeed there can be little point in doing local pilots, since the economics of the web may make it as cheap to launch on a national or continental scale. Marginal costs close to zero accelerate the growth phase – but also the phase of decline and disappearance.

Two necessary conditions for success are a propitious environment (for example, a market for the service on offer, or government interest in providing funding or contracts) and organisational capacity to grow. These are rare with social innovations. It may take decades to create the environmental conditions for growth – persuading consumers and public agencies to pay for something new. The organisational challenges are no less severe. In charities and social enterprises the founders who were just right for the organisation during its early years are unlikely to have the right mix of skills and attitudes for a period of growth and consolidation (this is also one of the ways in which an over-individualistic model of change may have become an impediment to the field). Often, founders cling on too long – and trustees, funders and stakeholders do not impose necessary changes.

By comparison, in business the early phases of fast-growing enterprises often involve ruthless turnover of managers and executives. Indeed, growth in all sectors nearly always involves *outgrowing* founders. Wise founders therefore put in place robust succession plans (and very few successfully remain in executive roles for much more than a decade). Similar considerations apply to organisations which create other organisations. Christian Aid, CAFOD and Tearfund, for example, are all social innovations with global reach today that outgrew their founders and founding institutions (the British Council of Churches, the Catholic Women's League and the Evangelical Alliance, respectively).

In business, the experience of companies such as Microsoft, Google, Facebook and Amazon suggests that pioneers who create markets through radical innovation are almost never the companies that go on to scale up and dominate them. None of these companies invented the idea that made it so successful; all were highly efficient followers rather than first movers. The skills and mindsets required for creating a radically new market not only differ from, but actively conflict with, those needed to grow and consolidate. Big companies are often better placed to take new ideas from niche markets to mass markets, and many have concluded that they should subcontract the creation of new and radical products to start-up firms and concentrate their own efforts on consolidating markets or buying up companies or licences that they see as promising.[24]

For innovators themselves one of the key lessons from all sectors is that ideas spread more quickly when credit is shared, and when at least some of the 'trees' can claim ownership. As Harry Truman said, 'It is amazing what you can achieve if you don't care who gets the credit.'[25]

Learning and evolving

In a fourth stage, innovations continue to change: learning and adaptation turn the ideas into forms that may be very different from the expectations of the pioneers. Experience may show unintended consequences or unexpected applications. In professions, in competitive markets and in the public sector there is an increasingly sophisticated understanding of how learning takes place. New models such as the collaboratives in health (pioneered in New England and later used by the NHS to improve innovation and practice in fields like cancer and primary care) and closed research groups (used, for example, by a number of major cities to analyse their transport strategies) have helped to embed innovation and improvement in fairly conservative professions.

These highlight the degree to which all processes of innovation can be understood as types of learning, rather than as eureka moments of lone geniuses. Instead, ideas start off as possibilities that are only incompletely understood by their inventors. They evolve by becoming more explicit and more formalised as best practice is worked out and as organisations develop experience in how to make them work. This phase involves consolidation around a few core principles which can be easily communicated. Then, as the idea is implemented in new contexts it evolves further, and in new combinations, with the learning once again more tacit, held within organisations, until another set of simpler syntheses emerge.

This linear account of innovation is a useful simplification. But it should already be clear that the stages are not always consecutive. Sometimes action precedes understanding. Sometimes doing things catalyses new ideas. There are also feedback loops between every stage, which make real innovations more like multiple spirals than straight lines. Real-life innovation is a discovery process that often leaves ideas transformed and mutated, and sometimes sees them jump from one sector to another. So, for example, innovations to reduce obesity can be found in public health programmes funded by taxpayers, in self-help groups and in large commercial organisations like Weight Watchers. Sometimes innovations are progressive for a period and then become problematic: like France's HLM system (*habitation à loyer modéré*), which for a time provided vital cheap housing for people in need, but became isolated ghettos.

Common patterns of success and failure

Social innovation doesn't always happen easily, even though people are naturally inventive and curious. In some societies social innovations are strangled at birth, particularly societies where power is tightly monopolised, where free communication is inhibited, or where there are no independent sources of money. Generally, social innovation is much more likely to happen when the right background conditions are present. For social movements, basic legal protections and open media are key. In business, social innovation (for example, the spread of organic food, complementary medicine or Linux software) can be driven by competition, open cultures and accessible capital, and will be impeded where capital is monopolised by elites or government. In politics and government, the conditions are likely to include competing parties, think-tanks, innovation funds, contestable markets and plentiful pilots, as well as creative leaders like

Jaime Lerner in Curitiba, Ada Colau in Barcelona, Won Soon Park in Seoul or Stephen Goldsmith in New York.[26] In social organisations the acceleration of social innovation is aided by practitioner networks, allies in politics, strong civic organisations (from trade unions to hospitals) and the support of progressive foundations and philanthropists. And in every field global links make it much easier to learn lessons and share ideas at an early stage, with ideas moving in every direction (for example, the movement of restorative justice from Maori New Zealand to mainstream practice around the world).

Most innovations in business and technology fail. So do most social innovations. Sometimes there are good reasons for failure. An idea may be too expensive; not wanted; insufficiently useful; not good enough relative to the alternatives; or flawed by unforeseen side-effects. But many ideas fail not because of inherent flaws but because of the lack of adequate mechanisms to promote them, adapt them and then scale them up. In business there is a reasonable flow of good innovations, in part because of the pull of competitive markets, but also because of public subsidy of technology and private investment in incubators, venture capital and start-ups. The equivalent potential supports for social innovation – foundations, public agencies and investors – are much weaker.

Having reviewed some of the steps that ideas take on the journey from being an idea to a large-scale reality, let me briefly touch on some of the dilemmas that surround these patterns.

The innovators' dilemmas

For the innovators themselves every step is fraught with uncertainty and difficult choices. How far do you compromise with incumbents or funders? How fiercely should you stick to a pure model of your idea? Do you fight within the system, fight against the system or create alternatives? Buckminster Fuller, the great 20th-century inventor and visionary, argued that 'you never change things by fighting the existing reality. To change something, build a new model that makes the existing model obsolete.'[27] But that's not always an option, especially if you're poor and powerless.

Then there's the dilemma of who has the right to act. Social change isn't something that can be done by one group of people for others – a belief that has undermined the credibility of charity from 19th-century paternalism to 21st-century venture philanthropy.[28] But are people suffering injustice the only ones with a right to act for their own redemption? Most lasting social change has come about from below as well as above, through alliances between the victims of injustice and more privileged others bringing the additional knowledge, power and money they lack.

Do you then avoid structures or build them? Many innovations start out in what David Graeber has called organisational 'bubbles of freedom'[29] that reject any links to formal politics or the state, let alone big business. But all at some point either have to create more permanent structures or risk going the way of bubbles and bursting or just fading away (a century ago Georg Simmel wrote brilliantly about how the very moment of success can so often feel like a disappointment, as the passions of the movement translate into solid institutional form).[30]

The dilemmas of government

What, then, of the dilemmas for anyone dealing with the state or working within it? Most governments are instinctively hostile to social innovation. The Saudi government, which in 2018 legalised women driving and simultaneously locked up the women who had campaigned for women's right to drive, exemplifies these ugly habits: resisting reform and then, when it proves irresistible, demanding the credit.

But in recent years, for the first time, many governments have introduced explicit policies to promote social innovation, from Korea and Canada to the UK and France. President Obama created an Office for Social Innovation in the White House, and a range of funds to scale promising projects. The European Commission went further, backing funds, incubators, networks and research, including on newer topics like digital social innovation.

Governments have many motives, from the need to respond to pressure from assertive civil societies to a genuine wish to find novel solutions to intractable problems. The social economy has become a significant source of jobs and wealth and over the next 20 years the biggest growth in jobs is likely to come in fields like health, education and care, whose shares of gross domestic product (GDP) are already much greater than cars or telecoms, steel or biotech. These are fields in which commercial, voluntary and public organisations all deliver services, in which public policy plays a key role and in which consumers co-create value alongside producers (no teacher can force a student to learn if they don't want to). Without systematic innovation there's a high risk of stagnation.[31]

Governments' challenge is to link the multiple micro examples of innovation to the scale of impacts they need. They typically provide some 30–40% of NGO finance in countries like the US, Germany, UK, France and Japan – but are generally poor at recognising and replicating good innovations, particularly when these come from other sectors. It is notoriously difficult for government to close its own failing programmes and services, and there are few incentives for either politicians or officials to take up new ideas. Failure to adapt is rarely career threatening, and anyone who does promote innovations risks upsetting powerful vested interests. It's all too easy to conclude that the apparently promising new idea is too dependent on particular circumstances – such as a charismatic individual – or that the evidence just isn't strong enough (the threshold for evidence on existing programmes tends to be much lower).

As a result, social innovators generally find governments unresponsive. Governments have a bias to the big and powerful; they like predictability; and they generally prefer hardware and physical things to the subtler tasks of social change. China's Belt and Road Initiative is a good current example: far more focused on ports, roads and rail than on the less tangible wellsprings of development.

But there are sometimes good reasons for public sectors to be cautious about innovation. Innovation must involve failure – and appetites for failure are bound to be limited in very accountable organisations, or where people's lives depend on reliability (for example, around traffic light systems, or delivery of welfare payments). Most public services, like most NGO service delivery, have to concentrate primarily on the better management and performance of existing models rather than the invention of new ones.

Innovation is therefore easier where the risks are contained; where current approaches are clearly failing; where users have choice (so that they can choose a radically different model of school or doctor, rather than having it forced on them); and where expectations are carefully managed (for example, through politicians being open to the fact that many models are being tried out and that some are likely to fail). More generally, innovation is likely to be easier when contracts for services reward outcomes achieved rather than outputs or activities, or when there is competition or contestability rather than monopoly provision by the state.

Governments aren't monoliths and there are now many good examples of successful collaboration between radical movements and state policy that give the lie to lazy clichés about government. A good example has been the reorganisation of social care as self-directed support, in response to the disability movement.[32] Another is the rise of recycling. These examples confirm that how public sectors 'dock' with the social or non-profit sector is important, particularly given that public funding tends to overshadow other revenue sources for many innovations. Funding the outcomes rather than the activities helps; so too does funding directed to genuinely risk-taking ideas, experiments and trials. But, at root, what matters is a mindset that's open and willing to collaborate.

The deeper issue, however, is how governments engage with the more strategic, maximalist versions of social innovation. Roberto Mangabeira Unger put it well: the maximalist view is concerned with 'the whole of society, of its institutional arrangements, and of its dominant forms of consciousness ... at its maximalist best, the social innovation movement [undertakes] the small initiatives that have the greatest potential to foreshadow, by persuasive example, the transformation of those arrangements and of that consciousness'.[33] That requires a degree of openness, and humility, that is rare in the history of government.

The dilemmas of knowledge

What do we need to know? And where are the biggest gaps in knowledge? More serious research on social innovation has been growing since the 1990s.[34] Some comes out of the study of NGOs, others out of business schools and the wider field of innovation studies,[35] and there is now a growing literature straddling many disciplines.[36]

Most of this is focused on the more minimalist interpretations of social innovation. But even within this more modest space we are still some way short of a truly mature field of research, with really rigorous research testing out hypotheses and using data, or one that is truly global. The research community is still separated into distinct regional cultures. The most prominent journal covering social innovation – the *Stanford Social Innovation Review* – has grown out of the study of US NGOs, tends to rely on case studies and has been dominated by a few US consultancies (Bridgespan, McKinsey, FSG) and a handful of US universities. In other countries there are very different traditions and reference points. In Quebec and France, for example, social innovation and its research has tended to be associated with the socialist Left; in other parts of Europe it's focused on territorial development.[37] In Germany it has tended to be closer to the Green and radical movements, and to Schumpeterian ideas in economics;[38] Italy has a range of traditions, some rooted in the social economy and cooperatives, others in design;[39] in Canada there has been an emphasis on complexity and resilience;[40] in India thinking on social innovation often draws on Gandhian ideas.

While we await more truly global perspectives, a lot of research has sought to learn from neighbouring fields, primarily in the Western academic tradition. The expanding field of research on business innovation provides useful frameworks like the distinctions between total, expansionary and evolutionary innovations;[41] or between incremental, radical and systematic ones.[42] There is useful research on how competition influences innovation;[43] the sociological work on the role of intermediaries who help to make markets work more efficiently, spotting connections and opportunities;[44] the analyses of how much innovation is best understood as creative reinterpretation;[45] and the work pioneered by Everett Rogers on diffusion.[46]

Often the insights from business pose important challenges to social innovators. We know, for example, that in some sectors the best market structure for innovation is a combination of oligopolistic competition between a few big companies and a much larger penumbra of smaller firms (the model that exists in sectors such as microchips, software, cars and retailing). Yet, in most social fields monopolistic governments sit alongside units which are too small to innovate radically (schools, doctors' surgeries, police stations), which may be one reason why far-reaching innovations are so rare.

We know that disaggregated industries tend to adapt better to volatility, and big structures to stable conditions. And we know how serendipitous innovation often is – seeking one solution, firms stumble on another, quite different one. The organisational choices faced by social and commercial organisations also run in parallel. Some companies organise innovation largely in-house as part of their mainstream business (like 3M); some create semi-autonomous corporate venture units (like Nokia); some grow through acquisition of other innovative companies as well as their own innovation (Cisco, for example); others use widespread networks (like the original design manufacturing companies in China). Again, in the social field there are similar advantages and disadvantages in keeping innovation in-house; integrating innovative NGOs into big public systems (as has often happened in housing); or using networks (the traditional method of innovation in fields as diverse as public health and urban planning).

In other fields social organisations have been ahead of business. The fashion for user networks in business innovation emulates long-standing practices in NGOs (Michael Young pioneered patient-led health innovations in the 1980s, including what became the Expert Patients Programme in the NHS); similarly the open source movement took models from academia and civic organisations directly into the heart of business.[47] We now know that household innovation is pervasive – and a series of studies prompted by Eric von Hippel (the first of which was commissioned by Nesta for the UK in 2010) revealed some 60 million household innovators around the world. Some of their work resulted in commercial start-ups, but most were doing innovation to meet their own needs.

Research of this kind points to some of the important differences that separate social innovation from innovation in business. There are likely to be very different motives, which may include material incentives but will almost certainly go far wider, to include motives of recognition, compassion, identity, autonomy and care. The critical resources are likely to be different: in businesses money provides the bottom line, but social innovations usually seek out a different mix of resources, including political recognition and support, voluntary labour and philanthropic commitment. Social organisations tend to have different patterns of growth: as a rule, they don't grow as fast as private ones, but they also tend to be more resilient. Judging success is also bound to be very different. Scale or market share may matter little for a social innovation concerned with a very intense but contained need.

Looking to the future, there are many promising areas for research. One of the most important is more systematic use of data to track how innovations emerge, spread and evolve (covered more in the piece on 'A representational theory of social innovation' in Part VI). Another is better understanding of how top-down processes intersect with bottom-up ones to achieve genuinely systemic change, for example to cut carbon emissions or to reduce isolation.

Why what we don't know matters

The practice of social innovation remains roughly at the point where science was more than a century ago, when invention and innovation were left to the enthusiasm and energy of determined individuals like Alexander Graham Bell who beavered away in their laboratories until the occasional eureka moment gave the world a new invention. For science that era is long gone, thanks to figures like Thomas Edison who brought industrial methods to innovation. As it came to be understood just how important science was to the economy (and to warfare), invention and innovation were taken out of the attics and garden sheds, and backed with large-scale public funding and by R&D

departments in big companies and university departments, and by the systematic testing of new ideas. Today we live with the results of that revolution, and a stream of new products that come onto the market every year. Social innovation has yet to pass through a similar revolution. But it may be coming, and if it does, it will be fuelled both by detailed knowledge of how to grow ideas and by a different way of thinking about progress. I turn to this in the next chapter.

2

The roots of social innovation and the fragile springs of social generativity

> True generosity to the future lies in giving your all to the present.[1]

How can a society imagine, create and evolve? How can it be more alive? How can it grow in social and psychological terms, not just materially? Here I share ways of thinking about social creativity, generativity[2] and innovation – their ethics and aesthetics as well as their tools and systems. I analyse the uneven dynamics of social systems – which allow some to innovate intensively, while others do not; I describe the ethos and culture of social innovation; and I look at where social innovation happens on the boundaries of states, markets, civil society and the household.

Worlds in motion

Our current era is unusual in its enthusiasm for innovation. In ancient Greek, innovation or *kainotomia* was a largely political concept, while in Latin *in novo* was a theological idea, meaning renewal or a return to the original soul, which related to Christian concepts of rebirth or regeneration. In a later period, innovation came to refer to things that had to be crushed. In the mid-16th century the English king Edward VI issued a famous proclamation 'Against Those That Doeth Innovate'[3]; innovation meant heresy. When, several centuries later, the term 'innovation' was linked to the word 'social' for the first time, the combination was intended to be pejorative: William Sargant's *Social Innovators and Their Scheme*, published in 1858, used the term as a stick to criticise reformers who wanted to overthrow the social order and private property. Innovations were designs, but designs in the sense of conspiracies or plots.[4]

So, how did innovation become a good thing, and one that could be usefully extended to society? The simple answer is that modernity in its broadest sense has lent any discussion of social innovation a very different tone to any equivalent discussion in medieval Europe or ancient China. Since the 18th century the world has been in motion both in its physical facts and in its mentalities entirely because of innovation. The charts show this dramatically. Many measures before around 1800 show very little change over centuries and millennia, despite empires rising and falling. Then they start pointing up, the lines twitching into an inverted 'J' of near-exponential rises in material prosperity; life expectancy; energy use; communications; mobility; population. Less desirable numbers shoot up with equal vigour: pollution, depletion of resources and carbon emissions, to mention just a few.

This change was brought about through a harnessing of knowledge that had many components – science, technology, engineering, markets, universities and cultures of tinkering and everyday invention. It's now clear that the world had stumbled onto a kind of perpetual motion machine: the cumulative, progressive acquisition of applied knowledge through experiment, discovery and continuous improvement, in which states as well as businesses played decisive roles.

This feature of the Enlightenment transformed the organisation of the material world. But its implications for the social world, as opposed to the world of things, were always more ambiguous. Some advocated a comparable scientific, experimental approach in society as in engineering; there are hints in Francis Bacon, John Stuart Mill and others. But nowhere was there a coherent programme for social innovation as opposed to technological innovation. In any case, in nations that were scarcely democracies it wasn't clear who should design and run experiments, where the money would come from or what might count as success. Novel knowledge was disruptive and threatening.

Conservatives were happy to promote technological innovation if it meant military prowess or profit. But they had little appetite for social change.[5]

Past eras had had social analysis and description (such as Ibn Khaldun's) and social prescription (from Plato to Kautilya and Confucius). But conscious and deliberate social imagination is much rarer, and much more recent, dating only from the 18th and 19th centuries.[6]

Indeed, it was only in the late 20th century that the idea started to take hold that societies could consciously and deliberately cultivate the capacity to reinvent themselves and so become better at both defining their goals and achieving them. That idea – of an autopoietic, self-creating society, able to reshape itself without the need for cathartic crisis – grew out of earlier traditions of pragmatism, reform and evolution. It stood against, or at least in tension with, the utopian view of an end point to history, imagined as a steady state. It stood against the view of mainstream economics which assumed the market to be self-organising but assumed society to be a follower, and against technological determinists who assumed there would be a flow of new science and technology to which society could only respond.

The radical alternative view, which generalises the ideas of social innovation into a broader account of social change, views the good society not as a teleology but, rather, as a process and movement: a perpetual motion of continuous renewal that is guided not so much by blueprints as by experiments, by imagination more than disciplines, by dialectical emergence rather than linear plans. It relies not so much on periodic structural reforms but on a constant reinvention of systems and structures (through 'structure-denying structures', in the words of Roberto Mangabeira Unger).[7] It asserts, in other words, a deeper ideal of human freedom and potential, contained by human-made laws and rules but not imprisoned by them in perpetuity.[8]

The motives for systematic innovation

Humans are curious and creative beings. But much human ingenuity and creativity goes to waste because our many motives for inventing or trying new things only become effective if they are harnessed, channelled and organised. Through most of human history only three main motives have been linked to organised innovation.

The first motive was victory, for the military and the states they served or captured: finding an edge in warfare through metals, siege engines or warships. This was the primary motive for kings and emperors to devote scarce resources to trying new ideas. Even at the start of the 21st century more than half of all public funding for R&D in the US goes to the military (the sums declined for a time in other countries such as the UK, as a brief peace dividend was realised before the harsher climate of the late 2010s pushed the numbers up again). In many countries it's taken for granted that emerging technologies such as artificial intelligence are primarily the domain of the military long before they pass into commerce and society.

The second motive for organised innovation has been glory: from the pyramids to space exploration, innovation was used to add lustre to a leader or a state. For the wealthy there was experiment in extravagant displays – from water features and fireworks to grand palaces and buildings designed to inspire awe in their observers and works of culture to serve the pleasure and interest of the rich. As Joel Mokyr wrote, in a society with a small, unproductive elite, creativity is directed to their needs, not those of the population: 'the Austrian empire produced Haydn and Mozart but no industrial revolution'.[9] Glory still has its place even in apparently mature democracies, and it's under-rated as a motive for nations building space programmes or seeking a place at the frontier of science.

The third motive has been profit, for the business enterprise and the investor. In the 19th and 20th centuries profit became a more important motive for innovation. From the railways and factories, through chemicals to pharmaceuticals, aerospace to computers, the aim was to achieve returns for investors and owners, which in turn required mass markets and mass consumption. Modern markets have systematised innovation of all kinds: classic research and development of the kind found in industries like pharmaceuticals; design innovation for companies like Apple; service innovation in airlines or banks; and process innovation in firms like Amazon.

In relation to each of these three motives for innovation the mass of the public remained as passive observers. They were sometimes beneficiaries of breakthroughs – from mills to steam power, whether as consumers or citizens. But this was as much a matter of chance as design, since neither their interests nor their voices were a primary motivation for experiment.

Throughout all of these periods there was of course imagination, experiment and discovery in every sphere of society. People continually reimagined their clothing and dance, music and craft. Humans are naturally cooperative and creative and have often created elaborate systems for cooperating at scale. But innovation in civil society lacked the resources, the concentration of effort, brains and money that is so essential to growing ideas and that marks innovation driven by the three primary motives of victory, glory and profit. And so, the fourth cluster of motives for innovation – a social or public benefit – remained confined and weak.

Subsystems with uneven capacities to create

The pattern that took shape was a pattern of uneven development, and its unevenness shaped the modern world. The head of India's central bank, Raghu Rajan, made a similar point when he warned that society is underpinned by three pillars – the market, the state and the community[10] – but that too great a focus on the first two pillars led to a neglect of the third.

We can analyse any society as made up of subsystems – economy, justice, media, civil society, household – each with its own logic and language. Some subsystems have strong feedback loops that reward and encourage innovation and improvements, while others do not. The former progress, sometimes fast. The latter stagnate. And, over time, imbalances grow between the sectors that are intrinsically dynamic and those that are not. The former develop ways of categorising ideas as promising, potentially useful and so worthy of incubation and investment. The slower-moving subsystems, by contrast, lack categories of this kind and the associated supports. New ideas are more likely to be seen as anomalies to suppress or marginalise.

In contemporary Western societies the strongest feedback loops have been found in science-, business- and technology-intensive sectors, fuelled by heavy public subsidy. Science systems were primarily funded by the military until the late 19th century, but then won for themselves strategic support from states that allowed a much broader approach to discovery.

Scientific imagination was in full flood in the 19th century. But it took time to create institutions that could harness that imagination: funds, universities, laboratories, corporate R&D, initially in and around the military but spreading out into the economy. In Germany this took place under the influence of Friedrich List, and half a century later in the US under the influence of Vannevar Bush. A similar pattern transformed medicine, at least in so far as new drugs or clinical procedures are concerned. In these fields evolution was effectively accelerated: not just the invention of new forms, mutations, inventions, but also the organisation of environments that could recognise and then adopt the best ones.

In them there was a line of sight from the conception of an idea through its birth and growth; systems in place that were capable of using and absorbing those ideas; money looking for ideas to fund; and people with jobs to support, measure and manage ideas on their journey, from accountants to lawyers to administrators. In other fields the rewards were much smaller, and the resources available for experiment much more meagre.

Some social goods are supported by fields with at least a degree of formal organisation and therefore some capacity to absorb innovations: childcare, schooling and welfare all were organised not unlike industries, with standards, training and policy systems. Other fields of social activity, by contrast, have lacked anything comparable: the issue of loneliness; the pursuit of happiness; and until recently issues of sexuality or domestic violence.

Social innovation was not unknown in the 19th and 20th centuries and was helped by philanthropy, trusts, foundations, and by more formal social experiments run by municipalities and central governments. But it lagged far behind the deliberate orchestration of innovation in the military and business, hence the imbalance. Social generativity and growth was constrained essentially by lack of organisation, not imagination, so ideas failed to develop and flourish. What this meant was an uneven capability to create viable futures – to imagine, to try out and grow ideas, whether small or large. The social world of civil society instead saw a constant stream of lost futures, conceived but never born, imagined but never built. Other fields – from physics to space exploration, from banking to retail – by contrast, had access to the means to nurture and grow their ideas and their visions of the future.

This imbalance remains very visible today. Contrast, for example, the huge sums invested in technology-driven visions of the future smart city with the meagre investment in future visions that are motivated by notions of social value.

The net result has been predicted: a widening gap between the fast-moving, innovating and experimenting subsystems and the rest. The former pull in surplus resources and talented individuals, and win prestige. The latter stagnate and fail to translate imagination into results, and experience a dissipation of creativity and entropy.

This has big implications for how we think about the social. It explains why societies often feel that they have been left behind. There may be social imagination in generous supply, but without the resources to test, refine and learn, it lacks expression. Alternative ways of organising money, work, care or housing linger as ideas, possibilities that remain latent. Some do succeed in changing the landscape – movements that over time become a common sense, transforming laws as well as daily life. But the great majority do not realise their potential. And so we get growth without happiness, hardware progressing without the corresponding social software and a sense of technologies out of control. We get phenomena like sharp rises in suicide (up a quarter in the US in the first 15 years of this century) along with economic growth.

What follows is a challenge: how to design institutions that can address the misallocation of money and brainpower and access to attention, and help the birth of the new, its incubation and growth.

Cultures of social innovation

Joel Mokyr in his classic account of the Industrial Revolution puts culture centre stage, gently chiding those who claimed that institutions were enough to explain economic growth. Using one of the classic definitions of culture – a 'set of beliefs, values and preferences, capable of affecting behaviour, that are socially (not genetically) transmitted and that are shared by some subset of society'[11] – he shows how these were essential to promote widespread participation not just in invention but also in adoption.

Monarchs exemplify this shift. Queen Elizabeth I responded to being shown a knitting machine by asking: 'Consider you what the invention could do to my poor subjects; it would assuredly bring to them ruin by depriving them of employment.'[12] Her successor, the next Queen Elizabeth, four centuries later, took an opposite view, praising inventors and entrepreneurs and showering them with honours, regardless of how many jobs were destroyed or created.

Institutions matter, Mokyr argued, but 'an economy that grows as a result of favourable institutions' requires more: 'contracts, law and order, a low level of opportunism and rent-seeking, a high degree of inclusion in political decision-making and the benefits of growth, and a political organisation in which power and wealth are as separate as humanly possible'.[13] These in turn are aspects of culture.

Mokyr's writing describes in detail the attitudes and norms that made it easy for people to invest, speculate and invent. There are very equivalent cultures in the social field, patterns of ethos that give shape to the spirit of social change.

How ideas and thoughts are transformed

These cultures have some overlaps with the cultures of economic innovation: openness to ideas; curiosity; a willingness to tinker and experiment; and an admiration for risk takers. Their pioneers are, perhaps even more than in other fields, cantankerous, opinionated, brazen and difficult. Their relative weakness can be a strength, certainly when up against big institutions: as Carl Schmitt put it, 'victory ends curiosity'.[14] Strength breeds complacency. But the innovators also have other distinct characteristics that make the milieux of social innovation different from others. Here I mention a few of the defining cultures of social innovation.

- *Bearing witness*: A first feature of this culture is that it values moving phenomena from invisibility to visibility as the precursor to action. This has happened with experiences of disability, loneliness or abuse that were disguised, covered up and ignored and then, thanks to passionate activism, uncovered and made public. This role of making things visible is helped by marginal and then mainstream media and by campaigns and social organisations that transform private or invisible phenomena into public, social facts. One example of many is Ushahidi, a highly successful digital social innovator, which takes its name from the Swahili for 'testimony'.
- *Frugality*: Civil society has generally been poor, even if charity has often been funded from the largesse, vanity or shame of the very rich. Social innovation tends to value frugal ways of doing things: the lean and cheap, the workaround, the clever ways of making small sums of money go a long way. It favours an aesthetic of simple necessity – plain woods and bricks, without much that's garish or garnishing. Waste is abhorred.
- *Dialectics*: Social innovation is dialectical in nature. Anyone who thought in too linear a way would give up when they faced the inevitable barriers (Michael Young advised innovators to take the response 'no' as a question, not an answer). So we see repeated patterns, starting with externalisation, taking an idea out of and away from the mainstream so that it can grow on its own terms, before it is then reintegrated. This allows imagination to be amplified and then harnessed, learning to see things not as they are but as they could be. Indeed, recognising the liquidness of things is essential to creative social change.
- *Relational growth*: Radical social innovations leave behind transformed social relationships, with more possibility, more equity and more potential liberated. A striking pattern of all progressive social change is that people discover, and then

collaborate with, strangers. They form friendships and fall in love and later leave behind structures that allow similar relationships of trust to be reproduced.

- *Holism*: Unlike the innovation cultures of the military or business, there is a tendency to holism. Looking at things through the experience of individuals, rather than that of the state or a business, emphasises the connection between things, the whole life. As a result, social innovation tends towards dietetics (from the Greek root *diaita*, 'way of life, mode of living' in its widest sense) rather than being concerned only with products or services. So, we see innovators trying to connect the many elements needed for a carbon-free world or a full sense of health and wellbeing.
- *Giving*: Giving is preferred to buying or commanding. The sense of being in a chain provides an ethical anchoring. It means acknowledging inheritances and passing something on, whether that is the inheritance of a rich family or simply the sense of being the beneficiary of the collective richness of a culture or ecology. This drive to belong, to be part of something larger, also connects to the gift of presence and listening: seeing people not just as victims, deficits or lacks but as potentials and assets, so that any gift relationship is reciprocal.
- *Enaction*: In the beginning is the deed, as Goethe wrote, and social innovation has an ethos of learning by doing rather than of theoretical speculation. Francisco Varela suggested the idea of 'enaction', laying a path down by walking it, which describes this ethos too among artists who often say that they only discover what they want to draw or paint through the act of drawing or painting, and something similar happens in social change. Action generates or hardens ideas which rarely grow fully formed in theory.
- *Peace*: Social innovators tend to abhor violence. They draw strength from non-violent ideas: *ahimsa* and *satyagraha* in the Gandhian tradition; the ideas of Tolstoy, Thoreau and other Western writers that so influenced him; and the later practice of figures like Martin Luther King, asserting an ethical power against the guns and an alternative to revolutionary violence.

- *Livingness*: Social innovation emphasises 'livingness' and challenges the greyness and soullessness of bureaucracy and corporate life. Christopher Alexander wrote of places that could be seen as more or less alive, and there is an equivalent in the social domain.[15] Social innovators often want to cultivate joy and then transmit it; to promote dancing, music, the carnival and festival more than the sermon; and to resist what Max Weber called 'specialists without spirit, sensualists without heart'.[16]

These cultural characteristics, which are about aesthetics as well as ethics, shape the qualities of social innovation: its complexity, its wave-like qualities, its sense of motion. They explain why it often rubs against bureaucratic, hierarchical systems which require stable categories and concepts.

Motivations and actors

Who makes things happen? Alice Walker wrote that activism is the rent we pay for living on the earth, but it's a rent we can choose not to pay, and relatively few take it on themselves to be agents of social change in a deep way.[17]

The motivations of people who commit their lives to social change are complex. The positive view of the change makers draws on an earlier tradition in psychoanalytic literature interested in the 'generative personality', and sees these as the people with an integrated maturity. But just as many are motivated by unhappiness, frustration and blockage, and in wealthy societies they include some at least prompted by anomie: the people who 'tick all the boxes but don't feel they exist', with a partner, job and home but without these roles being adequately integrated into a viable sense of the self. Activism offers an alternative to the 'fatigue of being oneself',[18] a route to both social recognition and more enriched individuality.

Much recent writing on social innovation has emphasised the role of individuals: social entrepreneurs, activists and innovators who are given a heroic role in driving change. This narrative tends to trouble others who see the primacy of structures and systems. They view the individual focus at best as distorting and at worst as a diversion from the harder and necessarily collective nature of change.

It's certainly true that invention is rarely the work of only one individual, even though the stories often turn out that way. Innovations tend to swarm – converging on similar ideas at similar times (which is one reason why it is so hard to attribute causation – successful innovations are highly social in nature and have many parents). But without individuals nothing happens, and the purely structural and social accounts fall down on close examination. They are ahistorical in denying the role of detail, the particular chronologies of the lives of people who chose the path of rebellion over comfort and conformism.

So, society has to cultivate rebellious, independent people who distance themselves from the whole in order to help it grow and renew itself, forming alternatives that are first externalised and then later reinternalised. This is a common pattern – with the details of family, history, circumstance, rejection and opportunity making some people idiosyncratic, willing to threaten, challenge and annoy, and to take on the viewpoint of the society and its inner needs.

Individual innovators dominate the stories. But equally important are their supporters and fellow travellers: the enablers who may be philanthropists, civil servants or politicians, who nurture and protect the space for the new, and for the innovators, providing money and moral support, especially when things go wrong, as they inevitably do. Both groups are vehicles for the collective, but are framed by their individual context (which in turn may reflect a grievance, values, guilt or privilege).

Favourable systems

The design question, then, is how their work can be made easier, how to multiply the number of individuals devoting their life to social change and how to improve the odds that they will succeed. Here a useful analogy is with the invisible hand of the market, which creates a reward for the divergent entrepreneur if they can connect to the spending power of consumers, a hand that depends on many supportive institutions, including fair laws, competition authorities and often generous public subsidy for research and development. What societies generally lack, but need, is a comparable invisible hand that can give expression and reward to a self-organising civil society: like the invisible hand of the market, with laws, taxes and institutions that can enable new ideas to grow and spread, but in this case harnessing other motivations of care, giving and belonging.

These supports can take many forms, as they do in science and business: funds (from philanthropy or government); incubators and laboratories; research that's opened up to social innovation; universities providing courses and research programmes; social movements generating their own momentum, from shops and products to model communities. These are easier where there are strong structures linked to the production of social goods, staffed by people whose job it is to run parks, schools, welfare centres or public health programmes; it is harder when these are missing.

When?

What contexts make it more likely that these cultures and systems will take shape? The current growth of interest in social innovation has been helped by crisis, the widespread acknowledgement of problems that existing structures and policies have found it impossible to crack – such as climate change, the world-wide epidemic of chronic disease and widening inequality. These are all issues which cut across the boundaries between the state, the market and the household, between different parts of the state and between national states themselves. As a result, the classic tools of government policy, on the one hand, and market solutions, on the other, have proved inadequate.

Attention also turns to social innovation because the prospective cost of dealing with these threatens to swamp public budgets – and in the case of climate change, or healthcare in the US, private budgets as well. In health, as in climate change, pollution control, waste reduction, poverty and welfare programmes, and other fields such as criminal justice or traffic congestion, the most effective policies are preventive. 'End of pipe' measures are costly. But effective prevention has been notoriously difficult to introduce, in spite of its transparent economic and social benefits.

As in earlier technological and social transformations, there is a disjunction between the structures and institutions formed in a previous period and the requirements of the new. This is as true for the private as for the social economy. New paradigms tend to flourish in areas where the institutions are most open to them, and where the forces of the old are weak. So, for example, there is more innovation around self-management of diseases and public health than around hospitals; more innovation around recycling and energy efficiency than around large-scale energy production; more innovation around public participation than in parliaments and assemblies; more innovation around active ageing than around pensions provision; more innovation around new kinds of money, using blockchain and other technology, than around monetary policy.

Where?

Where does social innovation thrive? Traditionally, those social tasks for which the private market is inadequate have fallen to three quite different economies: the state, the household and the grant economy. Each has its own means of obtaining resources, each its own structures of control and allocation, its own rules and customs for the distribution of its outputs, and its principles of reciprocity. In the industrial economies of the 20th century, nations reached different settlements about the border lines and responsibilities of each. In Western Europe and Canada, the state played the leading role. In the US a tradition of resistance to 'big government' left households to manage as best they could, with a greater role played by charitable foundations (though still with a large state, by historical standards, and one that has played a role in funding a number of major commercial innovations).

Each is problematic when seen through the social innovation lens. The state is associated with coercion; the market with blindness to social value; the traditional gift economy with an unacceptable inequality of power and respect between giver and beneficiary. Yet each can also be a space for innovation, as governments create labs, as businesses create corporate social innovation programmes and old foundations take on the language of empowerment.

So, social innovation refers not to any particular sector of the economy but to innovation in the creation of social outputs and outcomes regardless of where they spring from (the shaded area in Figure 2.1), stretching far beyond the traditional third sector or civil society.

It leads to new questions. How can markets be reshaped so that they meet the goals of the social economy and aren't incentivised to dump costs onto society and the environment? This has been the mission of much recent environmental policy that seeks to internalise costs and benefits that were previously external, reframing regulations and incentives to this end. It has also influenced policies around disability (for example, requiring employers to take on a percentage of disabled employees); training (requiring investment in employees' human capital); or in India, where a share of profits has to be directed to social projects.

Within the state it prompts questions about procurement (how open, how disaggregated); about the shape of delivery (from networks like Buurtzorg to social movements in health); and

Figure 2.1: The spaces for social innovation

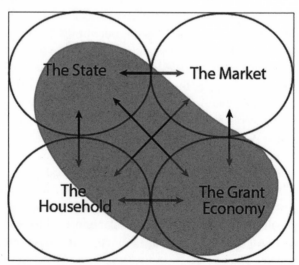

about the role of the citizen (how much to prioritise mobilising volunteers to enhance public services).

Within the market, the pressures for social innovation lead to questions of business model and growth. How should business collaborate with social movements – for example, around plastics in the oceans or improving support for mental health in the workplace? How big a role should there be for social enterprises (like the Mondragon group of cooperatives in Spain or BRAC, now the world's largest NGO); for new methods like the open source software which underpins much of the internet;[19] or for 'platform cooperativism', which offers ways to provide care, taxis or housing through internet-based worker or consumer cooperatives rather than traditional companies?

Within the household there is also a changed view of what is possible. The consumer changes from a passive to an active player, not only as a navigator of exuberant choice but as a producer in their own right.[20] Retail purchases that have been cast as the end point of the linear process of mass production are part of a circular process of household production and reproduction. The consumer doubles as a domestic producer – a cook, a parent, a carer, a shopper, a driver, a nurse, a gardener, a teacher or student and sometimes an innovator too.

This domestic sphere, previously seen as outside the economy, as too complex and ungovernable, comes to be recognised as critical economically, with all the needs of support, tools, skills and advice that being a producer entails. Moreover, if we accept that working hours are likely to continue their very long decline, the household may also be the place where we all spend more time in the future, including in old age. The world's population has never been older. But the world's population has also never had as many years left to live.

Once again, though, the household is also the site for conflicting visions. One is symbolised by the smart home, using the tools of Amazon, Google or Samsung to make the home as efficient as an office or factory in harvesting data and optimising processes. An alternative view sees the home as a place for creation: home learning, cultural production or craft as well as digital making (photography, video, music, for example), families that talk to each other and do things together rather than living separate lives within their own digital bubbles.[21]

Looking at these fields, the relationships between them are as significant as the relationships within them. The first interface is between the various sections of the state and the civil economy. Central to this first interface is the way finance crosses the borders, inwards in the form of taxation and fees, and outwards in the form of grants, procurement and investment. There are many others, including the regulatory, fiscal and legal conditions determined by the state, and the platforms and tools provided by the state for the actors in other parts of the social economy. These are vital for innovation – and have also been a field of innovation themselves (for example, in new types of social investment, outcome-based budgeting, commissioning or support for platforms).

The second interface is between the private market and the household. In the private market this is well-worn terrain, since it is where firms operate, selling products and services to households and trying to influence the work, still mainly done by women, that sustains homes and families. The extent to which social networks and a gift economy operate in the sphere of consumption has long been remarked on by anthropologists, for example (from Christmas presents to buying rounds of beer).[22]

There is then the subject of household time and how it relates to social production and innovation. This is partly a question of visibility, and acknowledgement of the voluntary time contributed by the household sector, either individually or collectively, in some form of credits for cash or public rights and reduced obligations.

Systemic change and circuits

To overcome the resistance of the old requires systemic change: often an interaction of social movements, new laws, newly shaped markets and technologies that allow a new system to act and coordinate in novel ways.

The pioneers of the current technological revolution did not have to worry about the context for putting their ideas into practice. While much of the finance for the fundamental ideas came from the state, and the investment in turning them into viable products came from venture capital, that context was the market, with all its established structures to promote innovation: individual property rights, trademarks and patents, joint stock companies and capital markets, accountancy rules, financial regulations and so on. Firms could start small, accumulate capital, take over other firms or be taken over, sell their services to others and buy in other services. Each one of these has its history (and controversies), but to an entrepreneur in Silicon Valley they have been 'naturalised'. They are part of the economic fabric and fall outside an individual company's sphere of concern.

When it comes to the state, innovation is harder. In a market, the point of exchange transfers goods and services from one party to another, and transfers money in return; the amount of money that is returned – the price – becomes a signal and provides the incentive and discipline for the economic actors involved. These three functions, unified in the process of exchange, are separated in the state. The state is structured as a system of levies and bounties. The transfer of money and the delivery of services are no longer part of a single, individual transaction but are social aggregations. Services are provided free, and their cost is funded by compulsory levies (taxation). Because this is not a commodity economy there are no prices, and the determination of the magnitude of the taxes raised, the allocation of the revenues and the overall provision of public services – in other words, the function of guidance and discipline of the public economy – requires a separate structure of governance and accountability through politicians.

The public economy is aggregated and centralised. It offers strong incentives not to take risks, and fuzzy links at best between actions and results or rewards. What is remarkable – given these structures – is how much innovation there has been in the public sphere. Globally, examples range from the NASA moon landing to CERN and the creation of the World Wide Web; from innovative welfare-to-work programmes to childcare; from holistic public health to smart cards. Contemporary examples range from the hugely ambitious Aadhaar identity system in India to China's social credit system; from Estonia's creation of e-citizenship for non-residents to Taiwan's reimagining of democracy as collective intelligence in vTaiwan. In the UK, state pensions, the BBC, the NHS and the Open University are only a fraction of the 20th-century public innovations that shape culture and society in Britain today. Yet a striking feature of these innovations is how many have come at the edges of the state, often at arm's length from the central structures, or below the radar of high politics.

Innovation is uncertain in its costs and effects. The potential costs and difficulties are unlikely to be counterbalanced by incentives, since the savings generated will rarely accrue to the innovators. All money is taxpayers' money, so that if anything goes wrong in any part of the public sphere it contaminates the whole. Given the degree of transparency for public finances and performance and the adversarial character of its politics, not only is there a disincentive to take risks, but there is also a pressure for the centre to keep a close eye on performance in every corner of government.

To open up public finance, to make its connections more tangible, more connected to those funding and those receiving public services, both funding and accountability need to be distributed. At one pole is the personalised budget – or, in its Danish form, the citizen's account, whereby each citizen has a public account, parallel to a bank account, to which they contribute, to which credits are allocated according to rights and which is debited according to the citizen's public expenditure.

Here accountability on the principles of allocation rests with the relevant level of government, but service accountability is directly to the user, as in a market, and the choice open to the user can act as a spur to innovation. But such methods can apply only where a service is individualised. For more inherently collective services – such as a park or community centre or regeneration programme – other methods are called for, like participatory budgeting or matched crowdfunding, that can introduce a comparable transparency, engagement and heat into the process of making decisions.

Data, knowledge and intelligence

The mirror of money as the fuel for action is the role of data, information and knowledge that support decisions and actions. Here we see a new battleground as well as new tools. The ubiquity of data can be a constraint on civic power as it is used in coercive ways by governments or in predatory ways by big companies.

But in other forms it makes new actions possible. It can make the financial operations of the state more visible – as OpenFisca has done in France. It can make new patterns visible – like the very localised effects of neighbourhoods on life chances in the US. It can usher in new forms of power – as when citizens generate data on such things as flooding in cities or gather data on corrupt officials. Combined with artificial intelligence, it can help to predict harms and needs, so that social programmes are better aimed where they can achieve most.

'Open data', 'AI for good', 'tech for good', 'digital social innovation' – these are some of the labels for emergent fields of civic innovation that in their most developed forms turn into comprehensive systems for collective intelligence, or what I call 'intelligence assemblies' that link together observation, analysis, prediction and action. Again, however, they are easier to progress on the boundaries of the state – one step away from the ferocious gaze of daily media or adversarial politics.

Threat and challenge

All innovation systems risk stagnation. They can become comfortable. Our default is inertia. Elsewhere I have written about the forces that prevent change and how they can be overcome;[23] how the old becomes efficient, as institutions get used to each other; how it becomes locked into interests, mentalities and relationships. So that even those wanting to change find themselves repeating the refrain 'I'm so busy with my job, I have no time for the new'.

Only when an external threat appears is this inertia jolted. And so, a good design feature for any innovation system is that it should be contestable and challengeable.

Beyond the imbalances

Imbalances in capacities to innovate have marked modernity. Some sectors have evolved sophisticated means for finding, developing and growing new ideas, and have grown related cultures. Others have lagged behind.

But in the early 21st century society, in all its forms, is beginning to create a comparable alignment of culture, money, law and institutions to the systems created around material innovation in science and the economy. The common aim is to construct a more comprehensive invisible hand that can turn a range of social motivations into a public benefit – wellsprings of love, care, cooperation and hope.

These don't solve the manifold problems of conflict, distrust and messy compromise. But they do widen the space of possibility and they offer an answer to contrary forces that hark back to opposite ideals.

The heart of this more radical idea of social innovation is a deeper reimagining of democracy, with rule by the people also implying the capacity to create options and not just to choose between competing programmes, parties or leaders. In response to the manifold problems of modern democracy – the inadequacy of representation; the distortions of information and perception; the corruptions of party systems – it offers an amplification of agency, proposing the universal right to shape both the present and future, fuelled by associated tools, as well as knowledge, money and power.

Democracy, in short, is no longer only equated with state power, but is generalised, and also fused with innovation. The assumption is an untapped capability to govern, in the widest sense, that is dependent on an ecosystem of information, experience and knowledge.

In the novel *Light Years*, James Salter's narrator observes: 'Acts demolish their alternatives, that is the paradox.'[24] Social evolution narrows options. Social innovation, by contrast, aims to do the opposite.

Part II
Challenges, roadblocks and systems

In this part I turn to the political context for social innovation. In the 2000s it was riding a wave of relatively benign progress. Economic growth across much of the world coincided with reductions in poverty and other social harms, as well as the rapid spread of democracy.

A decade later, as the full shock of the financial crisis and austerity had taken their toll, politics was moving in a much less favourable direction.

3

The political context for social innovation now: Thesis, antithesis and synthesis

Introduction

In the heady days of 1989, with communism collapsing and the Cold War seemingly over, the political theorist Francis Fukuyama declared that we were witnessing the 'end of history',[1] which had culminated in the triumph of liberal democracy and the free market, aided by a succession of powerful technologies. Fukuyama was drawing on the ideas of Hegel, but of course history didn't come to an end, and the Cold War was just sleeping, not dead.[2]

Now we're at a very different turning point, which many are trying to make sense of. I want to suggest that we can again usefully turn to Hegel, but this time to his idea that history evolves in dialectical ways, with successive phases of thesis, antithesis and synthesis. He (and Marx after him) implied that we should see history, and progress, not as a straight line but, rather, as a zigzag, shaped by the ways in which people bump into barriers or face disappointments and then readjust their course.

This framework helps to make sense of where we stand today. The 'thesis' that has dominated mainstream politics for the last generation – and continues to be articulated shrilly by many proponents – is the claim that the combination of globalisation, technological progress and liberalisation empowers the great majority. Some parts of the social innovation field allied with this claim, advocating the application of markets and managerial principles to ever more fields, confident that for every social problem there was a ready-made solution that needed only to be found and scaled.

The antithesis, which, in part, fuelled the votes for Brexit and Trump, as well as the rise of populist parties and populist authoritarian leaders in Europe and beyond, is the argument that this technocratic combination merely empowers a minority and disempowers the majority of citizens. The job of governments is therefore to take us back to a safer world, with secure boundaries, a strong sense of nationhood and an economy providing well-paid jobs, predominantly in manufacturing.

A more progressive synthesis, which I outline, addresses the flaws of the thesis and the grievances of the antithesis in fields ranging from education and health to democracy and migration, dealing head on with questions of power and its distribution: questions both about who has power and about who feels powerful. It articulates how a knowledge economy can be truly inclusive and how society can learn to solve its own problems. This is the broader political context for social innovation, the maximalist complement to the minimalist promise of small projects and grassroots ideas.

The thesis

The thesis, in essence, was simple: increasing globalisation and liberalisation, combined with waves of new technology would empower everyone. The more we acceded to this, the faster the benefits would spread. Better jobs, more money, greater freedoms, increased opportunities … everyone would be a winner in the end, even if many had to find new skills along the way.

Since the 1970s this was the message from political and corporate leaders, in speeches and opinion pieces, conferences and talks. Books by journalists and business gurus breathlessly proclaimed that the world was now flat, borderless and open, rendering old attachments irrelevant. It was an article of faith that more openness, and more flows (of capital, people, goods and information), would contribute to the public good.

The internet was a great symbol of this, bringing information and data across boundaries and connecting huge swathes of the world's population. Social media would end isolation. Smart machine-learning tools would solve problems, with artificial intelligence applied not just to search engines but also to healthcare, criminal justice, climate change and humanitarian disasters.

The thesis was symbolised in futuristic visions of hypermobility, where fleets of flying cars and drones would overcome barriers of physical distance. As consumers we'd find goods and services at the beck and call of our mobile devices, while Amazon would drop parcels in our front gardens, taking us to a seamless future where life would become effortless and frictionless.

The optimists could point to extraordinary achievements. The years since 1950 have indeed seen unprecedented advances in prosperity: dramatic rises in life expectancy (up 40 years during the 20th century); greater democracy; and falls in poverty (to less than 10% of the world's population). Sunny forecasts that these trends would continue were given confidence by the continuing falls in the price of computing and genomics, and by the rising ambitions of hundreds of millions in India, China and elsewhere.

For the business world, the dramatically declining costs of starting a new firm – particularly in the digital economy – offered the prospect of a far more open and inclusive economy in which you could sell your ideas or wares, taking advantage of platforms, whether from your bedroom or in a remote rural area.

It seemed obvious that we could extrapolate to a future of ever more integration and ever more benefits from floods of new technologies, from virtual and augmented reality to gene sequencing. This was a positive and optimistic story about where the world was going, and a story with plenty of hard evidence to support it.

The antithesis

The counter to these arguments was also simple. In its more coherent forms it accepted some of the thesis, but argued that the combination of globalisation, technology and liberalisation empowered a small, wealthy and mobile 'elite' but did little or nothing for the majority and, in fact, often damaged their interests, threatening their jobs and communities.

This antithesis found its voice in politics, everyday conversation and social media. It claimed that large minorities had seen their incomes stagnate. Even larger numbers feared that their children would be worse off than them, and probably jobless, thanks to the combination of migration and automation. The antithesis could point to trends in technology which continue to be capital-biased, meaning a declining share of income for labour, compounded by lax treatment of corporate taxation by governments, which were often run by political parties directly funded by big business and finance.

It could show that, to the extent that jobs were being created, they were concentrating in particular areas – those with high levels of graduates – benefiting the highly educated and well-connected but doing little for the low-skilled.

The famous 'elephant chart' (from Lakner–Milanovic)[3] showed this at a global level: although the poor and middle classes of China and India had seen extraordinary gains in prosperity, and the global rich got richer, the relatively poor of the developed world had seen their incomes stagnate and even fall. Though the detail could be challenged, the bigger story was clearly accurate.

Within the rich countries, GDP and productivity growth no longer correlated with job growth – the 'jaw of the snake' shown in another much-discussed diagram from the US Department of Labor[4] – and now there was the prospect of accelerating jobless growth. In the US, for example, in many states the most common job is that of truck driver, a role eminently vulnerable to larger versions of the kind of driverless vehicles that have appeared on the streets of Las Vegas and Pittsburgh.

Automation threatened millions of jobs. According to the Organisation for Economic Co-operation and Development (OECD), which has been sceptical of some of the bigger forecasts of job loss, many rich countries had only small proportions of their workforce in the kind of high-performance jobs that were least likely to be replaced by machines.

In this view, although holders of capital were set to do well, having already prospered massively from the huge infusions of credit that followed the financial crash, most of the population, often still on incomes lower than in 2007 and in less secure jobs, had little to look forward to.

The effects of these shifts were more than economic. Precariousness leads to both mental and physical ill-health. In the US, the Nobel Prize-winning economist Angus Deaton showed the rising mortality rates among middle-aged white men, and that 'deaths of despair' – from suicide, opioids and liver disease – had a strong correlation with areas voting for Donald Trump.

Peak employment might already have been reached, certainly for groups like middle-aged men. A parallel pattern could be seen in global trade: it had been assumed that it was bound to grow, but data from the mid-2010s suggests that we may have already passed a moment of peak trade, too.

The sense of a turning point against the thesis was evident even before Brexit and Trump. In May 2016, Jeff Immelt of General Electric, and one of the world's more thoughtful CEOs (chief executive officers), said: 'The globalisation I knew, based on trade and global integration, is changing, which is why it's time for a bold pivot. And in the face of a protectionist global environment ... we will localize ... We are going through a transformational change in globalisation, which will require fresh, new thinking.'[5]

Technology was another battle ground where remorseless trends might be turning around. The technologies that were meant to empower us could easily now be the enemy of freedom and opportunity. The internet was meant to be for everyone but was instead dominated by a handful of mega-companies that sell our data without our conscious consent. Billboards that read your face not just for your age, gender and ethnicity but also for your degree of attention are good symbols of this fusion of capitalism and Orwell's *1984*, in which the public are only passive, disempowered consumers.

At the very least, it's clear that the central economic and technological promise of the thesis was not being delivered for large minorities. But the problem wasn't only economic. Since 1989 it had seemed obvious that democracy was the only plausible governing model for advanced societies, and that its competitors (fascism, communism, dictatorship) had been defeated for good. Now that confidence had been shaken.

In the old democracies, where the forms of democracy have changed little since the 19th century, large minorities lost faith not just in politicians and political institutions but even in democracy itself. This was particularly true among younger age groups. Many social democratic parties which had been a vehicle for radical social hopes had compromised with global capitalism (Eduardo Galeano noted that 'power is like a violin you pick it up with your left hand and play it with your right'[6]). But that strategy had run out of steam, failing to deal with the new imbalances.

It had also seemed obvious that the world was becoming ever healthier. But now we were seeing a growing risk of epidemics and pandemics and the threat of rising antimicrobial resistance which could threaten tens of millions of lives by mid-century – in part an effect of a much more connected world with far more travel. And in some countries – including the UK – life expectancy had stalled or even started to fall by the early 2010s.

After a period when large parts of the world thought that war was a thing of the past, confrontation between heavily armed, technologically advanced countries became a serious prospect again, with Russia a belligerent aggressor around Europe, Saudi Arabia gaining a taste for military action and China flexing its muscles in Asia.

All these shifts affected large parts of the world. But they were most unsettling for Europe, which once thought of itself as the centre of the world. Now it was becoming marginal, with its share of global population shrinking rapidly (from 22% of world population in 1950 to 12% in 2000 and a forecast 6% in 2100).

The net result of all these trends is anxiety and powerlessness. People were promised that the currents of change – economic, social and technological – would make them feel powerful. Instead they see decisions being made by political and corporate leaders ever further away from them. They feel like observers, not participants. Indeed, according to one Edelman poll in early 2019[7] only one in five of the 33,000 people surveyed in 27 countries felt the system was working for them and over 70% voiced a desire for change and a sense of injustice about the status quo.

Trust in the powerful

One response is to project hopes onto powerful leaders who promise to fix things. Our powerlessness is solved vicariously through faith, as has happened so often in human history. And so, we see the rising tide of populist authoritarian nationalism in every region of the world, in the US (Trump), Russia (Putin) and parts of Europe (from Marine Le Pen in France to Lega Nord in Italy and Alternativ für Deutschland in Germany), echoed in China under President Xi, India under Prime Minister Modi and Japan under Prime Minister Abe.

Other countries have yet to follow them, but with polling suggesting that large majorities believe their countries to be heading in the 'wrong direction' it's easy to see how that list could extend quickly.

These authoritarian leaders are less afraid of taking state action. But populists tend to be better at opposition than governing and often burn out fast. So how should we respond? What is a more constructive response to the current situation?

Simply to assert the old thesis ever more stridently doesn't work, though it has been a comforting response for media outlets, thought leaders and politicians. Instead, we need to design a new synthesis which, in true Hegelian fashion, adapts the thesis in light of the antithesis. It needs to avoid both nostalgia and the fetishisation of globalisation and technological advance as ends in themselves, rather than as means. And it needs to take seriously the complaints of the bypassed and excluded, the hundreds of millions who feel left behind in a slow lane while the rest of the world hurtles off into a future that's not for them.

Zombie orthodoxies

A starting point should be a ruthless willingness to do away with zombie orthodoxies. An oddity of the modern world is that policy approaches that don't work often survive because of inertia. Here is Paul Romer, then newly appointed Chief Economist of the World Bank, speaking candidly in September 2016 about the limits of his own profession: 'For more than three decades, macroeconomics has gone backwards ... respect for highly regarded leaders evolves into a deference to authority that displaces objective fact from its position as the ultimate determinant of scientific truth.'[8] Similar comments could be made about other fields, or indeed about political parties that so easily get trapped in their own zombie orthodoxies, certainties that survive decades longer than they deserve to.

Many attitudes, cultures and institutions have survived long after the conditions in which they made sense: the belief in growth as a good in itself; institutions devoted to the preservation of arcane beliefs; vestiges of feudalism.

The power test and the potential test

Social innovation is, at root, a promise of power: power not only to receive but also to shape.

If the main source of the strident antithesis is a sense of disempowerment, then this is where an alternative must start – not only shifting power to the people, but also ensuring that people feel that power as well. Social innovation encourages us, in other words, to apply a power test to each area of public policy or social action: does it share power? Is it designed in ways that will help people to feel power over their own lives?

In what follows I briefly map out some directions of travel in a dozen fields stretching from education through health and democracy to the ways government works. In each case what's needed is not a blueprint but, rather, a combination of top-down reform, using the unique powers of the state, with bottom-up experimentation and creativity.

Recasting the knowledge economy

In the economy the goal desired by many countries is easy to describe: a high-productivity, high-knowledge and learning society, providing plenty of opportunities for good jobs. But achieving this is much harder, or at least harder in an inclusive way.

There is no plausible route map to economic growth in the 21st century that doesn't involve a further advance of the knowledge economy. This is true whether you care nothing about climate change or whether you see it as the central challenge of our times. In either case progress requires a greater deployment of knowledge of all kinds, embodied in goods, production processes and people.

Many nations and cities have learned how to cultivate dynamic vanguards; creative quarters; knowledge industries; universities buzzing with spin-offs; technology hubs and incubators. But far fewer have spread the benefits widely. Instead the knowledge economy has become contained: concentrated in the biggest cities, with the gap between them and the rest widening, just as the gap between the most productive firms and the rest has widened and the gap between the highest paid and the average has widened too. Within markets information and knowledge encourage economies of scale, since the marginal costs of products and services tend to zero; hence the new dynamics of monopoly. The same applies to places, where the agglomeration of talent and knowledge creation creates a dynamic that widens the gap with the left-behind. There are also powerful new economies of scope, particularly for the dominant platforms that can diversify, rapidly extending their power from one industry to another – as Google has done, from search to cars, and as Amazon has done, moving into every field of retailing and then into cloud services.

As people grapple with these new concentrations it's not surprising that education has become a vector of political disagreement. Those excluded from the knowledge economy are the most likely to reject it, as is shown by strong correlations between education levels and votes for Trump, Brexit and the populist Right in Europe.

So, we need to maintain the momentum of a deepening knowledge economy, but with a different distributional effect. We need to maintain the dynamism of the vanguard groups, places and firms, but with much more effective ways to spread the opportunities.

How is that to be done?

Some of the tools are familiar. They can involve more aggressive competition policy; more deliberate industrial policies to spread adoption of new tools, like data analytics or artificial intelligence

(AI). Others are newer, like more encouragement of open source technologies, or tougher requirements on big firms to open up their data, or reimagining the internet as a publicly accountable public service.

Perhaps the biggest shift needed is to reverse the priorities that so shaped late 20th-century technology. The dominant model, established by Vannevar Bush in the US and adopted elsewhere, fuelled research and development primarily through the military. Whether it was aviation, computing or sensors, the first priority was to upgrade the military; next came spin-offs to business; and only many years later did attention turn to possible social uses. In the US, DARPA (the Defense Advanced Research Projects Agency) takes credit for many of the innovations that we use today: not just the internet but also innovations, from graphical user interfaces to speech recognition, from LCDs (liquid crystal displays) to AI, all funded first for their military potential. Another government programme, the Small Business Innovation Research programme, is the largest source of early-stage funding for hi-tech companies in the US; 97% of its funding comes from national security agencies. The result of this history is that the world has some extraordinarily sophisticated military forces, able to deploy missiles with remarkable precision, but, by contrast, has made far less progress in dealing with basic social tasks, such as care for the elderly.

At least three other fundamental shifts will also be needed. The first is to support the wider distribution and adoption of the tools and capabilities of the 21st-century economy. The 21st century brought a concentration of funding on venture capital, urban hubs and top universities. That was a necessary phase for many countries that otherwise risked losing out on the generation of high-growth start-ups, particularly in digital industries. But it now needs to be matched by an equally energetic approach to the distribution of skills and tools, helping smaller businesses and social enterprises, or businesses in outlying regions, to become equally adept at using tools like data or AI.

This is not an entirely new task; it was key to German industrial policy in the late 19th century, and to US industrial policy in various phases of both the 19th and 20th centuries. But their lessons have generally been forgotten. If the knowledge economy isn't present and relevant, and accessible to all, we shouldn't be surprised if voters are attracted by anachronistic promises of a return to a previous model of economic life.

New approaches to industrial policy are also becoming necessary. There are signs of diminishing competition; more 'winner takes all' markets, with the most successful achieving wider margins and buying up competitors more than before. So much of industrial policy is having to be rethought. Earlier ideas about mission-led investment don't quite work when new concentrations of power consolidate so quickly. Instead, we need more activist competition policy that requires big firms to open up their data to allow challengers to grow.

The other great challenge concerns the material economy. Some have learned to shift towards a circular economy where materials are reused, greatly reducing carbon emissions and energy use through regulation, supply chain reorganisation, use of standards and so on. China has made this an ever more central priority for government, even as the US has wobbled. The overall goal is to amplify the growth of immaterial elements and to slow down and then reverse growth in material use.

Some of this can be achieved through big redirections of R&D: some through laws, taxes and regulations, and some through directing the new tools of 'anticipatory regulation' to trying out new approaches. But perhaps the most interesting challenge for next-generation industrial policy is how to accelerate complementary innovations. Technologies evolve in relation to other technologies, not alone, and this is particularly true of the most fundamental ones. Just as important, technological innovations generally rely on complementary social and institutional innovations to really work.

The car is a good example. Why did it take from the 1880s to the 1950s before it really had a big effect on society and the economy? Some of the reasons had to do with technical improvements in engine performance. But the more important reasons had to do with the slow pace of complementary innovations: tyres, materials, petrol production and refining, garages, driving schools, speed restrictions, social norms (for example, around drink-driving), urban planning that favoured suburbs and so on.

The same was true of electricity. Again, it faced technical challenges, but just as important was the growth of complementary industries: white goods, skyscrapers, a transformed gender division of labour, models for regulating utilities and hundreds of other innovations.

Why does this matter? It matters because it's a fair guess that some of the biggest productivity advances of the near future will depend on precisely equivalent complementary elements, including social innovations.

Driverless cars are an obvious example. They don't just need AI that actually works and that can cope with everyday challenges like rain and snow. They also need new rules on liability; charging patterns (both energy and financial) and business models; rules on how they move between areas they know well and areas they don't; and a thousand and one other details. Drones are the same. To become part of the mainstream of city life they need new rules on noise, where they can fly, how they land, and they also need business models for retail delivery or human transport and protocols for handling data in real time.

The use of AI in healthcare is just as profound an example that not only depends on progressing the technology but also on new rules, and probably on institutions for data (Who owns it? What are the penalties for abuse? What transparency is there for algorithms?). It will mean new habits for doctors, nurses and patients; new processes for linking narrowly defined health data to related data sets ranging from genomics to finance; and new rights for the beneficiaries. For all of these reasons the narrow thinking of classic industrial policy is now obsolete.

Education that grows makers and shapers

Every survey of current and future skills needs in the workforce confirms that education has to be about more than the transmission of knowledge, important as this is. It needs to also cultivate the ability to solve problems, to work in teams and to create and invent.

That's why we need schooling models that give young people experience of agency, of making the world around them rather than just observing it. Education that passes the power test will also be better aligned with the needs of the economy and social mobility.

Programmes to teach coding are of limited direct use (not least because much of the work of coding will be done by AI in the near future). But they have an indirect value in helping children to think, helping them to understand the digital world around them and how to be a maker, not just a consumer. Project-based learning, entrepreneurship embedded into schooling – the sort of models promoted by High Tech High in the US, Lumiar in Brazil or studio schools in England – are a response to feelings of disempowerment. They are also aligned with what we know labour markets will be demanding in the future – more ability to work in teams, solve problems and create. This should be obvious. But education policy in many countries is running in an opposite direction.

Adult skills taken seriously

Few doubt that millions of jobs will either disappear or change as a result of automation and other pressures. As that reality dawns, attention will turn to adult education and retraining to help the millions at risk of losing their jobs adapt to growing industries.

Some countries like the UK lack mature systems for supporting lifelong learning, despite great traditions – from the Workers' Educational Association to the Open University. But even in these countries with stronger infrastructures governments will need to do much more. One is to provide funding and new entitlements. Singapore and France show one way forward, offering adults personal accounts with which they can buy training (through SkillsFuture in Singapore and France's Compte Personnel de Formation). The scales are modest – an annual 150 hours entitlement for each adult in France and $500 in Singapore – but the levels of support are set to rise. Tax changes are also needed. Some countries (again including Singapore) use the tax system to encourage firms to invest more in their lower-paid workers. Public finance is also likely to be needed to help people on low incomes take time out of work to upgrade their skills.

To reinforce these, the state will need to be much more active in providing tools to help people navigate their way through new skills and careers in the light of what's known about likely patterns of job growth and destruction.[9] No country has got this right, though Scandinavia has some fine traditions of adult education. But some countries, including the UK, which cut funding for adult skills by nearly 50% in the 2010s, have got this particularly wrong.

People-powered health

Similar considerations apply in health. We need the best possible healthcare, provided by experts using the best available technologies. But we also need patients and the public to take more power and responsibility for their own health.

Contemporary healthcare reflects a huge imbalance of funding over the 20th century. There has been very welcome investment in R&D to find new drugs, new clinical procedures and new medical technologies. But there has been vastly less investment to discover answers to what we know are the bigger causes of premature death: environmental, social and behavioural factors. Meanwhile the effectiveness of R&D spend in pharmaceuticals has been on a steady downward slope since 1950, soaking up ever more money and delivering ever fewer useful drugs.[10]

One necessary shift is a big redirection of resources to experimentation and evidence gathering around social health. A parallel shift is needed in care itself. Nesta has supported many of these under the label 'people powered health': peer-to-peer mutual support; digital tools to help people manage their own conditions and those of others around them; promoting social movements; and showing how digital technologies can amplify people's feelings of power over health and how people with Parkinson's disease or dementia can become more active in shaping research and practice.

As a result of the work of pioneers all over the world there are now plausible alternative visions of future healthcare – with less activity centred in large hospitals; more care at home or in the workplace; more use of digital technology and genomics; and more mobilisation of social resources to help.

This should be obvious. But the way healthcare is presented, and argued about in politics, leaves the public as angry, disempowered observers looking on as hospitals are shut or services are changed, rather than as collaborators.

Welfare to address risk and precarity

All over the world welfare is in flux, and for very different reasons (I set out in the next chapter some of the reforms needed). The crucial question is whether welfare addresses the most important current needs, and whether it uses the most effective current tools. In many countries welfare fails both tests. It doesn't adequately address burgeoning needs for eldercare, or security in precarious labour markets. And it makes little use of digital tools that could make it feasible for governments to offer a much wider range of financial supports, including loans repaid over the recipient's lifetime.

The current experiments in basic income in Finland, the Netherlands and Canada are welcome in showing a willingness to think more creatively. But they don't address the most important risks and needs, and may not be legitimate. They are a standardised response to needs that are by their nature very diverse (thanks to varied family size, levels of disability, age and so on). But although basic income is the wrong answer to the right question we need more, not less, experiment, and parts of the answer will probably look quite like a basic income, but aimed at particular groups.

Some of that experiment could point the way to a more comprehensive national care service that provides transparent, comprehensible rights to care for the frail elderly. Creativity is also needed around precarity: for example, in 19 of the OECD countries the self-employed are not entitled to unemployment benefit, and in ten they are not insured for accidents. New tools to insure against and to pool risk are clearly needed as the digital economy fragments the very nature of work.

Open and inclusive innovation

Dynamic innovation has to play a decisive role in creating new opportunities and jobs. But some rightly fear that, done wrong, it can widen divisions, with a wealthy few in small clusters enjoying unprecedented opportunities, and little trickling down or out. That's why many countries need to consider how to make innovation policy itself both more dynamic and more inclusive.

An important recent study demonstrated this in relation to inventive capacity. Analysing 1.2 million inventors in the US over a 20-year period, it showed a very strong correlation between parental influence, direct experience of invention and quality of schooling and the likelihood of a child's ending up as an inventor. Children born into wealthy families where the parents had direct involvement in science and technology were far more likely to become inventors themselves. The implication was that the majority of bright children's potential was going to waste. This led the researchers to argue that shifting public resources from tax incentives towards subsidising more opportunities for invention in early childhood would amplify the creative and economic potential of the US.[11] The study also showed geographical effects: growing up in an area with a large and innovative industry made it more likely that children would become inventors.

Innovation policy in most countries is primarily about big companies, top universities and research centres. These will inevitably dominate. But if they monopolise money and attention it's hardly surprising that the public may feel that the future is being done to them rather than for them. And if the decisions are mainly made by men (only 2% of venture capital funding in the US went to female-run start-ups in 2017, only 0.0006% of venture capital funding since 2019[12] went to firms started by black women, while in the UK only 8% of patents are awarded to women) it's hardly surprising that billions of women feel disempowered.

The fourth industrial revolution reoriented to needs that matter

The idea of a fourth industrial revolution (4IR) has been in play for 20 years. It usually refers to a convergence and interpenetration of technologies: bio, nano, info and things. It's a catch-all for many different technological trends – from prosthetic devices to the Internet of Things and new models of advanced manufacturing.

On the present trajectory the 4IR promises great benefits. But it also risks a widening divide between vanguards and the rest, accelerating job destruction ahead of job creation and introducing potentially big threats to personal privacy and cybersecurity.

So how could this path be shifted? How could the benefits of extraordinary new technological possibilities be spread more widely? How could many more people have the opportunity to be makers and shapers, entrepreneurs and innovators of this revolution, rather than passive observers?

Some of the answers lie in mobilising the powerful new platforms of the 21st century to use resources far more efficiently. The existing sharing-economy models point the way: not just the commercial variants like Uber and Airbnb but also many more citizen-owned ones like Peerby and Streetbank, or the cooperatives being promoted in Bologna.[13] Similar ideas can be used in the public sector – for example, to organise volunteer emergency services to enhance the health service (as in GoodSAM,[14] which has tens of thousands of volunteer medics in the UK and around the world linked by smartphone to complement ambulance services).

Platforms of this kind can greatly increase utilisation rates across society and the economy – using not just things (land, buildings, vehicles) but also people in more efficient ways. But to get there requires fresh thinking about regulation, supply chains, taxation and law. It takes us to new ideas like Sweden's recently introduced tax breaks for the maintenance of consumer durables like washing machines – an attempt to shift the economy away from waste, while also creating jobs; and to some of the technological possibilities around blockchain. But the promise is an economy that can create value, and opportunities, for many more people than before.

Democracy upgraded

The most problematic part of the current situation is the stagnation of democracy encouraged by the widespread view that all politicians are corrupt and self-interested. This fuels the passive anger of electorates who then revert to faith in populist leaders as the solution to disempowerment.

The alternative is to reshape democracy so that it does provide more genuine power to citizens. That's not easy, and there have been many false starts and false promises of push-button instant democracy. But there are now many examples of more considered, practical routes to empowerment.

Cities have been in the lead, for example with the CONSUL open source tools[15] (now in use in 90 cities worldwide)[16] that enable citizens to be kept informed on the subjects that matter to them (for example, when their local council or parliament is debating a topic); allow them to propose and debate ideas and legislation; provide voting opportunities and scrutiny of implementation.

There are many similar examples around the world. Better Reykjavik[17] has had hundreds of thousands of users proposing and voting on improvements to the public realm. Paris[18] has a large participatory budgeting scheme, as does Portugal[19] at a national level. Taiwan has shown how many more people can be brought rapidly into decision making.[20]

The best of these schemes make government more like a collaborative, reflective process of deliberation than a permanent referendum. They have the virtue of not only involving the public but also educating them along the way so that, for example, the trade-offs of any decision can be made clear. Reforms to upgrade democracy must be part of the new synthesis too, as a counter to the trends towards a democracy built around spin, deceit and bluster.

Data and the internet

The management of data isn't yet at the top of the political agenda. But it's an issue that is bound to become more important – partly because data now plays such a big role in the economy and partly because it has become so central to the ways we live our lives.

The internet and World Wide Web (WWW) were born out of the hope that they could, in the words of Tim Berners-Lee, inventor of the WWW, be for everyone an open, free and shared resource. Some of that original spirit survives, but much of today's reality is very different.

Power has been consolidated in a very small number of commercial firms. Amazon intermediates our relationship to products; Facebook our friendships; Google our relationship to information. They've grown huge, thanks to business models that rely substantially on how they use and sell our data, and to network effects which mean that the ones that first became big then tended to become enormous, because the marginal cost of another user was so much lower for them than for their competitors. That's why we live in a world where the dominance of the big Silicon Valley firms is so much greater than that of their equivalents in previous industrial eras.

As consumers we've done well out of a deal that offered us free services in exchange for handing over our data. But such consolidation of power is problematic in all sorts of ways. Our most important infrastructures are now unaccountable, driven by incentives that are often against our interests (we're not their customers but, rather, a commodity which they sell). We have very little control over our own data. Meanwhile, much of the potential value of the internet is not being realised because it doesn't fit the dominant business models.

That's why the search for very different models of the internet is bound to become more prominent over the next few years. How can the citizen control more of the data that matters to them? How can these great new infrastructures be more accountable? Part of the answer will be a new family of data trusts to curate, protect and make the most of data in accountable ways. None exists today. Many will before long.[21]

Migration and democracy

Feelings of loss of control have had a big influence on the drive to populist authoritarianism. Many people feel that they have no control over migration, that their communities and places have been taken away from them.

There's clearly a tension between democracy and open borders. Democracy means a community having control over who is welcomed in and on what terms. But the more ardent advocates of the thesis with which the chapter began often sought to override democracy, and treated free movement as an absolute principle, even though in practice it has always been qualified.

We know a lot about what makes people belong. All humans are well designed to read the feedback messages from their environment about whether they are at home or not. We can spot whether the labour market can offer jobs to people like us, whether politics speaks in our language, whether public culture reflects our values and interests or whether policing and other public services reflect our needs.

When the messages are negative, people feel insecure and that they don't belong. That's what happens to many new minorities. But it has also increasingly been the experience of older working-class communities, which consequently feel a sense of loss and rejection. Chapter 11, on belonging and the practical ways it can be nurtured, provides some practical pointers for local and national governments.

The new synthesis will have to include more overt democratic control over the terms of migration: who comes in and on what terms, whether as worker, student, tourist or patient. The only kinds of democracy we know are based in places, and so it's not surprising that control over place is so important to feelings of empowerment.

Democracies can – and should – choose to be generous to refugees and attend to the suffering of the world. But these choices have to be consciously made in an inclusive way, not imposed.

Government experimentation and adaptation

To achieve ambitious goals and restore trust, government itself needs to be recast. One of the disappointing features of the current wave of authoritarian populists is that they appear to have few if any ideas about how to improve the machinery of government – and often want to turn the clock back.

Yet this is a time when almost every aspect of government can be improved: changing how intangible resources like data, information and knowledge are used; using money in more creative ways; tapping into public expertise to shape and adapt policy. The emerging field of collective intelligence shows some of the tools being used by governments around the world – and provides a far more attractive future picture for government than posturing populism.

Some governments have committed themselves to systematic experimentation: Finland, Canada and the United Arab Emirates in particular have tried to apply the simple principle that ideas should be tested out on a small scale before being implemented on a large scale. Others are developing the idea of government as a platform – providing resources and information, but allowing society or a market to organise provision and use. A related trend is experiment around uses of money – grants, loans, equity, challenge prizes, social impact bonds, matched crowdfunding – many of them allowing for hybrid approaches in which more social intelligence is integrated into the workings of the state.

New platforms and infrastructures for the public

Since the 1970s many infrastructures have been privatised, broken up and regulated, sometimes successfully and sometimes at a high cost. But there are many infrastructural roles that only government can perform, and over the next few years we may see much more activism as this is recognised. A good example is India's creation of a universal ID (UID) card with biometric identity. Now in use by well over a billion people, it has massively opened up financial services for the very poor. It also appears to be cutting corruption of all kinds and is experienced as empowering, despite plenty of practical challenges that have accompanied its implementation. Countries such as Singapore and Denmark have created personal accounts for citizens, making possible much more creative ways of providing welfare.

Another example is the idea of opening up central banking to offer cheaper mortgages and other financial products to the public. Both the UID and these ideas suggest a potential future in which governments can offer much more flexible kinds of welfare – lending money for a first home, for acquiring new skills or a university degree, with repayments through the tax system spread over a full working life. Done right, these can greatly enhance freedom, economic security and feelings of power.

They provide a base infrastructure on top of which a plurality of services – mutual, peer to peer, social as well as commercial – can sit, and represent a political articulation of one of the core ideas of social innovation, with policy as a complement to grassroots creativity rather than its enemy.

These are just a few building blocks of what could become new syntheses. They are far from comprehensive. There will also need to be more attention to tax – including fairer taxation of business and wealth to respond to class and generational imbalances. We may also need to return to the role of the state as employer of last resort, though the challenge will be to create work that has respect and dignity. Cybersecurity is bound to become more visible as an issue. And overhanging everything may be a more aggressive geopolitical climate, with more direct attacks by nations such as Russia on the institutions of the democratic West.

Fleshing out programmes of this kind won't be easy. It requires us to think dialectically, achieving a balance between conflicting ideas rather than taking them to their logical conclusions – the consistent mistake of the more extreme partisans of globalisation. It also requires us to reject the opposite option – simply caving in to ugly, regressive ideas which are at odds with the best values of tolerance, enlightenment and compassion.

There's plenty of political space in between, space that aligns with the values and interests of most of the public in most democracies. John Maynard Keynes is often reputed to have said, 'When the facts change, I change my mind. What do you do, sir?'[22] Now some, at least, of the facts have changed.

4

Structural change and new social contracts: How innovation in welfare can address changing needs

Introduction

What connects the hundreds of millions of people in India who have received biometric ID cards, the hundreds of thousands marching on the streets of cities like Paris to protest about pensions reform and the millions of families receiving conditional cash transfers in Latin America?

All are experiencing the rapid pace of change in welfare states that are adapting to new conditions. The pressures for change vary greatly. In some parts of the world welfare is in crisis. The German chancellor Angela Merkel regularly repeated a stylised fact that summarises the problem for some parts of the world: Europe accounts for 8% of world population, 25% of GDP and 50% of welfare spending. The well-rehearsed challenges of ageing populations, disappearing jobs, welfare dependency and possibly declining willingness to pay in more diverse societies now combine with shorter-term pressures to cut deficits. As a result, the most prominent accounts of the future of welfare emphasise only retrenchment, salami-slicing cuts and a shift of responsibility from the state to citizens.

But in many countries welfare is expanding. Every developing country has had to build up new welfare rights – to healthcare, pensions and unemployment insurance. Some have done so very fast, like South Korea and Thailand. Others are doing so from a much lower base, including India and China. So long as economies continue to grow, there is no obvious reason why welfare can't grow too. The perspective of the richest 10% of the world, experiencing a time of crisis, can distort the bigger picture in which risk is being socialised and managed at larger scales than ever before. It can also disguise some of the bigger trends – including the ways that 100-year lives and 70-year careers will mean a big increase in how much time each individual can work, even if they also take much more time out for leisure or for volunteering.

But how welfare is organised is bound to change. Needs have changed, as have the available tools. A huge concentration of wealth has widened inequality, coinciding with growing returns to capital relative to labour, and often ferocious destruction of jobs.

It follows that there is an imperative to renegotiate social contracts. The precise forms these contracts will take are only partly visible through the mist of reform and experiment. They may include new variants of basic income (now being tested in several European countries); new personal accounts for financial dealings with states and citizens (already in place in some of the most advanced governments); credits or frameworks for human capital and lifelong learning; rights to care; and new ways of handling everything from personal data to health. But what can't be in doubt is that the changing contexts – of continued deindustrialisation, fragmented family structures and much greater ethnic diversity in open societies – will demand creativity, both technical and political.

In what follows I suggest some of the building blocks that can be assembled in different ways, according to context and culture, to revive and reform welfare. I show where the state needs to be more active in direct ways, deliberately providing new infrastructures for payment and support, where it needs to enable rather than provide and where it needs to step back.

What is welfare for?

Welfare states are not new inventions. There is a very long history of government involvement in welfare, which stretches back to ancient Sumeria (where the first-ever organised state was primarily a welfare state, organised around the distribution of grain to its citizens).[1] Rome provided bread. Ancient India provided alms as well as healthcare; and pre-industrial England was one of many countries with a comprehensive, albeit very imperfect, system for alleviating poverty.

The modern welfare states we are now used to emerged in successive bursts of invention responding to the needs of dense, newly industrialised urban societies in the late 19th century. They were born out of a combination of three main factors: first, politics and public demand, as recently empowered citizens called for a share of rising wealth to address the risks they couldn't address on their own; second, the importance of productivity and the impact of strong evidence that poor health, as well as poor education, undermined the economy; and, third, the arrival of new technologies of provision, in particular large-scale national bureaucracies which were able to manage complex assessment and payment systems.

At first welfare played a much smaller role in states than warfare. In Britain in 1910, for example, the cost of building warships was more than the cost of old age pensions. But by the second half of the century welfare had come to dominate public finance.

These welfare states grew up to socialise a small number of risks which had previously been seen as the responsibility of the individual, the family or the church. They included poverty in old age, unemployment and ill-health. At the same time states were investing heavily in social productive capacity through education systems and infrastructures. What is now called social investment was a major theme of early welfare design; so was 'pre-distribution' – the provision of universal education, maternity and other services to reduce inequalities (and prepare a productive population). In many countries, too, social contracts were agreed that involved substantial obligations on employers.

It was obvious that individuals, families and communities could not address many risks alone. Yet it was also generally assumed that they would be better placed than the state to deal with many other risks and needs, including emotional needs, mental health, most child rearing and eldercare.

The new landscape of risks and needs

If we stand back and look at today's needs, we see a landscape that is very different:

- much longer periods of old age, and infirmity in old age, requiring means for shifting income across the life cycle and organising care on a much larger scale;
- continued challenges of unemployment, requiring not only help for short periods out of work but also action to address deeper problems of structural unemployment and obsolete skills;
- rising incidence of mental illness, with atomised societies often less able to provide informal support, friendship and care;
- related to this, rising incidence of loneliness and isolation;
- rising incidence of long-term health conditions and disability, partly the result of medical advances;
- risks that are the result of genetic bad luck, as well as risks that are the result of behaviour and life-style choices;
- the worsening challenges of transition facing young people needing a reliable job and a home.

The new landscape of tools

Very different tools are now available for the daily delivery of welfare, and what we could call new 'operating systems' for welfare. These include:

- predictive algorithms, of the kind already used in health services and criminal justice to predict who will be at greatest risk of such events as emergency hospital admission or reoffending (being used in Saskatchewan in Canada and Allegheny in the US, for example, to guide children's services);
- technology platforms allowing not just direct payments into bank accounts but also virtual monies and internet-based payments, secure identities and personal accounts;
- digital tools allowing states to orchestrate marketplaces for provision, for example, of care supports or learning, using credits provided by the state alongside personal contributions;

- blockchain-based exchanges of money, time or property of different kinds as an alternative to centralised databases;
- multiple feedback channels, and much easier tools to enable peer support;
- formal and informal 'collaboratives' to help partnerships and cooperation across professional and organisational boundaries;
- new contracts, conditions and 'commitment' devices;
- financing tools such as social impact bonds to incentivise outcomes.

Any plausible account of the future of welfare needs to address both the content and the forms. In what follows I suggest 12 ways in which welfare could evolve, addressing both form and content. The central purpose of welfare remains as in the past: to protect people from risks they cannot easily manage on their own. Some of those risks are long-lasting ones (like the facts of old age) and some relate to periods of transition. But risks change, and the biggest challenge for reform is how to shift resources from the problems of the past to the problems of the present and future. Here, then, are prompts, or building blocks, for reformers to draw on.

Reasserting pooled protection against risks beyond the control of the individual

For more than a century states have attempted to fund welfare through insurance. There are some risks for which insurance makes sense. But insurance markets have well-analysed weaknesses. They work best for the providers when purchasers are ignorant, when the majority of payers don't make claims and when insurers can avoid the highest-risk and highest-cost payers. Bismarck's welfare state was a prime example, designed to pay pensions only for the small minority who lived several years more than the then average life expectancy (he took up Emperor Joseph II's slogan 'Everything for the people, but nothing through the people').[2]

Today a wide range of critical risks are essentially about luck and fate, for example: diseases whose main causes are genetic, and chronic problems of old age, such as dementia, that are the result of bad luck and for which there are few credible cures. For these it makes far more sense to pool risk; insurance systems create unnecessary cost and bureaucracy. I expect that we shall see a reassertion of some very basic ideas about welfare for some types of issue, with fully pooled risk, provision according to need and funding through taxation.

Reasserting personal responsibility for risks over which individuals and families have some control, and incentivising pro-social actions

The corollary of greater pooled risk for problems that are the result of bad luck is a greater stress on personal and family responsibility for risks which can be influenced: risks associated with poor diet, smoking, laziness and risky living. In all of these cases support can be made partly conditional, and adjusted according to desert. Much welfare has always been conditional on various statuses (unemployment, disability) or on certain actions (willingness to be available for work). Sometimes conditionality overshoots and, like life, punishes children for the errors of their parents. Some countries have used conditionality more creatively – the better welfare-to-work policies of Scandinavia; the Bolsa Familial and related programmes in the developing South that reward parents if their children attend school. All aim to make more explicit the implicit social contracts that underpin welfare, and the deep human commitment to reciprocity. How far these go is bound to be controversial: should missed doctors' appointments carry a cost? Should health provision be conditional on signing up for smoking cessation? But some conditionality is essential to avoid perverse incentives and moral hazard.

Cultivating resilience: Predictive algorithms and new supports

The most cutting critiques of late 20th-century welfare focused on its tendency to promote dependency and to address symptoms rather than causes, leaving recipients less, rather than more, able to thrive. This critique was often overdone, since much welfare necessarily has to be tied to needs and many people are unavoidably dependent. But it contained important truths. So, welfare has to be reshaped to help people become more resilient, rather than just supporting needs. That involves an orientation towards assets to fall back on; it requires welfare to include more learning, including both formal skills and the skills needed to be resilient in life, from financial literacy to non-cognitive skills; and it's partly about promoting social networks.

More powerful predictive tools are likely to become more popular. Already algorithms can predict the risk of an older person entering hospital in the next year, or the risk of a former prisoner reoffending. Companies providing labour market support routinely use their own algorithms to help with triage. The more that large data sets are made open, the more sophisticated these are likely to become, providing guidance to individuals on how they can reduce their own risk factors, as well as guidance to the state and professionals about what interventions can be most effective in preventing future problems.

These can be controversial. The UK's attempt to create a comprehensive database of children at risk so as to guide preventive action was closed down by the Conservative-led government in the 2010s. *Minority Report*-style forecasting of who is likely to be a future criminal raises a host of ethical and practical issues. But the promise of more effective, targeted and timely welfare interventions is likely to be attractive to many.

If resilience is the goal, new types of intervention are likely to follow. Some will be about early childhood, and helping children to grow up confident, rounded and smart. Others will focus on older age groups. For example, schools can emphasise non-cognitive skills such as teamwork, motivation and grit alongside more familiar skills in maths or science. They're not formally part of the welfare state, but any welfare system that aims to reduce youth unemployment needs something similar.

Another example is health programmes that deliberately mobilise support networks for mental health, or 'social prescribing' for patients with long-term conditions, to offer companionship, peer support or activity rather than drugs prescriptions. These are much talked about, and there is strong evidence that they can be highly effective in enhancing resilience. But they are rarely made central – perhaps because they require very different ways of organising support, different skills for front-line staff and different metrics of success.

Co-production as well as provision, and the integration of formal and informal support

Welfare systems that promote resilience are also more likely to complement provision of money and services with more deliberate co-creation of welfare. This is most obvious in healthcare, where long-term conditions now make up the majority of health needs and require self-management and peer support as well as good doctors and hospitals. Turning the home and workplace into places for healthcare requires services with a very different method of delivery, including a much bigger role for coaches and mentors, and orchestrators of networks of support. This is part of what I have called the 'relational state': a government that organises its roles, its staff and its success metrics in terms of relationships as well as entitlements and outputs.[3]

The classic welfare state was conceived primarily in terms of the distribution of money and the provision of services by paid professionals. In reality it was always much more of a partnership with the public, who might volunteer as drivers, carers or tutors. Fiscal pressures, particularly since the financial crisis, have restored interest in the combination of formal and informal support. Again, healthcare is a good example, where care models try to link together the formal support of the hospital and the engagement of family and friends, or, in the case of dementia, with trained volunteers in the community. Nesta's Centre for Social Action Innovation Fund backed dozens of projects that were doing this effectively, with tutors for school students, volunteers in hospitals and business coaches for unemployed young people. GoodSAM, for example, provided a volunteer ambulance service based on smartphones which rapidly spread all across the world, providing a complement to existing services. Social media technology makes it much easier to orchestrate these. Barcelona's ambitious plans for circles of support for isolated older people could become a model for others to follow.

These all point to a very different way of thinking about the state. Instead of conceiving its resources as limited to paid staff, and the buildings it owns, the state can think of a much wider pool of community resources to draw on. The Bookshare project captures the difference. Instead of a library consisting solely of the resources within the library building, Bookshare allows citizens to put their book and DVD collections onto the library database, simultaneously expanding its resources and building social capital.[4] In business, the many ventures of the collaborative economy are showing how the internet can mobilise distributed resources through firms like Airbnb, Buzzcar and many others. The city of Seoul is using the same principle to reorganise how its assets are managed.

Personal and family budgets and welfare marketplaces

In some fields the most efficient way to organise welfare is to give credits to claimants and let them decide how to spend the money, within constraints. This is how personal budgets already work in many fields, such as care for disability. A similar principle has been explored with individual learning accounts. Getting the detail right is all-important – with the right balance of openness and accreditation/regulation. Some of these budgets are similar to parallel currencies, and smartcard technologies have long made it possible for a welfare agency to distribute money with limits on what can be bought (for example, to preclude spending on drink or drugs). The other side of this development is the deliberate organisation of marketplaces of support, for example, training agencies providing skills, personal care services and alternative provision of healthcare.

In principle, tools of this kind can empower groups of citizens to produce and purchase their own services, transforming the power dynamic between professional providers and beneficiaries.

New parallel currencies to mobilise under-used resources

The world is full of parallel currencies sitting alongside traditional fiat money. At times welfare states have provided some of these through credits that are like monies – food vouchers, for example. Non-state monies include big currencies like the WIR in Switzerland,[5] and there are many thousands of timebanks, local exchange trading systems (LETs)[6] and others, like the Sardex in Sardinia or the Bristol Pound.[7] Often, when the mainstream economy has broken down, new currencies of this kind have grown up to fill the space – from Argentina in the early 2000s to Greece in the early 2010s. One weakness of these is the lack of involvement of the state as guarantor or manager of value, which limits their scale and usefulness. That is why attention has turned to the potential for the state to sponsor parallel currencies as part of reformed welfare systems, for example very local currencies to encourage circulation of value in towns, rural areas or poor neighbourhoods; currencies linking marginal public resources; specialised currencies for care or education. The radical potential is for cities or small nations to offer pay and receive tax in a mix of formal money and parallel currency, creating a parallel market for firms to support the civil economy. Such parallel currencies could in time become a fundamental pillar of welfare systems; and technologies make it possible to manage money in very different ways – from mobile payments platforms like M-Pesa, to digital currencies like bitcoin and Ven.

Identities and integrated accounts that make new welfare products possible

Another building block of the future welfare system will be guaranteed management of identities. India's Universal Identification programme is an interesting pointer to the future – a state-sponsored, biometric identifier which can be used to underpin the provision of bank accounts and other commercial services. States may be better placed to provide trusted and authenticated identification services than private companies – and, if they do so, they can support mixed economies of welfare. A good example is the scope for governments to offer mortgages that are secured over lifetime earnings, with the power of tax agencies to ensure repayment. It should be possible for states to offer these at significantly lower cost, and risk, than private firms, because of their superior capacity to avoid default and because they already have a working infrastructure to manage payments in the tax system. Other types of welfare product would include loans to pay for higher education, apprenticeships or training. In all of these cases a 21st-century state should have major advantages in terms of economies of scale and scope and should be able to move some parts of welfare from grants to loans, thus allowing money to go further.

Transparency, simplicity and visible welfare

A general, if difficult, principle for reform may be to make welfare as transparent as possible, with every recipient clear on what they are entitled to, with easy access to self-assessment and planning tools. This would mean a drive for legibility and simplicity rather than technical perfection. Welfare needs to be comprehensible so as to be legitimate, yet for now welfare remains extraordinarily opaque. A telling moment for me was working with programmers to design online platforms for claimants to assess their own entitlements – which in the UK context turned out to be almost impossible. Single accounts of the kind developed by Denmark may be pointers to the future, allowing citizens to see more clearly all of their payments and receipts from the state, as well as some of their lifetime entitlements. Australia has long adopted a principle of simplicity in its policy design, a principle enforced by its Treasury, which, among other things, led to one of the simplest systems for paying taxes in the world. At the very least, cognitive overload for citizens should be avoided.

Navigation support: Helping citizens make sense of welfare, and sometimes nudging them to change their behaviour

A more open and complex welfare provision system will require correspondingly better support to help people navigate their way through it. Some of this can be done online; some has to be face to face or phone based. There are simple self-assessment tools already. But coming over the horizon are more sophisticated supports – for example, to help plan curriculum or training choices using big data sets showing pay-offs or career options. There are also possible new nudges and prompts. Most people are already bombarded with data-shaped communications from business, and the scope for more targeted communications of all kinds is immense. But how would we feel if the government sent SMS or equivalent messages to warn us that we weren't saving enough for our pensions, that our failure to maintain our skills threatened unemployment, that our children were obese or that we really should be volunteering more in our community?

Commitment devices

Much has been learned about how to encourage choices and behaviours that support the interests of the individual, their family and the community. Many of the points previously described are essentially about better aligning how welfare works to these findings. Commitment devices of various kinds have been widely used in welfare-to-work, encouraging or requiring claimants to set out a personal plan; home–school contracts to encourage parents to help with their children's education; personal plans in health, agreed with a doctor. Social media technologies make it possible to extend these, and many already encourage people to set goals for themselves that are visible to a circle of friends and family.

Budgets for impact: Prevention, outcomes and contracts

Public finance is not well suited to the needs of 21st-century welfare. It tends to be driven largely by demand; to be managed in terms of inputs, not outputs or outcomes; and to be time neutral. Very different ways of organising finance include outcome-based funding like payment-by-results schemes, or social impact bonds, that release certain categories of money only where outcomes are achieved. These are most appropriate for transitional welfare rather than ongoing support, for example for unemployment or transitions to adulthood or programmes aiming to improve health behaviour. Another example is preventive funding with life-cycle budgeting. Governments already use life-cycle budgeting for some categories such as buildings, but it is hardly used at all for people. The alternative is to look at cohorts, and groups of interventions, in terms of both current cost and the mix of costs and benefits over many decades. This is particularly relevant for preventive health, education and labour market policies.

Linking both outcome and preventive funding, some countries have experimented with contracts between different tiers of government, providing funding for investments (for example, into early years provision), but with the lower tier taking some of the risk of failing to achieve outcomes (Australia's Council of Australian Governments [COAG], the structure for coordinating national and state-level governments, is a structure which has the potential to do this in a much more sophisticated way).

Experimentalism and evidence

Welfare states have tended to be set up by decree – with policies designed in ministries in capital cities and enshrined in laws and entitlements. There are good reasons why welfare should be stable, predictable and law based. But there are risks as well: that welfare will not be sufficiently evidence based or sufficiently flexible to adapt to new needs and new tools. That is why around the core welfare state there is a strong argument for experimentalism: systematic trials of new ways of organising such things as public health, eldercare or skills.

A batch of experiments around basic incomes are good examples: in Finland, Barcelona, Canada, Scotland, the Netherlands and Kenya. They have many weaknesses. Almost none of the experiments is for a pure basic income (instead they are targeted at the unemployed); most are testing only one variant; and there are major challenges of scale. But the willingness to use experimental methods is very much to be welcomed.

Basic income has many weaknesses as an idea: it offers a one-size-fits-all solution to widely varying needs, and it faces huge challenges of maths and politics, being either cheap and mean or generous and extremely costly. But experimental testing of alternatives will at least accelerate serious debate about what kinds of welfare will actually work and be legitimate.

The same imperative is also why more systematic use of evidence is needed, along the lines of the What Works centres in the UK that provide easily used guidance on the state of global knowledge. Great care needs to be taken in how risks are handled; no one wants to be a guinea pig for ill-conceived welfare ideas. But, in the long run, a more experimental approach to welfare, combined with more systematic synthesis of evidence, can lead to much higher performance.

Bricolage

These are building blocks, not prescriptions. It would be very surprising if the same answers made sense in every environment. Welfare systems reflect history and culture, the battles of the past as well as the present. What evolutionary biology calls 'fitness' landscapes may explain why what works in one country is bound to fail in another. Or, to put it another way, not everyone could become Denmark even if they wanted to.

But one lesson of history is that there often has been convergence – whether of new tools like income tax, national insurance or welfare-to-work programmes – and it's likely there will be in the future too. Welfare systems are by their nature slow to change – and there is a virtue in keeping them reasonably stable. But the fiscal pressures in the North, and the demographic and political pressures in the South, mean that speed of adaptation will be increasingly important. We badly need thinking about welfare to become more creative and open, and less formulaic and rhetorical. And we badly need to recognise that this era can be as much one of invention as of retrenchment, with a bigger role for social innovation to complement the top-down designs of the state.

5

Social production systems: What is the best unit for analysis and action?

Introduction

Are the roadblocks described earlier best dealt with at the level of a whole nation or at a more granular scale? In this chapter I suggest the value of action in particular sectors in particular places.[1]

One of the big hopes in social entrepreneurship was that a wave of productivity-improving innovations would transform how well societies dealt with social and public problems. Social entrepreneurs would be far more dynamic than governments, tap the energy of markets and cut through the constraints of bureaucracy. The hope was that expenditures in philanthropy and government could then be shifted from less to more productive ends.

But, for the most part, that seems not to have happened. To the extent that data exist, productivity improvements have been marginal in most social fields. Although many individual social entrepreneurs have achieved a lot, both the diagnosis and the prescription were inadequate. The time is ripe therefore for a rethink.

The approach I take here draws on Joseph Schumpeter's views of innovation and productivity gains and the work of Robin Murray on social and industrial sectors. It means applying the insights of the field of industrial organisation to the industries responsible for producing and improving such things as child rearing, health, education, care and readiness for work, and reducing various harms, from homelessness and excessive use of plastics to drug addiction and crime.

What is the best unit of analysis and action?

Successful social action requires the right level of granularity. Most analysis, advocacy and funding focuses on:

- the individual social entrepreneur, providing them with money and freedoms;
- the enterprise or NGO, helping it to grow;
- the individual innovation, helping it to spread and scale.

Meanwhile, at the opposite end of the spectrum much energy has gone into very generic approaches, such as encouraging all businesses to adopt corporate social responsibility obligations, or 'bottom of the pyramid' ideas, new tax incentives or legal forms.

These different levels of action and analysis all matter. But they may miss out the most crucial ones. Here I suggest that the most important unit of analysis and action is what in economics would be called the industry or production system: the capabilities that together produce such things as democratic voice, education or care for the elderly.

The production system

In any place these can be analysed as a production system. They bring together inputs of money, time and skill; organisations that are capable of producing outputs and outcomes; and purchasers or funders. All are in turn influenced by environments, shaped by laws and cultures and by specific conditions of competition and cooperation.

The characteristics of these social production systems are often strongly shaped by politics and the state and their view of what things are valuable and needed. As a result, these sectors or production systems are usually:

- complex combinations of commercial, voluntary and government-managed enterprises;

- shaped by third-party payments from government or contributions from the voluntary sector (whether money, actions or volunteer labour), which are more important than money controlled by beneficiaries;
- dependent on a mix of paid work, voluntary work and labour by clients or beneficiaries themselves;
- powerfully shaped by the regulatory authority of the state, operating on the demand side, and less directly by social movements and political pressures which generate willingness to pay and influence rights;
- designed to produce outputs and outcomes that are often as much relational as material.

These characteristics make them different from most other sectors and industries, and also different from the internal workings of the state.

Analysing production systems

Seen through this lens, it's possible to analyse the structures and processes of an industry in a particular place and time. We can ask what levels of investment there are (usually these are low because of poorly functioning capital markets). How well do they adopt new technologies or techniques (usually not well, because of deficits of skill and capital)? What are their margins (again, these are usually low because of an ethos of service)? Are there new entrants, and if not why not? Are there patterns of vertical or horizontal integration? Do they benchmark against, and learn from, other sectors?

Often, we'll find unhealthy patterns – poor skills and little spending on training; slow adoption of technologies; ferocious competition driving down margins or, alternatively, local monopolies. From this kind of analysis it will often not be too difficult to suggest ways of improving the functioning of the production system.

The problem then is the lack of entities with the capability and legitimacy to act at this more systemic level. What is often needed is a combination of regulator, developer, investor and commissioner – a systems curator that can act at the level of the sector or production system.

The task for action

If this is an important unit for understanding what happens, it follows that there will sometimes need to be action at this level rather than at the level of individual innovations, people or enterprises. For example, if a major city wants to drive up productivity in its systems for helping the unemployed into work, or tackling homelessness or drug addiction, more systemic action will be needed.

That will generally require a collaborative approach on the part of the organisations with some power to shape the systems, including public authorities and foundations. They will need to come to some agreement about what needs to be done and what success would look like. They may need to pool resources, to jointly commit to aligned actions and to jointly measure effectiveness.

Several decades of area-based initiatives linking governments, NGOs and foundations have shown how this can be done. But, as I discuss in the next chapter on collective impact, many of the most prominent current methods not only miss what was learned from previous experiments but also miss the insights that come from looking at production systems through the lens of industrial organisation. They emphasise targets, metrics and performance management, but have little or nothing to say about:

- competition or new entrants;
- the scope for shifting purchasing power into the hands of beneficiaries or outcome-based contracts;
- the role of R&D to finance experiment in more radical options;
- the role of regulation (such as the 'anticipatory regulation' methods that make it easier for new entrants to enter the system with different business models, and which have been pioneered in finance).

As a result, they tend to reinforce incumbents and existing models, and often end up with disappointing results.

An example: The production system for connectedness

Many of the outputs of the social sector are relational as well as material. This makes it harder to understand them in economic terms. But the example of isolation among the frail elderly shows that it is meaningful to think in terms of productivity and systems, even for very human issues of this kind.

First, there is a good, and well-tested, metric – the Revised UCLA (University of California , Los Angeles) Loneliness Scale, which can be asked at the beginning of a programme and later, for example after six months and 18 months. The scale includes four questions that ask about a participant's feelings related to loneliness, for example 'How often do you lack companionship?' and assigns an overall loneliness score (from 4 to 12).

Second, there are some fairly evidence-based interventions – mainly through local voluntary services connecting people with community organisations in sustainable ways, for example through lunch clubs and knitting groups, all tailored to the background of individuals to ensure they'll not only be interested but stay interested. Local delivery partners that are well connected and empathic are key.

Third, it is possible to design financing systems that can address isolation. In the West of England, for example, a large municipality leads a consortium which pays for proven reductions in loneliness, which it's assumed will lead to reductions in spending on social services and hospitals. Payments are tied to loneliness points reduced – which means that there can be quite a precise measurement of productivity.[2]

Fourth, the production system for reducing isolation will tend to be quite complex and messy in any particular place, with its combination of voluntary effort and professionals. But differences between places will be determined by how well they are orchestrated, by issues such as the use of new technological tools (such as digital alerts, neighbourhood sites) and by organisational structures.

Looking ahead

The production system approach could prove more useful than focusing solely on the level of individuals and enterprises, and more actionable than the sometimes vague discussions of systems change. It can help clarify the ways in which different levels evolve with often different logics (as happens in biology). The evolutionary pressures at the level of the individual enterprise will be very different from those at the level of the production system or the nation.

But it will require focused research, analysis and design of tools for action if the full potential gains are to be achieved, and a new family of institutions to guide action. As I show in the next chapter, it can also be helped by bringing the people who constitute the system together to think, and then act, as a system.

6

Place-based systems change: How can governments, funders and civil society achieve more together?

Introduction

In this chapter I turn to the broader experience of cross-sector collaboration to shift whole systems. How does social innovation become more than a series of interesting pilots and projects? How can the whole be more than the sum of the parts? How can whole systems be transformed – to better care for the old or young, or to solve serious problems, from crime to carbon emissions, through the kinds of action described in the last chapter?

There is a long history of experiments to align the actions of many different organisations across the public sector, civil society and business that are trying to achieve some kind of social change – better early years education; less violence; improved public health or urban regeneration. These have usually involved some combination of shared plans, targets and commitments. They have had many names. Many books have been written about them, and many universities have run courses to make people better collaborators. Responsible funders naturally want to find ways to make their money go further, and recognise that this is bound to involve collaboration – pooling resources of all kinds with others.

Yet one of the oddities of the field is that there is not much cumulative learning. I have regularly come across reports and articles, and outputs from consultancies, claiming to have invented new ways of doing this. They're perfectly well intentioned, and many are doing important work. But they rarely make much, if any, mention of past experiences, and often appear to be unaware of the lessons learned.

In this chapter I describe what collaboration and collective impact are, what has been learned and how practice could improve.

Why now?

The topic of how to achieve large-scale, cross-sector collaboration to deal with social problems in places is an old one. Many big tasks require cross-sector, multi-partner, multi-stakeholder collaboration, whether in a geographic area or in a sector. Many tasks also require some shared institutional capacity to coordinate and drive actions.

The good news is that there are thousands of examples of systems change in practice.[1] Some have been truly global, like the World Health Organization strategy to eliminate smallpox in the 1960s, the collaborations on vaccines in GAVI (The Vaccines Alliance), and the strategy to fight malaria in the 2000s. Some have been national, like the National Community Development Initiative (NCDI) in the US in the 1990s, or the successful strategies to cut rough sleeping or teenage pregnancy in the UK in the 2000s, or for that matter China's strategies to cut poverty.[2]

Much of the action has been in cities: the commonest partnerships have been found in cities trying to turn around deindustrialising places like Cleveland in the US, or Manchester in the UK, and there are standout examples of sustained multi-sector collaboration, like Bilbao in Spain. The 1990s also saw many attempts to package up methods under brand names: one which was visible for a while was Communities that Care. A more recent one is Collective Impact, and there are now many live examples, from Memphis and Cincinnati's Strive to the Harlem Children's Zone (HCZ) in the US.

Some of the most ambitious ones were public sector-led, such as Total Place and the London Collaborative. Although most of these are hard to evaluate because of the sheer number of variables involved, and because they often don't last long enough for serious assessment, there are some good stories to tell (see, for example, the debates about the effectiveness of the HCZ[3] and the long-term impact of holistic urban regeneration schemes[4]). There has also been plenty of serious academic analysis in the field, including classics like Eugene Bardach's work on cross-agency collaboration,[5] or Elinor Ostrom's work on the key requirements for managing common resources which led to her famous list of the eight principles essential for successful management of commons (such as participation rights for everyone affected by decisions, graduated sanctions, effective monitoring and nested tiers taking responsibility).[6]

The NCDI[7] was one of the most interesting US examples, partly because it straddled philanthropy, finance and government and took advantage of legislation (the Community Reinvestment Act, which forced banks to change lending policies). In the 1990s the NCDI pooled the budgets of a group of foundations, banks and others to create an infrastructure of community finance across the US, both at a national level and in multiple poor communities. It directly committed $250 million from seven foundations and private partners, and leveraged around $2 billion, creating a network of hundreds of community development corporations and national bodies like LISC (Local Communities Support Corporation) and the Enterprise Foundation (the Rockefeller Foundation has kept its work alive in the Living Cities programme).

I've been involved in schemes of this kind since the early 1990s, most recently through Nesta. In recent years we've been particularly interested in methods that inject urgency into partnerships and reduce the risk of them becoming empty talking shops. Our thinking draws on experience of systems change,[8] and the work around the world to make systems thinking practical.[9] A good example is how these methods have been used in health systems. The approach is in some respects quite simple, even if its execution isn't. It brings the players in a system together – for example, all the people acting on the health of the frail elderly in an area, or school-to-work transitions (often they haven't met before); it secures the commitment of the leaders of the main organisations, sets stretching targets and then provides active support to them in collectively reshaping how the system works to meet targets over 100-day sprints. When these work well they tap into the deep knowledge of practitioners, inject urgency and, above all, forge a network of strong relationships. The system becomes aware of itself and redesigns itself to work better.

The tools

If you want to get the players in a city or sector to collaborate, there are many tools available. All will involve some joint activity to diagnose the problem, which then leads on to commitments towards action to solve it, and then some way to monitor results and adjust. This isn't rocket science and has been described in many very similar frameworks and diagrams. These are fairly similar to the better standard policy-design methods, though, as I show later, there's also now a wide array of digital methods available to support collaboration.

But, although the job of deciding on tasks, defining metrics and following them through with performance management tools can seem easy, in practice each of these steps brings challenges, and the greater the mismatch between the shape of the problem and the shape of the organisations with some power to act on it, the greater the challenge of coordination. It's a problem if the basic diagnosis is flawed; a problem if the actions committed to aren't the right ones; a problem if the participants look at issues through radically different frames; a problem if the commitments are weak; a problem if there isn't sufficient implementation capacity; a problem if street-level cultures aren't right; a problem if the metrics don't capture what's important.

These are the usual challenges of any kind of complex problem solving. They require a heavy dose of humility, along with the commitment to work through them. They also require very particular skills. The ability to curate, facilitate and nudge a disparate group towards a common purpose is extraordinarily important, requiring tact, wisdom, strength and an odd mix of charisma and quietness.

Light or heavy?

The tools then run in a continuum, from the light to the heavy. The light ones involve mutual coordination: public commitments but without legal force, and some use of open data collection and shared metrics. This is roughly what the European Union (EU) does at a national level: the principle of open coordination is that explicit targets and transparent actions will encourage convergent actions. It's also what most of the recent projects labelled 'collective impact' do. They are coalitions that work so long as the partners are willing. The heavier tools formally combine budgets, targets, teams and reporting requirements over long periods of time with legally binding obligations. Many of the urban regeneration collaborations were heavy in this sense, with formal powers and rewards to incentivise sustained collaborations – including models like the Single Regeneration Budget,[10] New Deal for Communities[11] and Total Place[12] in the UK. NCDI in the US was another example of a relatively strong tool, with formally pooled money. The many EU-funded collaborations also tend to be strong in this sense (even if they are often, in reality, quite cosmetic).

A common lesson is that, although structures and processes matter greatly, cultures matter more. This is often a blind spot for the more technocratic, or mechanistic, approaches to collaboration. So, in one view, the best collaborations are grown more as movements than as coordinated performance management; the main focus of work is on relationships and trust building. Nesta's work on systems change in health, described in Chapter 3, has prioritised this sort of work – strengthening horizontal links and confidence between public sector staff, professionals, NGOs and others – as a vital complement to top-down authorisation from leaders and the use of formal metrics. This was also an emphasis for the London Collaborative – building much stronger informal networks and trust to complement the formal structures and processes.

Equal partners or dominant players: What role for government?

The tools also run in a continuum from those that are government dominated to those that wholly bypass government. For most social problems government is likely to be better suited (in theory) to acting on the problem, having more resources, greater legitimacy and better information. But this primacy can become a problem if government is inflexible, wedded to old solutions or poor at partnering. It's also bound to be fragmented itself, especially where two or three different tiers of government are involved. So, a lot of subtle knowledge has built up over the years about how to get the benefits of collaboration without government smothering everything. There are many interesting examples of attempts to square this circle. One unusual recent example was Delivering Social Change in Northern Ireland, substantially funded by Atlantic Philanthropy but implemented by government, which aimed at tackling a range of issues including dementia and integrated schooling.[13]

Structure, process and culture (and why actions may be a better starting point than principles)

The general lesson from most of these exercises is that structures help but are less important than processes, and that these in turn are less important than cultures. Announcing the collaboration and getting the principals to turn up is (relatively) easy. So is the paraphernalia of shared metrics and reporting. But lasting impact depends on much deeper-rooted habits of collaboration, for example between key professions on the ground. This tends to take a lot longer. The joined-up-government method has thrown up lots of options for all of these – joint boards, teams, reviews, policy making, implementation teams, targets, budgets, double and triple keys. But these tend to have most impact when they are given enough time to become embedded in everyday cultures and are reinforced by the main drivers of behaviour, from how leaders act to appraisal and pay systems.

Another common lesson is more counter-intuitive. Organisers of collaboration often want the participants to get back to first principles and then move logically on to actions. A great deal of experience, and political science, show that this approach is mistaken. It is much harder to get a disparate group to agree on underlying principles and values than it is to get them to agree on actions.

Why collaboration is hard – and not always desirable

Collaboration can be frustrating, imperfect and time consuming. The literature which makes it sound neat and logical is misleading. Herding cats may well be easier than the job of getting disparate organisations, with radically different cultures and accountability arrangements, to work in harmony. But there are also more fundamental challenges in collaboration, barely mentioned in the recent literature.

The first is that collaboration brings costs as well as benefits. Silos exist for a reason, and reinforce themselves for good reasons too: it's not possible for everyone to talk to everyone all the time. Any anti-silo measure brings its own trade-offs, and its own new handovers. In the 1990s the joke used to be that the only thing worse than organisations never talking to each other was organisations doing nothing but talk to each other. The critical question for any horizontal collaboration is whether it adds more than it subtracts, since it inevitably creates new boundaries, and new problems of coordination.

A second critical issue is that, when radical innovation is required, bringing incumbents into collaboration can slow down necessary change. Imagine a cross-sectoral collaboration to improve the book-retailing business in a city. If all the bookshops and libraries had been included it would almost certainly have tried to crush new innovations like Amazon. Similarly, a collaboration of existing banks to improve financial services would be highly likely to exclude competing peer-to-peer and alternative finance tools. So, collaborations work best when there aren't fundamental clashes of interest.

The third challenge is democracy. All jurisdictions will have an existing legitimate authority – a municipal or regional government. Some collaborations are interwoven with democratic power and defer to elected leaders. Others try to circumvent them. Often, community leaders claim a competing legitimacy to that of elected politicians. Since collaborations often bring in unaccountable philanthropic money, this can create any number of tensions and problems.

A final challenge concerns argument. Any kind of partnership encourages people to form a consensus. That can be very healthy. But often the best thinking depends on vigorous, robust argument. A common finding of partnership boards is that they brush difficult issues under the carpet and don't cultivate the kind of hard argument that is found within the best organisations.

Making collaboration easier

Several recent technology trends could be making large-scale coordination easier. Open data allows for more systematic scrutiny of funding decisions and actions. Nesta and other foundations are part of the 360Giving[14] group in the UK, which is promoting the provision of machine-readable data on all grants, their purposes and locations. WASHfunders[15] points in the same direction, mapping projects and programmes around access to water. This sort of openness is still very far from being the norm in most countries. But it is a significant help to serious coordination because it allows more independent, and rigorous, assessment of whether collaboration is really happening in terms of actions.

Perhaps the most powerful aids to collaboration now come from the digital world. There are many more online tools to help dispersed groups work together, from simple ones like Google Docs or Slack to complex ones like Genius. Some older ones still look impressive – such as the tool developed by Rosabeth Moss Kanter with IBM in the early 2000s for helping a whole system to navigate change. We've learned that these online tools are complements to, not substitutes for, face-to-face engagement. But they've improved a lot and they can embed the habits of collaboration.

There are also digital tools for self-assessing collaborations. I was influenced in the 2000s by social network analysis, which seemed the perfect method for mapping the reality of partnerships by asking several hundred people working in a system at city level – for example, the system delivering secondary education, or for cutting domestic violence – who they found had been helpful to them in their daily work.[16] These methods remain uniquely well suited to showing the reality of collaboration, but they are very rarely used, perhaps because they often show up when collaboration is only cosmetic.

Better collaboration could also be helped by other, non-technological trends. One is the spread of common languages for evidence. The temptation for any programme of this kind is to use self-generated data, which then allows all the partners to pat themselves on the back for the numbers of jobs created or skills learned. But, without independent validation and a common, rigorous framework for thinking about evidence, these rarely stand up to scrutiny. The wider use of common standards should improve the performance of partnerships.

A related trend is the spread of cross-cutting leadership development programmes. There are now lots of organisations skilled in training leaders from across sectors to cultivate a shared sense of responsibility. In the UK, Common Purpose has been doing this for decades. Quite a few universities now offer tri-sector leadership courses. Organisations like UpRising[17] do this for a slightly younger age group. All try to inculcate familiarity with collaboration, as well as personal links, and to address the cultural underpinnings of collaboration.

Problems

What can go wrong with collaborations or collective-impact projects? Apart from lots of talk and not much action, or waning commitment – for example, as the leadership changes in key organisations – or a major change in the environment (like a recession), several typical problems often affect collective-impact projects. They include too much focus on what's easily measured rather than what matters, and actions to cut bureaucracy that end up increasing bureaucracy as they create new committees and processes while the existing ones continue in parallel. They may also create new, competing forms of multi-functional governance – but without the direct democratic accountability of the municipality.

Where next?

It's natural that innovators should want their work to feed into something larger, and it has to be right for organisations with the power and money to collaborate, to focus on outcomes, not activities, and to make themselves accountable for the results.

But this is a field that needs to become better at learning – with critical case studies, sharper analysis and more hypotheses to be tested. Precisely because collaboration is obviously a good thing, it risks being talked about uncritically. But bad collaboration, and cosmetic collaboration, could be worse than no collaboration at all. There won't be any neat formulae to guide the future collaborations of governments, funders and civil society. But this is space where we should set our ambitions higher and be less accepting of prescriptions that haven't bothered to draw on what's already known.

Part III
Sources, ideas and ways of seeing

7

The theoretical foundations of social innovation: Sources, ideas and future directions

Introduction

The field of social innovation has grown up primarily as a field of practice.[1] There has been surprisingly little attention to theory, or to history, and at times even a disdain for intellectual input. Although there has been much promising research work, no major thinker has yet written about the topic; there are no clearly defined schools of thought, no continuing theoretical arguments and few major research programmes to test theories against the evidence.

But, to mature as a field, social innovation needs to shore up its theoretical foundations, the frames with which it thinks and makes sense of the world. Sharper theory will help to clarify what is and isn't known, the points of argument as well as agreement. It will help in the generation of testable hypotheses.

Above all, it may help to guide practice. Social theories, unlike theories in fields like physics, are inseparable from their purposes and their uses. Not all innovations are good, nor are all social innovations. So, theory needs to fuse three things: rigorous and objective analysis of patterns, causes and dynamics; normative analysis of social change from an ethical perspective; and guidance on how practitioners can do better in improving wellbeing, alleviating poverty or widening distributions of power.

Here I suggest some of the main theoretical currents that have flowed into the broad river of social innovation; I suggest how they may be synthesised, and the contribution that other fields may make. To summarise, I suggest that together these theoretical foundations show:

- that social innovations tend to originate in contradictions, tensions and dissatisfactions that are caused by new knowledge, new demands and new needs that make the transition from being personal to being recognised as social in their causes and solutions;
- that they then depend on a wide array of actors, including social entrepreneurs, movements, governments, foundations, teams, networks, businesses and political organisations, each with different ways of working, motivations and capacities, but united by a belief in plasticity and what I call (drawing on Albert Hirschman), the 'rhetorics of progress';[2]
- that innovations gain traction only when they can attract vital resources, which include money, time, attention and power;
- that the processes whereby innovations develop have strong analogies with a much wider family of evolutionary processes that multiply options and select and then grow those best suited to changing environments;
- that innovations gain impact through being formalised as pilots, ventures and programmes, and through dynamic processes of externalisation and internalisation that may often leave their creators redundant and alienated;
- that innovations gain resonance, and wider impact, when they achieve a fit with wider patterns of historical change, including techno-economic paradigms and situations of political hegemony;
- that the fundamental goals of social innovation include the creation of socially recognised value, the promotion of greater wellbeing and the cultivation of capabilities, and that these provide increasingly rigorous tests for social innovations that are helping the field to mature beyond its earlier phase of anecdote and celebration; and, finally,
- that the nature of the knowledge created through social innovation is historically and spatially contextual, specific and liable to decay.

Definitions: The boundaries of the field

Social innovation, like social entrepreneurship, has struggled with definitions and boundaries.[3] Some people feel anxious talking about anything without a precise definition; others fear that excessive rigidity obscures more than it reveals.[4] This is not the place for a detailed discussion of definitions.[5] There are many in circulation (from sources including Stanford University, the OECD and Nesta), describing the field of social innovation as concerned with ideas, products and services that are for the public good. Some of the definitions are long. My preferred definition, which is simpler and shorter, defines the field as concerned with innovations that are social both in their ends and in their means. In other words, it covers new ideas (products, services and models) that aim simultaneously to meet socially recognised social needs (more effectively than alternatives) *and* to create new social relationships or collaborations that both are good for society *and* enhance society's capacity to act. This definition helps to capture the dual quality of much of the theoretical literature on which the field has drawn, which is a literature about means as well as ends, about notions of value as well as values and about capacities as well as products and services. The definition also internalises within itself the conflict that is inevitable in the use of the word 'social': what counts as good, or as a socially recognised need, is constantly contested, and this very contest provides some of the dynamic energy that drives the field.[6]

Plasticity and progress

The premise of any social innovation is that the world is imperfect, that our knowledge of the world is incomplete, that creative innovation can achieve improvement and that the best way to discover improvements lies in experiment rather than revelation or deduction. These premises may seem obvious. But right from the start they set social innovation at odds with many other traditions. They imply a view of society as engaged in its own self-creation. They see the invention of the future as a natural part of human action and extend the Enlightenment belief that the world is malleable, plastic and amenable to reform.

In all of these senses social innovation is a progressive approach (in the widest sense), clearly at odds with what Albert Hirschman called the 'rhetoric of reaction',[7] the theories and arguments that present all attempts at conscious social progress as liable to futility (they simply won't work), jeopardy (if they have any effect at all it will be to destroy something we value) and perversity (the claim that if any attempts at improvement had effects these would not be the ones intended, so that, for example, wars on poverty leave behind a dependent underclass). Social innovation tends to ally itself, by contrast, with the mirror rhetorics of progress:[8] these include arguments for righting wrongs and meeting needs, whether these are, for example, for pensions or affordable housing, which draw on fundamental moral senses of fairness. They draw on claims that change is cumulative and dynamic and that new reforms are needed to reinforce old ones, or to prevent backsliding. So, for example, new rights to maternity leave are essential to make a reality of past laws outlawing gender discrimination. And they use claims of tractability: that social action works and that, whether the problem is unemployment or climate change, the right mix of actions can solve it.

These optimistic views about the potential for change, and their related claim that the future can be found in the present, in embryo, are highly political stances that are largely inconceivable outside the contexts of active democracy and civil society. They connect social innovation to a deep democratic belief in the virtue of empowering society to shape society, and a view that the more broadly power is spread, the greater the capacity for good to prevail.

Ideas of this kind are central to the liberal democratic view of the world, but alien to many strands of conservatism, rigid Marxism–Leninism, theocracy and to any belief in autocratic rule. They also run counter to many of the claims of the Austrian school of philosophy and economics which, as I show later, have contributed important insights to social innovation, but whose fundamental stance was much closer to the rhetorics of reaction than to those of progress.

Perhaps the most interesting contemporary exponent of this view of the connection between social innovation and progress is the Brazilian theorist, professor of law at Harvard, and former minister, Roberto Mangabeira Unger, who in a series of works analysed the 'plasticity' of the world, and the role of law in processes of social change. His book *The Self Awakened* presents arguably the boldest attempt to provide a philosophical foundation for social innovation.[9] In it Unger argues that individuals and communities are not contained by their present circumstance: 'the habitual settings for action and thought, especially as organised by the institutions of society and the conventions of culture, are incapable of containing us ... this transcendence of self over its formative circumstances occurs in every department of human experience.'[10] From this, Unger deduces a more fundamental argument about the potential for systemic change: 'we can do more than innovate in the content of our social and cultural contexts: we can innovate as well in the character of our relation to them: we can change the extent to which they imprison us.'[11] Unger draws on the pragmatist traditions of Peirce and Dewey (which I discuss later), but gives them a modern, political edge.

This belief in plasticity is allied, in Unger's work and that of many others, to pluralism, opposing the claims of Marxism and the more assertive strands of modern economics that societies are singular, organised according to a single coherent logic. Instead Unger and others argue that, even if everything connects, they do so only loosely. Attempts to fit all things into a single frame of logic lead to pathologies and errors. This is the pluralism explored by figures such as Daniel Bell, who showed how advanced capitalist societies are made up of spheres with very different logics, languages and rhythms of change.[12] In a different way this was the idea explored by Jane Jacobs, who showed how healthy societies contain within themselves often contradictory moral syndromes (and whose work on cities, as I show later, provided some of the mental frameworks for innovators).[13] Bruno Latour's development of actor-network theory is also a very useful corrective to the notion that there is a coherent entity called a society, which has views and interests.[14]

In short, at the foundation of social innovation is a belief in people's capacity to create, to shape and experiment, and a bias against both over-confident top-down control or planning and the fatalistic view that nothing works.

Life and forms and the dialectics of change

Our next set of sources go into the nature of innovation itself and the exploration of plasticity. The philosopher and sociologist Georg Simmel provided one of the most compelling accounts that resonates with the experience of innovators themselves. After writing some of the definitive works of modern sociology, Simmel became increasingly interested in life and its processes.[15] Life, he wrote, is about flux, freedom and exploration. Yet life constantly creates forms, and it is through forms that action is organised. So, genetic mutations lead to the form of the body and the cell; musical experiment leads to forms like the symphony or the three-minute pop song; social action leads to the creation of new institutions. Yet it is in the nature of forms that they are almost opposite to life: they are fixed, permanent, limited by rules. And so, forms both express life and also stand against it.

Simmel used this insight to develop a remarkable set of ideas that went on to influence leading thinkers from Martin Heidegger to Jürgen Habermas. His account echoes the common experience of innovators themselves. Out of engagement with the world they come up with ideas, usually through messy processes of trial and error, kneading the dough again and again until it takes the right form. Then ideas become formalised, codified and defined. Then, in time, they become new organisations and practices. But, having become forms of this kind, they also begin to become new orthodoxies. The greatest aspiration of the innovator is in this sense, paradoxically, to stop innovation, so that their idea can be scaled or mainstreamed. Not surprisingly, many innovators experience ambivalence when they see their ideas translated into formal organisations. Some fall out with their creations; some have to be moved to one side by their organisation as the necessary condition for it to grow (since growth usually involves further formalisation).

Philosophy also points us to some other similarly dialectical features of innovation in practice. In Hegel's account of change, as in Simmel's, it takes place through processes of differentiation: by becoming different from what exists, or even negating it, we create the new and define our own identity. These processes of dialectical change are sometimes summarised in the famous triad of thesis, antithesis and synthesis, which can be a rough description of some of the history of social innovation with its common patterns of inversion in which peasants become bankers or patients become doctors or readers become the editors of encyclopaedias, usually on the way to new syntheses which combine elements of the old as well as the new. Dialectics can also (more accurately) be understood as a method for finding unity in opposites, ideas and practices that hold in balance apparently divergent forces, like the pressure to be simultaneously commercial and social.

But, even more relevant to the experience of social innovation is Hegel's account of the dynamics of externalisation and internalisation, mentioned earlier.[16] Often, ideas have to be extracted from daily life, taken from tacit knowledge and formally shaped before they can become powerful. In this externalised form they can then be processed and adapted – for example, defined as a business model or a business plan. But they become useful only if they are then reinserted into the practice of everyday life and internalised into the thinking of providers or citizens. Hegel's apparently abstract ideas were used to guide innovation in Japanese firms, notably through the theories of Ikujiro Nonaka,[17] who paid particular attention to the need for processes that drew out the insights of tacit knowledge among shop-floor workers, and then formalised them. They also fit with what we know about the processes of scaling and growth of social innovations. These are sometimes portrayed simply as diffusion or spread, or in terms of the growth of enterprises. But, without exception, social innovations with the greatest impact achieve their effects by changing how people think and how they see the world.

Evolution and complexity: Frames for thinking about the processes of innovation

Our next set of sources are present, if only implicitly, in any contemporary discussion of social change: the ideas of Charles Darwin and a century and a half of thinking about the nature of evolution. Innovation is in large part a process of evolution, with direct parallels with changes in the natural world. Evolutionary theory in particular helps us to focus on the three stages that are present in any process of innovation. One involves mutation – in evolutionary theory the random mutation of DNA that creates the potential for adaptation. Most mutations contribute little; and those that do contribute significant change generally fail. Sex is one of the devices which ensures a constant supply of new variants. Then comes selection – in evolutionary theory the focus is on fitness for environments: occasional mutations enable some organisms to outperform their predecessors and thus allow new types of organisms to flourish. Finally, there is replication – those mutations that pass the tests of selection will grow, displacing others and replicating their genes. Within evolutionary theory there are a huge range of sub-theories and metaphors that can be useful: such as the theories of predator–prey relationships and the many claims of evolutionary psychology which provide some insights into why certain kinds of innovation arise and then spread. The metaphor of the 'meme', the cultural equivalent of genes, has also proved influential, though it's not proved so useful for analysis.

In the social field today's interest is not in social Darwinism (which attempted in the late 19th century to apply evolutionary ideas directly to society) but, rather, using the inverted Darwinism of conscious action to advance evolution for human ends. By its nature social change cannot be comprehensively planned: but it can be pushed, nudged and guided. Where Darwinism focuses on how different organisms cope with changes to the environment, the inverted Darwinism of social innovation attends to how action can change the environment as well as the actors within it (so social innovators, for example, work to influence demand for their ideas as well as their supply).[18]

Other perspectives which are essentially evolutionary in nature have also shaped the field. Jane Jacobs, influenced by the work of Michael Young and others, used a variant of evolutionary thinking about cities as an antidote to the excesses of top-down planning. She favoured organic development, trial and error, and dispersed power, and in later writings extended this to a world-view of how economies and societies should be run.[19] More recently the open data and open source movements have advocated self-organising systems which use multiple horizontal links and complexity to solve problems.

In some of these fields there is growing attention to the importance of co-evolution. Biologists now emphasise the co-evolution of genes and cultures, making it meaningless to claim that a particular trait is X% caused by genes and Y% by culture. We know much more about the co-evolution of institutions and behaviours too – whether at the large scale of democracy and welfare states, or at the more granular level of public health programmes. Some of the difficulties experienced in spreading social innovations – such as Grameen's microcredit model or the public health models of Finland – can best be explained through this lens.

All of these insights have paralleled the emergence of complexity theory.[20] Complexity theory is neither a single theory nor wholly coherent and consistent. Rather, it is a family of concepts and insights that have been applied in many fields, sometimes extending the earlier insights of systems thinking and sometimes pointing in different directions. Its key concepts have been widely used: the role of feedback loops or, more broadly, feedback processes to understand why change sometimes accelerates but more often is inhibited; the idea of 'strange attractors'; the idea that societies are made up of both tightly and loosely coupled systems which respond very differently to shocks; the idea of organisations operating at 'the edge of chaos'; the idea of emergence, of complex structures and institutions emerging from very simple principles; and the idea of non-linearity, that many social processes do not follow linear relationships.

The insights of figures such as Ilya Prigogine, Brian Arthur, Stuart Kauffman and others have made this a rich and stimulating field.[21] It has certainly provided a very useful antidote to more simplistic currents of social innovation – anyone who has engaged with complexity theory is unlikely to talk glibly about 'solving social problems' or 'scaling' solutions. Instead, they are more likely to recognise that social challenges are messy, interconnected and not amenable to one-dimensional solutions. Complexity theory tends to force attention to the connections between things, to feed back and feed forward processes, to path dependence and to the many ways in which initial conditions can radically change outcomes. It tends to imply that policy should create generative rules rather than detailed, top-down prescription; that it should allow evolution and adaptation to local conditions; and that it should encourage the maximum feedback.

But it's less clear how useful these theories are beyond providing a rich menu of metaphors, and a mindset. The same has been true in economics. The work of figures like Benoit Mandelbrot successfully demolished the hubristic claims of financial forecasters – but offered little to replace them.[22] A good example of both the strengths and weaknesses is the case of the hugely successful campaign to halt the spread of AIDs in Uganda. The ABC campaign (abstain, be faithful, use condoms) has been described as an example of complexity theory in practice: ABC provided a few simple principles that could then be extended and adapted in many different ways. At the same time, the relative failure of attempts to replicate the ABC model confirms that complexity theory is rarely useful for prediction, or for shaping actions except at the most general level.[23] As Gareth Morgan suggested, these ideas may be useful mainly as ideas and frames rather than as tools which can directly guide action.[24]

Innovation studies

Innovation was not a central issue for the classical and neoclassical economists. Innovations were seen as exogenous or as a black box that didn't need to be explained. But since the 1950s, as its importance has become ever more obvious, a field of innovation studies has slowly taken shape. Some tried to make innovation more endogenous – this was the central theme of the work of Robert Solow (who analysed the contribution of new knowledge and innovation to economic growth) and of the endogenous growth theory associated with Paul Romer.[25] A cluster of loosely related bodies of research have put much more flesh on our understanding of innovation in general. These include William Baumol's accounts of capitalism as an innovation machine, as well as his work on the cost, disease, associated with activities like teaching and nursing, which can become a prompt for innovation.[26] Everett Rogers analysed diffusion patterns, both in business and beyond,[27] and was followed by an impressive school of successors.[28] Various other disciplines have also offered their insights, including the sociology of innovation (for example, Michael Piore's work on the decisive role played by interpretation[29]). Historians have studied both the transformational impact of some technologies (notably in Richard Nelson's work) and the longer sweep of technological change.[30] Arnold Pacey, for example, studied the roles of institutions as varied as monasteries and the military, and suggested that the most creative societies may have been those 'in which many types of institutions were active and in dialogue with each other', cutting across the different sectors and professions.[31]

There has been a great deal of work within business studies (from figures such as Rosabeth Moss Kanter, Gary Hamel and Clayton Christensen) addressing some of the common patterns of innovation, such as the relatively poor performance of very successful innovations in their early phases of competition with more mature and more optimised incumbents. Institutional analysis has mapped the behaviour of whole systems,[32] while the parallel study of scientific innovation has cross-fertilised with the economics of innovation, for example through the work of Nathan Rosenberg on non-linear processes in applied science,[33] and the ways in which end uses of innovations can be very different from the ones originally envisaged. There has also been a surge of interest in open innovation[34] and user-driven innovation,[35] both interesting examples of ideas from the social field being adapted to business.

The field of social innovation has, not surprisingly, drawn many useful insights from this literature, and it is common to find some uses of the basic concepts of innovation studies:

the distinctions between incremental and radical innovation; first mover and second mover advantage; the importance of absorptive capacity; and the ways in which innovation diffusion involves innovation too, since adopters will succeed best if they further enhance the innovations they adopt. In a later section I shall discuss the implications of perhaps the most impressive strand of innovation studies, the work undertaken over many years by Christopher Freeman, Giovanni Dosi, Luc Soete and others[36], which combined rigorous empirical analysis with theoretical creativity and which has direct implications for social innovation (for example, via the work of Ian Miles on innovation in services).

However, much of the work on business innovation is broadly descriptive rather than offering testable theses. The business literature has repeatedly been discredited for eulogising particular companies for their innovative genius at the very moment when they are about to hit crises. The more serious work may be hard to translate into the social field. For example, some research is suggestive of the links between market structures and innovation, pointing to the idea that sectors with oligopolistic cores and competitive edges may be more innovative than either monopolies or sectors made up of small competitors. But little serious analysis has been done on how much of this is applicable to social fields. Another example is the lack of any definitive view in the literature on whether businesses and other organisations benefit most from specialist innovation teams, funds and labs or from making innovation pervasive. There has been much analysis of the boundary between public returns and private returns in R&D, but this has proved hard to extend to the social field. Nor is there much clarity on how relevant intellectual property is. Clearly it is vital to innovation in technology. But it's rare for intellectual property to be easily protectable in the social field.[37]

Some of the most useful work has sought to interrogate widely assumed patterns. A good example is the work on tools for innovation,[38] which has challenged some of the claims made for radical 'out of the box' innovation made by business gurus and consultancies, showing how these are better understood as combinations of incremental steps which may therefore be easier for others to emulate.[39]

Theories of innovation and entrepreneurship

Our next set of sources concern the agents of change. In Adam Smith's classic account, the combination of markets, legal frameworks and property rights translates the self-interest and greed of millions of individuals into a force that promotes the prosperity of all.[40] The brilliance of the market mechanism is that it is automatic: by harnessing motives and energies which are already there, it avoids the need for a king or a commander to 'run' the economy. Instead, the economy runs itself and rewards both performance and innovation. In the 18th century Adam Smith was equally famous for a very different set of writings which looked at the 'moral sentiments' of sympathy and compassion which hold societies together.[41] Although he didn't put it in these terms, the two strands of his work can be brought together in the idea that all modern societies depend not only on the invisible hand of the market but also on another invisible hand: the legal and fiscal arrangements that serve to channel moral sentiments – the motivations of care, civic energy and social commitment – into practical form and thus into the service of the common good.[42] Just as markets draw on the energies and creativity of entrepreneurs willing to risk money and prestige, so too does social change draw on the often invisible fecundity of tens of thousands of individuals and small groups who spot needs and innovate solutions.

The most influential theorist who has been drawn on to make sense of these processes is Joseph Schumpeter, whose work, often overshadowed in the 20th century, has enjoyed a great revival of interest, partly thanks to the growing importance of innovation in the economy. This revival of interest has been helped by some superb books, such as *Prophet of Innovation*,[43] and by the vividness of much of Schumpeter's writings. Here are his words on the spirit of social pioneers:

> In the breast of one who wishes to do something new, the forces of habit rise up and bear witness against the embryonic project. A new and another kind of effort of will is therefore necessary in order to wrest, amidst the work and care of the daily round, scope and time for conceiving and working out the new

combination ... This mental freedom presupposes a great surplus force over the everyday demand and is something peculiar and by nature rare.[44]

Schumpeter's decisive contribution to economic theory was his attention to the role of entrepreneurs in driving change and pushing markets away from equilibrium. He claimed that 'stabilised capitalism is a contradiction in terms' and was interested in the dynamics of change.

The Schumpeterian view of how economies work has become much more widely accepted. In his account the entrepreneur is the decisive actor, seeking out opportunities, spotting under-served markets or unused assets, taking risks (with investors' money) and reaping rewards. His attention to the vital role of credit in providing funds for entrepreneurs to take risks has also become mainstream.

This perspective is very different in spirit to most of mainstream economics. It emphasises the search for what's not known, what's uncertain and what's unmeasurable. In perfect markets with perfect information there is no room for entrepreneurs. Instead, entrepreneurship highlights the difficultness of the world, its resistance to predictable plans and how we learn by bumping into things and then navigating around them. What entrepreneurs do is not wholly rational: in Schumpeter's words, 'the success of everything depends on intuition, the capacity of seeing things in a way which afterwards proves to be true, even though it cannot be established at the moment, and of grasping the essential fact, discarding the unessential, even though one can give no account of the principles by which this is done'.[45]

A very different view of entrepreneurship is associated with the work of Israel Kirzner,[46] who sees it not as the upsetter of equilibrium but as the creator of equilibrium, using information to take advantage of disequilibria and thus push the economy back into balance.[47] Like Schumpeter, Kirzner saw the entrepreneurial mind as distinct from rational management: it spots emerging patterns and 'weak signals', to use the current phrase; entrepreneurs demonstrate 'the ways in which the human agent can, by imaginative, bold leaps of faith, and determination, in fact create the future for which his present acts are designed'.[48]

Entrepreneurship thrives in fields of uncertainty, on the edges of industries and disciplines, and much less so in stable contexts or where risk can be calculated.

In either light, entrepreneurship is not peculiar to business, and the Austrian school of economists and philosophers, who were concerned with action in conditions of uncertainty, recognised this from the start. Schumpeter wrote of entrepreneurship in politics as well as business (and was for a brief period a minister) and saw entrepreneurship as a universal phenomenon, albeit one that was particularly dynamic in capitalist economies. Ludwig von Mises wrote that entrepreneurship 'is not the particular feature of a special group or class of men; it is inherent in every action and burdens every actor'.[49] So, it has been natural to extend Schumpeter's ideas to other fields, to see within universities some academics acting as entrepreneurs, assembling teams, spotting gaps, promoting the superiority of their ideas and bringing together whatever resources they can find to win allegiance; or to see the founders and builders of great religions as great entrepreneurs, pulling together belief, attraction and money.

Social entrepreneurship adapts the same ideas to civil society and social resources; it leads to an interest in the character of the entrepreneur, their motivations, the patterns of creating enterprises and then growing them; and, as with business entrepreneurs, the conflicts between them and the providers of capital, on the one hand, and the providers of labour, on the other.[50]

Just as Schumpeter's account encouraged a heroic view of the business entrepreneur battling against the resistance of society, so has the same happened with social entrepreneurs. At one point there were even claims (from one of the leading US support organisations) of a formula – one social entrepreneur for every million in the population (though, interestingly, it then went to the other extreme, with the more inclusive slogan 'everyone a changemaker'[51]). According to the radical individualistic view, the more that exceptional individuals could be provided with resources, and the more that any constraints could be removed, the more likely they would be to solve social problems.

By contrast, less attention has been paid to the other key actors in social innovation: the networks, teams, patrons and investors, even though, as in natural science, the more particular cases are studied in detail, the more it becomes apparent that individuals achieve great things only because of the complementary skills and institutions that surround them. It's interesting to note that Schumpeter in his later years became increasingly interested in 'cooperative entrepreneurship' within large firms and in the role of teams, and was convinced that this was a vital field for study.

He also recognised that profit was unlikely to be the only or even the main motivation for business entrepreneurs. Clearly for social entrepreneurs a wide range of motives intermingle, from altruism to recognition, from financial reward to the hunger for power.

However, neither Schumpeter nor Kirzner addressed the broader question of value. Both treat economic value as an unproblematic concept. Yet one of the keys to their wider use may be to link them to parallel developments in economic sociology, particularly the work of figures like Harrison White and David Stark. Drawing in creative ways on the work of Luc Boltanski,[52] they have shown how societies and economies are made up of systems of 'multiple worth', each with very different ways of thinking about value. Seen through this lens, entrepreneurship isn't just about spotting new opportunities for profit. Instead, in David Stark's words, it involves 'the ability to keep multiple orders of worth in play and to exploit the resulting ambiguity'.[53] In other words, it goes beyond the ability to exploit uncertainty rather than just calculable risk, and also entails arbitraging, or translating between, distinct fields. This is surely a good description of much social innovation and entrepreneurship, whose most successful practitioners are fluent across fields – medicine and business, voluntary action and education, law and politics – and were able to juggle multiple orders of worth. It may also be one of the crucial reasons why attempts to distil social value into single metrics have been unsuccessful: by denying the plurality of value systems, these attempt to bring certainty to actions that have to be ambiguous or multiple in nature.

How we think about entrepreneurship, and theorise it, has obvious practical implications. The idea of business entrepreneurship led in time to the idea that states should not only enable it through laws and (light) regulation but also support it, and many governments provide tax incentives, training courses and celebrations to encourage entrepreneurship. Social entrepreneurship, too, has encouraged various kinds of support from governments and foundations: prizes, funds and networks. As in business, sources of credit and investment are crucial, and this is the reason why, for example, specialised banks (such as Banca Prossima) or public investment funds for social entrepreneurs (such as the UK's UnLtd and Big Society Capital) matter so much.[54]

Techno-economic paradigms and the historical context for social innovation

Social innovation is powerfully shaped by historical context. What kinds of innovation will be possible at any point will be determined by prevailing technologies, institutions and mentalities. Wonderful ideas may simply be impossible at the wrong time. Some of the most influential and useful ideas for making sense of historical contexts have come from a group of academics led by Christopher Freeman and Carlota Perez[55] and from figures such as Luc Soete. Their aim was to understand the long waves of technological and economic change and to seek out common patterns and congruences between technologies, economics and social organisation.

Perhaps the most influential recent theorist of the connections between technological change and the economy is Carlota Perez, the Venezuelan economist who is a scholar of the successive techno-economic paradigms which define the shape of the economy. She has studied how these intersect with the financial cycles that have repeated themselves again and again during capitalism's relatively brief history. In Perez's account, which builds on the work of Nikolai Kondratiev and Schumpeter, the cycles begin with the emergence of new technologies and infrastructures that promise great wealth. These then fuel frenzies of speculative investment, with dramatic rises in stock and other prices, whether in the canal mania of the 1790s, the railway mania of the 1830s and 1840s, the surge of global infrastructures in the 1870s and 1880s, or the booms that accompanied the motorcar, electricity and telephone in the 1920s and of biotechnology and the internet in the 1990s and 2000s.[56]

During these phases of technological exuberance finance is in the ascendant and laissez-faire policies become the norm. Letting markets freely grow seems evidently wise when they are fuelling such visible explosions of wealth. Some investors and entrepreneurs become very rich very quickly. Exuberance in markets may be reflected in exuberance and a laissez-faire attitude in personal morals – a glittering world of parties, celebrities and gossip for the rest of the public to hang on to and experience vicariously. Entrepreneurs take wild risks and reap wild rewards. The economy appears to be a place for easy predation, offering rewards without too much work, and plenty of chances to siphon off surpluses. The booms then turn out to be bubbles and are followed by dramatic crashes. 1797, 1847, 1893, 1929 and 2008 are a few of the decisive years when crashes took stock markets tumbling and brought with them the dramatic bankruptcy of many of the most prominent companies of the booms, like so many railway companies in the later 19th century. Sometimes currencies collapse too.

After these crashes, and periods of turmoil, the potential of the new technologies and infrastructures is eventually realised. But that happens only once new social, political and economic institutions and regulations have come into being which are better aligned with the characteristics of the new economy and with the underlying desires of the society. Radical social innovation plays a key role in making possible much more widespread deployment of the key technologies. Once that has happened, economies then go through surges of growth as well as social progress, like the *belle époque* or the post–war miracle.

These patterns can be seen clearly in the Great Depression and its aftermath. Before the crisis of 1929 the elements of a new economy and a new society were already available. The promise of technologies like the motorcar and telephone encouraged the speculative bubbles of the 1920s. But they were not understood by the people in power nor were they embedded in institutions.

Then, during the 1930s, the economy transformed, in Perez's words, from one based on

> steel, heavy electrical equipment, great engineering works (canals, bridges, dams, tunnels) and heavy chemistry, mainly geared towards big spenders ... into a mass production system catering to consumers and the massive defence markets. Radical demand management and income redistribution innovations had to be made, of which the directly economic role of the state is perhaps the most important.

What resulted was the rise of mass consumerism, and an economy supported by ubiquitous infrastructures for electricity, roads and telecommunications and

> based on low cost oil and energy intensive materials (especially petrochemicals and synthetics), and led by giant oil, chemical and automobile and other mass durable goods producers. Its 'ideal' type of productive organisation at the plant levels was the continuous flow assembly-line ... the 'ideal' type of firm was the 'corporation' ... including in-house R&D and operating in oligopolistic markets in which advertising and marketing activities played a major role. It required large numbers of middle range skills in both blue- and white-collar areas ... a vast infrastructural network of motorways, service stations, airports, oil and petrol distribution systems ....[57]

The Great Depression helped to usher in new economic and welfare policies in countries like New Zealand and Sweden which later became part of the mainstream across the developed world. In the US it led to banking reform, the New Deal, social security and unemployment insurance (both backed by big business) and later the GI Bill of Rights 1944. As in Europe, big business could see advantages in the socialisation of risk: it ensured a more stable and efficient society and tended to raise costs more for small than for large firms. In Britain it was the

Depression, as much as war, that led to the creation of the welfare state and the NHS in the 1940s. Social innovation thrived in the wake of the Depression, with a surge of energy in many societies as welfare states were created, along with new arrangements at work and in politics. What emerged were more strongly bonded societies and new commitment devices – the large firm, the welfare state, as well as new and revitalised political parties, all of which were ways of getting people to pre-commit to actions and behaviours that then created value for them. Predatory extremes were reined in (in the US, marginal income tax rates peaked at 91% in the 1950s), and the dominant spirit in many countries emphasised fairness and fair chances.

An important dimension of these patterns is that phases of entrepreneurial exuberance tend to be followed by phases of consolidation and oligopoly. Industries become more ordered; the products and services they provide become more settled, and more reliable, alongside dominance by just a few firms. Bureaucracy wins out over buccaneering risk takers. This happened to the Hollywood film industry, telephony and cars in the 1920s, and then to software and computing 60 years later. Firms like Apple and Amazon are attempting a similar consolidation today, using business models that integrate vertically and lock in their customers. For them there are the benefits of monopoly, while for their customers there are the benefits of stability. Parallel patterns can be found in the social field: periods of intensive innovation and entrepreneurialism (such as the last decades of the 19th century) tend to be followed by periods of consolidation, as large NGOs become more bureaucratic and more managerial in approach.

Perez suggests that we may be on the verge of another great period of institutional innovation and experiment that will lead to new compromises between the claims of capital and the claims of society and of nature. The rise of a low-carbon economy, implying new kinds of arrangement for housing, transport and fuel, the maturing of a broadband economy, with ubiquitous social networks and open data, are all part of this story, and they provide some of the context for social innovations.

Here Perez's work intersects with parallel theories that have tried to make sense of the dynamics of societies based on information and communication. Manuel Castells's subtle and extensive accounts aim at a synthetic view that stretches from business to identity and social movements.[58] His work has shown the interrelationships between technological innovation, social innovation and power. Others, like Yann Moulier-Boutang, have tried to suggest a new phase of capitalism in which new kinds of enterprise (including ones based on common goods) are thriving.[59]

There is much to debate in these sweeping historical overviews. They can be criticised for being overdeterministic, or for exaggerating the influence of technology. But, as Eric Hobsbawm wrote of Kondratiev cycles, they have 'convinced many historians and even some economists that there is something in them, even if we don't know what.'[60]

Pragmatism: The epistemology of social innovation

The next family of ideas takes us back to philosophy and concerns the nature of the knowledge associated with social innovation. Here the most influential and useful set of ideas comes from the late 19th century, and in particular the pragmatist school of Charles Peirce, William James and John Dewey. They are of interest because they accurately describe the types of knowledge involved in social innovation, knowledge which is often rooted in practice and which is not timeless, universal or abstract in the way that knowledge about physics would be.

This is a good summary by one author of the nature of their ideas:

> ideas are not out there waiting to be discovered but are tools that people devise to cope with the world in which they find themselves ... ideas are produced not by individuals but are social ... ideas do not develop according to some inner logic of their own but are entirely dependent, like germs, on human careers and environment ... and since ideas are provisional responses to particular situations their survival depends on not on their immutability but on their adaptability.[61]

The pragmatists went out of fashion for a time. But it is striking how many of the most interesting contemporary thinkers have re-engaged with them. I have already mentioned Roberto Mangabeira Unger's use of their ideas. Bruno Latour, one of the world's leading thinkers on the place of science in society is another example of the creative reappropriation of this tradition, notably in his book on Walter Lippman and the 'phantom public', which explores the point, fundamental to much of the work of social innovation, that in processes of social change it may be necessary to create the public that becomes the subject of action.[62] In other words, it is not enough to have a good idea, to promote it or even to show its relevance. At each stage of social development, a new collective capacity may be needed which then calls forth the innovation.

On a more prosaic level, the growth of individual social innovations demonstrates a similar pattern. Innovations grow only if there is the right mix of effective supply, which means evidence that the innovation works, and effective demand, which means someone willing to pay for it. For innovators the implication may be that generating demand (for such things as drug treatments or eldercare) can often be more important than promoting supply; that, in turn, may require the creation of a new kind of public, a public that cares about cutting carbon emissions, that consciously stands for humanitarian intervention to alleviate famine and that is willing to put its savings into social investment products.

Pragmatism also links to what could be called 'experimentalism', the belief in constant experiment in social forms. The scientific method always intrigued social scientists as well as social reformers. Why couldn't society conduct experiments precisely analogous to those conducted by chemists or physicists? The economist Irving Fisher is generally credited as the inventor of randomised controlled trials (RCTs)[63] which he first used in agriculture. A couple of decades later Karl Popper suggested a grander philosophical account of experiment in his books *The Open Society and its Enemies* and *The Logic of Scientific Discovery*, advocating a vision of societies and science engaged in perpetual processes of experiment and disproof, with certainty always elusive, and openness to falsification the true mark of freedom.[64]

More recently, experiments and RCTs have again fired the imagination of social innovators and reformers, notably in fields like criminal justice and economic development. The practice hasn't always been sophisticated and has not caught up with the debates in medicine, where a more sceptical view of RCTs has been formed by experience. But the pragmatist spirit is as alive as ever.

Theoretical approaches to purpose and ends: Wellbeing and happiness

My final set of sources concerns the ends of social innovation: what it's for. For social movements, this was rarely problematic in the past: the goals of ending poverty or spreading rights seemed almost self-evident. But since 2000 more serious attention has been paid to what counts as societal progress.[65] This debate led in the past to the development of indices like the HDI – the Human Development Index – but the pace has accelerated since the year 2000, partly thanks to the work of the OECD under Enrico Giovannini in the 'Beyond GDP' project, which encouraged many statistical offices around the world to experiment with various combinations of indices and new measures of both economic prosperity and societal success.[66]

For some, the central question is how to measure capabilities, the means for people to exercise freedom (with figures such as Amartya Sen arguing that there will inevitably be discussion and disagreement over which capabilities are critical). Many social entrepreneurs and innovators describe their own work in this way, realising otherwise wasted potential. Expanding capabilities is a good in itself and allows people to decide on their ends for themselves. For others, the focus should be on measuring happiness and wellbeing, seeing these as the common goal for societies to aspire to.[67] There are many arguments to be had about how to deal with hedonic and eudaimonic measures, and the relationships between pleasure, fulfilment, meaning and other concepts of wellbeing.[68]

What connects all of these arguments is a view of value. Antonio Damasio has argued persuasively that there is a fundamental concept of biological value which is analytically robust, and which is prior to either economic or social value.[69] This is the value of survival and flourishing. Survival depends on homeostasis, preserving the conditions for our bodies to live, with the right temperature, food and water and physical safety. But Damasio argues that we can also extend from this basic value to recognise the conditions under which we are fully alive, mentally stimulated, socially engaged, loved and cared for: in other words, wellbeing is indeed a universal value and a solid foundation for constructing more specific measures in fields such as social innovation or action.

Perhaps the more interesting implications of this new field of theory and analysis are that it opens up novel questions: which kinds of consumption most contribute to happiness and which may diminish it? What kinds of work organisation are most conducive to wellbeing? Can philanthropy make up for the unhappiness of a very unequal society?

A few conclusions and a few gaps

Kurt Lewin famously said that there is nothing as useful as a good theory. So, which of these theories are useful and how? What can we extract from these very diverse and rich theoretical traditions? Clearly, social innovation is not contained or monopolised by any one of them. It cuts across disciplines, fields and areas of knowledge. But there are some common elements which have some clear implications for practice.

First, social innovation is an example of the much broader field of evolutionary change that takes place in biology, culture and societies, with some common patterns of mutation, selection and growth. Evolution happens at multiple levels with contradictory results – what's optimal at one level may not be so at another. Like any evolutionary process, innovation is not easy to plan or predict, but conscious action can make it easier for people and communities to self-organise and shape the direction of evolution. It follows that the most successful innovation systems will be marked by strong capacities to mutate, select and grow.

Second, the particular opportunities for social innovation will be heavily shaped by historical circumstance: prevailing types of institution and industry; prevailing technologies;

and the availability of freedom or spare capital. So, the specific circumstances of diffusing low-carbon technologies, globalisation, legitimation crises for governments and banks, are all part of the context. Understanding the specifics of context, with a wide peripheral vision and a sense of how the pieces fit together, is vital for anyone wanting to succeed as an investor, supporter or innovator.

Third, the motivations for social innovation will usually come from tensions, contradictions, dissatisfactions and the negation of what exists. We can draw from Hegel, Simmel and others the insight that these tensions are not unfortunate by-products of innovation; they are part of its nature, as are the disappointment and even alienation that innovation processes generate. The very act of innovation is also an act of rejection, and this colours its social and political nature and gives it a necessarily uneasy relationship with any fixed institutions, power structures and policies. The challenge, it follows, is to capture these tensions and contradictions within institutions rather than to try to iron them out.

Fourth, social innovation as a field seems inseparable from its underlying ethic, which is one of collaboration – acting with, rather than only to or for, a belief in rough equality, a cultural commitment to the idea of equality of communication (theorised in more depth by Jürgen Habermas) and perhaps an implicit idea that through collaboration we can discover our full humanity.

Fifth, the nature of the knowledge involved in social innovation is different from knowledge about physics or biology, or indeed the claims made for economic knowledge: it is more obviously contingent, temporary and often context bound. That evidence shows that something works in one place and one time does not imply that the same model will work in another place and another time. As Marx put it, we 'make the circumstances dance by singing to them their own melody'.[70]

Finally, there are signs that the growing interest in wellbeing could provide both the theoretical and the practical glue to hold social innovation practice together and provide a common measure of success.

There are many gaps in this account of theory, some of which are beginning to be filled. One is the very fertile work that has been done in recent years on commons and collective goods, led by Elinor Ostrom.[71] Much of this is suggestive for social innovators, particularly those interested in fields such as water conservation, land management or energy. The lively field of resilience studies shows how much practical use can be made of the best theories in this area.[72] But there has so far been little connection to research on the dynamics of social innovation. Another link with great potential is the social psychology of social innovation. The lively research that's been done in recent years on the dynamics of cooperation and reciprocity is suggestive of why certain kinds of social enterprise work: how they align hearts and minds, and how, through repeated interactions, they encourage people to behave in more collaborative ways. But it's waiting to be taken further in relation to particular cases and testable hypotheses.

Each of these is a space to watch and could become an important part of the network of ideas that will shape the social innovation mind. For now, we do not have a single theory of social innovation. But we do have the potential to begin joining the dots, linking this network of concepts more coherently together into a useful way of seeing the world.

8

Social science and intelligence design

In this chapter I turn to how social science can be adapted to the challenges and tools of the 2020s, becoming more data driven, more experimental and fuelled by more dynamic feedback between theory and practice.[1]

Social science at its grandest is the way societies understand themselves: why they cohere or fall apart; why some grow and others shrink; why some care and others hate; how big structural forces explain the apparently special facts of our own biographies. It observes but also shapes action, and then learns from those actions.

Starting with the idea of social science as collective self-knowledge, I describe how new approaches to intelligence of all kinds can help to reinvigorate it. I begin with data and computational social science and then move on to cover the idea of social R&D and experimentation, new ways for universities to link into practice, including social science parks, accelerators tied to social goals, challenge-based methods and social labs of all kinds, before concluding with the core argument: an account of how social science can engage with the emerging field of intelligence design. This is, I hope, a plausible and desirable direction of travel.

The rise of data-driven and computational social science

We are all familiar with the extraordinary explosion of new ways to observe social phenomena, which are bound to change how we ask social questions and how we answer them. Each of us leaves a data trail of whom we talk to, what we eat and where we go. It's easier than ever to survey people, to spot patterns, to scrape the web, to pick up data from sensors or to interpret moods from facial expressions. It's easier than ever to gather perceptions and emotions as well as material facts – for example, through sentiment analysis of public debates. And it's easier than ever for organisations to practise social science – whether it's investment organisations analysing market patterns, human resources departments using behavioural science or local authorities using ethnography.

These tools are not monopolised by professional social scientists. In cities, for example, offices of data analytics[2] link multiple data sets and governments use data to feed tools using AI – like Predpol or HART – to predict who is most likely to go to hospital or end up in prison.[3] The opening up of administrative data is set to have a big impact through new programmes like LEO (Longitudinal Education Outcomes), which links UK school data to tax records and could transform our understanding of social mobility.[4] Surprising patterns invariably emerge when data is combined in new ways – like the police discovery that the best predictor of domestic homicide is a previous suicide attempt (by the perpetrator).[5]

Within universities, computational social science has a slightly narrower definition, usually referring to social simulation, social network analysis and social media analysis. Huge data sets are being gathered on everything from human history and archaeology to image creation and literatures, building on the long tradition of longitudinal studies (from the Framingham Heart Study to the National Child Development Study). Large-scale (computational) social science projects include the Human Project[6] and Social Science One,[7] and very effective proponents of new research tools, such as Matthew Salganik,[8] now reach large audiences.

Social media provide a particularly fertile area for research, and some big companies are beginning to open up their data for researchers – for example, to understand the impact of social media on elections. There are strong umbrella bodies, conferences[9] and research programmes, and signs of a big shift coming in training for social scientists.

This revolution in data, experiment and prediction, and the spread of tools to observe, analyse and predict, bring with them all sorts of challenges, many of them ethical: how to ensure that enough data is open; how to get the right data, since many of the most important facts are not captured; how not to ignore the left-behind; how to avoid algorithms reflecting and then legitimising the biases of past actions.

But I suspect that the most profound challenge will be to develop better concepts and theories to make sense of data. We need, for example, much better theories of how large parts of economies can work without intellectual property; theories of place and belonging; theories to explain enduring inequalities; theories to explain unusual risks, and how social and economic systems can be prepared for the events that occurred once in a century or millennium but that may be happening more often.

In the natural sciences some argued in the 2000s that the growth of data would obviate the need for theory. Data would automatically show patterns. Theorists would become redundant.[10]

A counter-view, though, is that it's hard to make sense of any data without models or hypotheses and, interestingly, analysis of human cognition confirms that we start with models and then feed data in, rather than the other way around. Much as I welcome the way that disciplines like economics have become more empirical again, it's crucial that their engagement with data fuels creative generation of new theories and hypotheses. Otherwise we may just be left with better-informed confusion and the vice (which I describe later on) of being forever trapped in first-loop learning.

Social R&D and social innovation linked to social science: Learning through praxis

A key insight of social innovation is that societal self-knowledge often comes from praxis – the interplay of action and analysis, theory and practice – rather than from detached observation. Anything that doesn't yet exist (whether a new model welfare state or a novel way of providing eldercare) cannot easily be designed on the basis of backward-facing knowledge and data, hence the inherent tension between social creativity, on the one hand, and orthodox social science, on the other.

The field of social innovation, which claims to provide answers to this dilemma, has grown greatly over the last 10 or 20 years around the world both in research and in practice. Social innovation is now supported by many new funds provided by governments and foundations, new legal forms and capacity-building programmes, courses and research programmes in universities.[11] It's also now seriously engaging with the potential of data[12].

Social innovation both feeds off traditional social science – for example, insights into the impact of early years education – and challenges it, since often practice is ahead of theory. This means that the task for universities has been to make sense of, critique and analyse what's working in the real world, rather than following the models of traditional technology innovation where basic theories are developed in universities and then spread out into industry in a linear fashion.

An emerging strand within social innovation is social R&D. The idea crystallised in the late 19th century that R&D could be systematically funded and organised. Today, between 2% and 4% of GDP in most advanced economies is devoted to R&D, funded by government, foundations or businesses and carried out by universities, government labs and corporations of many kinds. We now take it for granted that systematic R&D is crucial to economic growth and prosperity, which is why it is supported by all sorts of subsidies and tax breaks. The basic idea is to do fundamental research and then, using experimental scientific methods, to turn the insights gained into new products and services which can be useful in the world, whether these are pharmaceutical drugs or new kinds of aeroplane.

The idea of social R&D, however, is much less common, and indeed most R&D funders around the world focus almost exclusively on hardware and using knowledge from the natural sciences rather than the social sciences.

At various points over the last century there have been attempts to apply R&D methods to social change (including by big US foundations like Ford and Rockefeller in the 1960s). Canada has been at the forefront of this, thinking through how public funders of research and big foundations could finance systematic research experimentation on social challenges such as homelessness, integration of refugees or youth unemployment.[13]

The mechanics of doing this are not so different from traditional R&D, involving funding at multiple stages running from fundamental research through the generation of practical ideas, testing, experiment, gathering of evidence and then, hopefully, the scaling and propagation of the models which work. However, there are still no examples of social R&D being done systematically and at scale, and this debate has hardly started in most countries.

There are many challenges in doing social R&D well. They include how to orchestrate experimentation; how to harvest insights and ensure they are used, whether in government policies or the practices of professions like teaching or social work; how to handle the ethical and political challenges of experiments involving people's lives; and how to avoid some of the risks of distortion, such as ignoring lived experience.

I have had some direct experience of applying R&D in new fields, through Nesta's digital R&D fund for the arts[14] and its Innovation Growth Lab, which pioneered systematic testing out of economic policy ideas. The Behavioural Insights Team (BIT),[15] which Nesta co-owns, uses similar methods in behavioural economics, running dozens of real-life experiments to find out what kinds of nudges actually work in encouraging people to pay their taxes on time, retrofit their homes or adopt healthier life-styles.

Experimentation has long been normal in health and is now mainstream in many parts of business, with companies like Amazon and Google doing A/B testing on new services of all kinds. Since 2010 there has been more use of experimentalism in governments, led by Canada, Finland, the United Arab Emirates and the UK, all of which in different ways have introduced more systematic approaches to testing out new policies on a small scale before they are implemented across the whole country.[16]

This new culture of experiment is influencing many professions and turning them into social scientists. This shift is helped in the UK by a network of What Works Centres (linked by the Alliance for Useful Evidence[17]). There's already a network of police officers using experimental methods – the Society of Evidence Based Policing[18] – to generate useful knowledge. In some countries school teachers see their role as combining both teaching and research, working with their peers to try out variations to curriculum or teaching methods (and the Educational Endowment Foundation[19] encourages and funds this). The new children's social care What Works Centre is mobilising thousands of social workers to generate and use evidence in a similar spirit. Many charities try to define a 'theory of change' and collect data to make sense of their impact, embedding into the everyday Karl Popper's vision of 'methods of trial and error, of inventing hypotheses which can be practically tested'[20]. Much of government and social action remains untouched by any of this. But systematic social R&D is no longer a pipe–dream.

New institutions linking practice and theory around the university: Social science parks, challenge-based learning and social accelerators

So, how should universities respond to this growing interest in learning by doing and active experiment? Here I summarise some emerging approaches that complement the classic activities of universities with others which generate insights through engagement with practice: social science parks, challenge-based learning, social labs and social accelerators.

The social science park

In the 1960s and the decades after, many universities created science parks next to them to provide a home for spin-off companies, larger businesses and laboratories. The notion was that science parks like this would help the translation of basic research from universities into business, and there are now literally thousands of these parks around the world. The social sciences were reluctant to develop similar models. Since 2010, however, several self-styled social science parks have arisen.

One of these is at Cardiff University[21] and brings together the university, Nesta's Y Lab and the What Works Centre for Public Policy in Wales. The idea is to create a space – which makes more sense in city centres than greenfield sites – where accelerators, labs and social ventures can grow, with active cross-pollination of practical knowledge and academic research.

The social labs

Over the last decade hundreds of new labs have been set up within governments and universities to pioneer public and social innovation.[22] They take many forms,[23] some using data, others design, still others citizen ideas, and they have varied relationships to formal structures.[24] Some of the most interesting ones sit on the edge of universities, providing a space for praxis, and they also increasingly connect to each other, creating global networks for rapid sharing on topics like joblessness or transport design.[25]

Challenge-based universities

A related trend is the rise of challenge-based university models. Here the idea is to base the work of the university more around problem solving than the propagation of established disciplines. These models mobilise undergraduates and graduates to work in teams, usually interdisciplinary, to solve real-life problems, whether in science and engineering or in the social life of their city. I've documented the many models in use around the world from Aalto in Finland to Stanford in California, from Olin in the US to Tsinghua in China[26], and shown how this method of working can be powerful as a pedagogical tool to help students not only to deepen their understanding of core disciplines but also to understand how the real world works, and how to collaborate and achieve change. With well over 150 million students in universities around the world there is huge scope to mobilise many more of them to work on real-life problems, for example, around the United Nations' Sustainable Development Goals.[27]

Social accelerators

Since the 1990s there has been a big expansion of business accelerators, some linked to universities and some in city centres, providing more systematic support to business start-ups,[28] with greater analysis of what makes them work and not work.[29] A more recent trend has been to apply similar models to achieving social impact.[30] These support start-up social enterprises, charities or for-purpose commercial enterprises which can achieve a reasonable financial return and a social goal. The rigour of having to create a viable venture forces attention to evidence and results, and universities have become increasingly interested in hosting accelerators of this kind as a way to put social science to work. Each of these approaches encourages social science to be engaged, practical and experimental, and each challenges traditional disciplinary boundaries.

Intelligence design and the role of collective intelligence

These new approaches offer new answers to the broader challenge for social science: how to truly live up to its role as society's collective self-knowledge, providing insights into everything from jobs to families, from war to happiness.

I believe the best answers lie in seeing social sciences through the lens of intelligence design and asking how well they orchestrate the different tools and elements that together make up a recognisably intelligent system or society.

If we look at intelligence in any serious large-scale system or organisation, it includes some of the following elements, all of which should be vital to a society's self-understanding:

- observation and data, which are quantitative and qualitative, relational and experiential;
- models of how the world works, which are vital for making sense of observations;
- analysis of patterns and dynamics as well as prediction;
- memory (including both history and memory of what works);
- creativity (including the link to social innovation);

- judgement and wisdom (in particular on the relationship between more general laws and particular contexts).

Any new social science discipline or sub-discipline that was being invented today would surely need an account of how it organises each of these functions (I showed in my book *Big Mind*,[31] for example, how economics could be reinterpreted in this way). The various methods mentioned earlier in this piece – from computational social science to experiments – fit in as parts of such an approach but lose much of their impact if they are seen only as methods in search of problems rather than starting with problems and working backwards to find the most suitable insights, theories and methods.[32]

Unfortunately, most disciplines have a quite unbalanced approach, often very strong on some parts, like observation or memory, and very weak on others. Moreover, I'm not aware of any with a coherent account of how they should mirror the crucial property of intelligence in individual human brains, which is the ability to connect these functions, from observations to judgement and creativity, ideally in close to real time.

These weaknesses become even more apparent if we situate social sciences within a broader story of societal learning. Intelligence in practice always involves learning loops: first-loop learning, which fits new data into existing models, paradigms and frameworks; second-loop learning, which generates new concepts and categories; and third-loop learning, which develops new ways of thinking. These together provide a good summary of what a healthy social science should look like (computational social science is itself a good example of third-loop learning, but is only as good as the second-loop learning it builds on). Yet some disciplines become trapped in the first loop, continuously seeking to feed new data into old models rather than generating new categories.

Thinking about social science as applied intelligence makes it more natural to straddle disciplinary boundaries, as many have advocated. For example, echoing E.O. Wilson and others, Nicholas Christakis has argued that, next to the data revolution and the rediscovery of experimentation, the key radical changes impacting on the social sciences today are huge advances in the biological sciences, specifically, discoveries in physiology, neuroscience and genetics (which have led to the emergence of new fields such as sociogenomics and biosocial science).[33] Others argue that it's the ability to think systemically that is crucial to the future of social science, learning from ecology and evolution, or reinvigorating its capabilities for design and imagination, which were quite strong in the 19th century but which were largely squeezed out by analytical orthodoxy in the 20th century.

In many fields there is an evident need for more synthetic approaches. For example, we still lack good accounts of feelings and moods and how these both influence, and are caused by, economic, social and political events. George Akerlof and Robert Schiller observed that: 'We will never really understand important economic events unless we confront the fact that their causes are largely mental in nature.'[34] But a viable synthesis of psychology and economics at both the individual and the collective level remains distant and the social sciences tend to resist change, to be inward looking, to be attached to particular methods, to be protective of boundaries, to be untroubled when the dominant models visibly fail and to be epistemologically conservative.

Collective intelligence

For social sciences, in particular, any interest in more conscious intelligence design quickly brings in questions of collective intelligence: how to harness social inputs, drawing on the hunger of many people to be creators of knowledge, not just users – generating information, running experiments and drawing conclusions. At the moment this shift to mass engagement in knowledge is most visible in neighbouring fields. Digital humanities mobilise many volunteers to input data and interpret texts – for example, making millions of ancient Arabic texts machine readable. Even more striking is the growth of citizen science: Galaxy Zoo has over a million volunteers scanning for new stars; eBird[35] gathers millions of reports; some 1.5 million people in the US monitor river streams and lakes, and SETI@home[36] has 5 million volunteers. In 2018 a University of Washington study estimated the economic value of citizen science at over $2.5 billion each year.[37]

This drive for people to become creators of knowledge that's relevant to them is very evident in healthcare, where patients' groups are now large, funding their own research and gathering data – like the Genetic Alliance,[38] representing patients with rare conditions. But so far there has been much less of this in social science, despite traditions like Mass Observation[39] and despite the fact that it is in many ways easier for people to observe and classify social phenomena than physical ones. Yet there are obvious parallels, and no shortage of fascination with social facts, that could prompt people to track what's happening on the streets, the prevalence of hate crime or speech and the emergence of new kinds of economic life.

If social science could become more embedded in daily life, then society could itself become more of a lab and more citizens could become part-time social scientists. Here we see a possible future in which the role of the specialist mutates into more of a coach and a partner, an aide to an intelligent society, more than a caste apart – a vision that would revive older social science traditions, including John Stuart Mill's belief in experimental progress, John Dewey's emphasis on how societies learn and, from the 1960s, Donald Campbell's advocacy of a truly experimental society, 'a process utopia, not a utopian social structure per se ... [that] seeks to implement Popper's recommendation of a social technology for piecemeal social engineering ...'.[40] We're all familiar with the old idea that it's better to teach a man to fish than just to give him fish. The implication of this long tradition is that it's better to skill up society's ability to do social science, rather than only giving it already-packaged social science conclusions.

Social scientists using collective intelligence

One of the most promising developments is the proliferation of tools to support social scientists, which allows them to act as something more like a collective intelligence. There are tools like Ureka to follow latest research, as well as ResearchGate, Academia.edu and Iris.ai[41] – research discovery with artificial intelligence. BenchFly, was set up to help researchers create and share videos; IN-PART to connect researchers with industry;

and others like SciLine, Linknovate, konfer, Pivot, Kolabtree, Academic Labs and Ohio Innovation Exchange.[42] There is Wonder,[43] to which you can e-mail questions and expert researchers will compile a list of resources for you. Thinklab[44] is an algorithm for distributing resources for comments and discussion by researchers and others, to reward engaging in difficult topics. Real Scientists[45] is a Twitter account where researchers and science journalists take over and talk about their life and outputs. The Conversation[46] provides news, while Nesta's Rhodonite and Clio search engines provide new ways to analyse trends in innovation, technology and social science at a global scale. All are attempts to apply intelligence design methods to the work of social science.

A brief conclusion

The main message of this chapter is that social sciences should more often start with problems rather than specific disciplinary approaches, situate their own tools within a broader theory of intelligence and build up a range of complementary methods alongside the classic ones of the academy (peer-reviewed journal, lecture and so on).

To me this seems an obvious direction of travel. But it rubs against tradition, inertia and the pull of status. The social sciences have quite a lot to say about why systems so often resist change. But they also show how, in time, new generations tend to break down the barriers.

9

Observation, interpretation and activism: Sociology's role in social change

Introduction

The decade after the financial crisis of 2007/08 saw many societies surprised by themselves: surprised by the return of apparently fading attitudes; surprised by anger and distrust; and surprised by the rise of new political forces.

These phenomena are social ones. But most of the leading commentators in many societies have struggled to make sense of them. They are reasonably proficient in economics, and can talk meaningfully about GDP or exports, inflation and unemployment. But they have little if any grounding in sociology or, for that matter, anthropology.

The public perception of sociology (in the UK, at least) was cruelly summed up a few years ago by an advertisement in which the actress Maureen Lipman talks on the phone to her grandson. He has just done his exams and tells her that he's failed. When asked if he's really failed everything, he says sheepishly: 'Well I did pass sociology', and she says, 'Oh an ology, you must be clever'.

The idea that sociology is too easy, too flimsy and too irrelevant has become commonplace. But many of the most compelling issues we now face can be understood only through a sociological lens; and the lack of sociological literacy among many decision makers has become a major impediment to effective policy.

Sociology's past and future became particularly pressing for me when I took over at the Young Foundation in the mid-

2000s. Fifty years before that, Michael Young and a small band of colleagues including Peter Wilmott and Peter Townsend had set up the Institute for Community Studies (ICS), the Young Foundation's precursor, in London's East End. Sociology was even then still something of an insurgent outsider, except in a few enlightened places like the London School of Economics, and was still excluded from older universities like Cambridge.

Young and his colleagues had a strong sense of mission for sociology. They felt even then that the universities were succumbing to jargon, turning inwards and failing to engage with the huge changes underway – including some of the unintended consequences of a new welfare state and the flawed urban planning that was displacing people to soulless estates on the edges of cities.

Their aim was to encourage an engaged social science founded on close observation of people's daily lives, tied to bigger theoretical explanations of society, connected to a vivid imagination about how society could change for the better and for the worse, and communicated in plain English to the widest possible audience of the people whose lives were being made sense of.

In much of what they did this mission was put into practice brilliantly: in the writings on family and kinship in east London, in the speculations on the downsides of a pure meritocracy, not to mention the practical work of building new institutions like the Open University.

That time – the late 1950s and early 1960s – was, in retrospect, the beginning of a golden age for sociology. In the 20 years after the ICS was founded, sociology went through a wave of extraordinary popularity: the number of academics mushroomed, hundreds of thousands of students sat through sociology courses and, for a time, social theorists became almost household names.

Yet, in retrospect, much of this opportunity was squandered. Too much of the work that resulted was thin; too much of the theory was bad theory, too vague to generate plausible and testable hypotheses; too much was driven by fashion and fads; and too much of the writing was obscure, marred by jargon.

The then prime minister, Harold Wilson, blamed the unrest of 1968 on sociology. But the problem of British sociology was not that it was too revolutionary but, rather, that it was too easy to ignore (and the same looks true for the US in the 2010s, and for much of Europe). It never became part of the mental furniture of people in power and with influence, and never matched the subtle intellectual power exercised by history and economics. As a result, when confronted by such things as urban riots, fake news, persistent truancy, drug use, stagnant happiness or the question of why some cities can absorb hundreds of thousands of foreigners without much problem while others have a fit over a few dozen, many highly educated and well-read people simply lack the intellectual tools to understand the problem.

This relative weakness is particularly striking, given that there has been a striking turn of intellectual and public attention to social issues – the interest in social capital; the rise, among economists, of interest in questions of happiness and of identity, belonging and alienation – which very quickly points to the paramount importance of social relationships and status. Yet sociologists have not always been in the forefront of these debates, and when sociologists have spoken up their colleagues have been slow to form a supporting chorus.

C. Wright Mills described the role of sociology as well as anyone in his great book *The Sociological Imagination* when he defined sociology as 'the idea that the individual can understand his own experience and gauge his own fate only by locating himself within his epoch and that he can know his own chances in life only by becoming aware of those of all individuals in his circumstances'.[1] In what follows I suggest seven of the elements that might contribute to a re-energised sociological imagination today.

Observation

The first is observation and description. To investigate social phenomena, we have to start by seeing things as they are – talking to people; undertaking the painstaking work of mapping behaviours and relationships – and using the methods of ethnography and the many tools of social analysis.

Close observation takes you a long way towards better understanding. It invariably throws up surprises: connections that were otherwise not obvious or insights into otherwise baffling behaviour. And it is usually inherently interesting, in its own right, to gain access to other people's lives.

Britain has a great tradition of observational sociology – from the great 19th-century surveys of Booth[2] and Rowntree[3] to modern examples like Dick Hobbs's work on crime and enterprise.[4] In the mid-2000s the update of Michael Young's classic, *Family and Kinship in East London*, titled *The New East End*,[5] showed the virtues of this quite traditional approach of patient interviewing and research in illuminating the complex dynamics of white working-class and Bangladeshi communities. And there are also great traditions in other countries that are still alive – from Bourdieu's work collected in *La Misère du Monde*[6] to Suzanne Keller's work on Twin Rivers in New Jersey,[7] both exemplary combinations of detailed observation with sophisticated theory.

Yet too much recent sociological work has relied on secondary materials, and it has been possible to pursue academic careers without ever doing primary research, observing a complex social phenomenon at first hand. Observation has come to be seen as somehow second class, even naïve, compared to the glamorous work of theory.

Sociology is not alone in this respect. It is possible to progress a long way in economics without ever having stepped into a factory, or observed at first hand how an office works, or how a real – as opposed to theoretical – market functions. But, without re-energising that fundamental work of documenting, recording and describing, there is little chance for sociology to reassert its position.

Public engagement

The second building block of a revived sociology is public engagement. In the past there was no firm dividing line between professionals and amateurs. Karl Marx had no post in any university. Booth and Rowntree were amateurs but immeasurably advanced sociology's understanding of poverty; and sociology has always been enriched by journalism (like Fran

Abrams's work on life on low pay[8]) and novels (like Rohinton Mistry's writings on India[9]).

There have been periodic attempts to cultivate a more popular sociology with more public engagement. In the UK the Mass Observation movement in the late 1930s was one example, the History Workshop movement in the 1970s another. But they were generally disdained by the academy and didn't become permanent.

All professions build walls, but those walls sometimes hold them in rather than holding others out. So it is with sociology.

Like astronomy, which has encouraged mass participation and greatly benefited from it, sociology should encourage a wider public to engage. Imagine what would happen if thousands of people regularly used ethnographic techniques to interview their neighbours, the otherwise nameless faces in the shopping centre or the young people sitting on street corners, asking them who they are, how they live, what gives meaning to their lives, or if tens of thousands of schoolchildren learned to become observers and mappers of the community around them, recording what is happening to power, or class, or families, and acting as social witnesses.

When dramatic events happen – like terrorist incidents – we see just how much the public enrich media coverage with blogs, video cameras and phones. But these are still not integrated into the discipline of sociology, whose primary medium is the text-based journal article.

Richer theory

Third, much of what went most wrong in the 1970s–1990s was an excess of theory – or, to be more precise, of the wrong kinds of theory. Libraries were filled with books devoid of any real people, any facts, any voices: these were books about other books, more literary theory than social analysis.

The answer to poor theory is not to have no theory but, rather, to have better theory. Kurt Lewin was right that there is nothing so practical as a good theory that generates new insights, new ways of looking and thinking and new hypotheses to be tested.[10]

That has been true of theories of risk, of social capital and opportunity hoarding, to name just a few. These theories are not equivalent to theories in physics. They are rooted in time and space with few general laws (and sociologists are too wise to make Larry Summers's misleading claim of economics, namely that its laws are eternal). Social theories are reflexive – part of the reality they interpret – and they are situated in time. As Max Weber put it, sociology can be an *Alterskunst*, an art from age, offering perspective and distance.

In recent years there has been nervousness about any general theories of social change. There are some good reasons for this, and we should be suspicious of any single theoretical framework that seeks to explain things as diverse as families, workplaces and political power.

But there are, nevertheless, some links between these diverse phenomena. There is now a hunger for better ways of understanding the dynamics of change, and particularly those big processes of change that have straddled the family, work and politics – like the transformation of gender relations.

Numbers and patterns

Fourth, much of life can never be captured by numbers. But numbers can generate insights. Quantitative analysis starts from careful description – defining categories, observing on a large scale, finding the regularities (and not moving too quickly, as John Goldthorpe has argued, to conceptualisations as an alternative to description) and then making sense of them.

In social science it is rarely possible to do controlled experiments, though random assignment methods in social policy do get close. Instead we have to rely on survey data, large-scale time series data, with which we are now much better supplied thanks to the British Household Panel Survey, cohort studies and hugely richer local data. These provide tools to test ideas, and, more than ever before, there are now plenty of opportunities for 'marrying a value-laden choice of issue with objective methods of data collection and analysis', as Chelly Halsey put it.[11]

Any users of numbers need to be sophisticated about their limits and the nature of categories. Numbers are socially formed, not pure and innocent, and they in turn shape how the world works and how people see things. But they offer counter-intuitive insights which are not accessible through any other means – for example, the surprising finding that the fear of crime correlates with social trust, not with levels of crime.

Communication

Fifth, we need to communicate all this to a public who are fascinated by the social world around them in all its complexity, as we can see in the TV audience ratings for *Faking It* and *Wife Swap*, even *Big Brother*, all of which are forms of sociological experiment using hyper-reality.

Enthusiasm to share insights should course through the veins of every social scientist. Yet this ability to communicate has been lost. It is very rarely taught or encouraged. It sometimes appears to be disdained as a sign of not being entirely serious.[12]

This is one of the reasons why sociology is rarely present in big contemporary debates. When reference is made to sociological work, it is often via interpreters – unlike natural science, whose leading figures have become adept at communicating their own work. The result is that there is far more distortion than there should be – as, for example, in debates over ethnic segregation.

Action

Sixth, Michael Young and his colleagues often linked research to action – creating new organisations and approaches in response to the needs they saw. The trick, as one commentator put it, 'was to look for small changes that have potentially big leverage' and then to push ideas through with 'sheer persistence, a kind of benign ruthlessness even, clutching onto an idea beyond the bitter end, always taking "no" as a question not as an answer'[13] (since 'no' was bound to be the response of power and money to any radical new idea).

Not all sociology should be concerned with action or needs to be policy relevant. And the motivation to achieve change has to be informed by understanding of the difficulty of achieving positive change (perhaps in the past sociology was too glib about the ease of prescription and reform). There are certainly plenty of good works that illuminate how hard change is, like David Robins's book *Tarnished Vision*.[14] It is not possible to read books like this and come away with blithe confidence about how problems can be solved. But work of this kind should help to direct energies more effectively, rather than providing excuses for inaction.

Ethical purpose

Finally, we need to reignite sociology's sense of mission. Sociological knowledge has never been divorced from its uses. In the past it was often directly commissioned by governments, and today social policy is necessarily tailored to the interests and needs of governments – for example, in fields like early years provision or welfare-to-work.

The mistake of some of the sociology of the 1960s was not that it was revolutionary but, rather, that it had such a narrow idea of revolution – one solely derived from the Marxist tradition. There has always been within sociology a strand of belief in what could be called a redemptive social enquiry, which aims to understand and reduce unnecessary human suffering that has social causes rather than personal ones – for example, conflict, poverty, exploitation or denigration of identities. This engaged sociology necessarily points towards action. It connects back to older traditions of civic sociology, including Patrick Geddes and Jane Adams in the US.

It can also offer insights into the more surprising aspects of human suffering. I am repeatedly struck by how many of the big systems in our society produce suffering as unintended side-effects of their operation. Thus, business in pursuit of profit squeezes family life; labour markets in pursuit of meritocracy produce more failures and greater feelings of inadequacy; glamour systems produce a dissatisfied public, suffering from low self-esteem and eating disorders.

It is rarely an option to do away with these systems, but that only makes it more important to try to mitigate, adjust and reform them.

None of this implies that the methods of sociology should be tailored to purposes. Weber – and more recently Bourdieu – managed to combine a strong commitment to a value-free science with personal involvement in social and political reform; the first was an epistemological stance, the second a social and ethical one. The ideal, in other words, is to be passionate about the ends of a better society, and utterly dispassionate about the means.

So, the time is ripe for a more confident sociology. Sociology should be more assertive about the progress it has achieved – understanding everything from the formation of identities to democratisation and mobility – and clearer that it should be a difficult discipline, necessarily more complex than economics, for example. It should not be shy about explaining some of the general patterns which are close to laws, for example, that smallness – in nations, towns, companies, organisations – tends to be associated with greater trust, or that health and happiness tend to be associated with a higher density of social support. And it should be militant in asserting that social phenomena cannot be understood without sociological concepts.

The mission of Young and others in the 1950s was an engaged social science, founded on close observation of people's daily lives, tied to bigger theoretical explanations of society, connected to a vivid imagination about how society could change for the better, and communicated in plain English to the widest possible audience of the people whose lives were being made sense of. That still seems a good description of what we need today.

10

Understanding how cultures change

There are very few thinkers who have changed how we see the world, and even fewer who have changed how we think about how we see the world. Mary Douglas was one of the very rare exceptions. Her field was culture, but she was as unlike the stereotypical cultural academic as one could imagine. A devout Catholic whose late husband was head of research at Conservative Central Office, she used the decades after she passed retirement age in an extraordinary flowering of enquiry that provided striking insights in fields as diverse as the study of the Old Testament and the politics of climate change.

She was a rare example of a public intellectual whose theoretical apparatus allowed her to think in original ways about almost any topic – for example, in her ideas on enclaves, the small groups which at their most extreme become terrorist cells. Where others emphasise their strengths, she emphasised their weaknesses: how prone they are to splits and sectarianism, and how hard it is for their founders to impose and enforce rules. To survive, they create around themselves what she called a 'wall of virtue' – the sense that they alone uphold justice, while all around them are suspect. Yet the very thing that binds them together encourages individuals to compete to demonstrate their own virtue and the failings of their peers. The only thing that can override this fragility is fear of the outside world – and so sects, whether political or religious, peaceful or violent, feed off the fear and hostility of states and societies, using it to reinforce their own solidarity and their own sense of virtue. The implication is clear, and challenging, for Western governments: in the long term, defeating terrorism depends on ratcheting fear down, not up, and on dismantling the 'walls of virtue' rather than attacking them head on with declarations of war.

This example is just one of many from a varied and fertile career that took Douglas from field work in the Congo to nuclear power. She was a 'genius of lateral thinking', in the words of another anthropologist, Adam Kuper. Her work was, however, shaped by a common thread: an interest in how societies shape the way people see the world, and a radically anti-individualistic account of how human cultures really work, in which people are better understood as bearers of the world-views of their institutions and cultures than the other way around.

Douglas's classic *Purity and Danger*[1] (ranked by the *Times Literary Supplement* as one of the 100 most influential books in the West since 1945), for example, showed how societies respond to the threatening nature of ambiguities with taboos and proscriptions – whether of foods or behaviours. Another strand of her work looked at the world of goods and showed how we use consumption to send messages to each other. An even more influential stream of books took on the question of risk – and showed how apparently irrational attitudes to nuclear power or genetically modified crops reflect deeper beliefs about what sort of society we want to live in, and which kinds of institutions we trust.

In each of these fields Douglas's work set in motion new schools of thought. Perhaps the most fertile of all of these is now being used to make sense of why so many well-intentioned policies fail, and why some others succeed even though they appear to work less well on paper. Her starting point is a deceptively simple framework which she repeatedly used to make sense of organisations and societies. It is a framework which should be part of the mental furniture of any educated person, as basic as the laws of supply and demand in economics, or the laws of thermodynamics.

Any culture, she argues, can be mapped on two dimensions. On one axis is what she calls the 'grid' – the extent to which behaviours and rules are defined and differentiated, for example by public rules deciding who can do what according to their age, race, gender or qualifications. Examples of a high grid would be a traditional corporation, a traditional agrarian society or families with clear demarcations of roles and times (when to eat, when to go to bed). On the other axis is what she calls 'group' – the extent to which people bond with each other and divide the world into insiders and outsiders. The more people do with a group of other people, the more they experience testing trials, or the more difficult the group is to get into, the higher the sense of group belonging will be.

These two dimensions come together to provide a simple two-by-two matrix: high grid and high group mean hierarchy; low grid and low group mean individualism; high group and low grid lead to egalitarianism; and low group and high grid result in fatalism. This very simple model has turned out to be a powerful tool for understanding social relations and for making sense of how people see the world. We may like to believe that we choose and shape our own beliefs, but Douglas, drawing on the work of Émile Durkheim and others, suggests that it's much easier to understand societies by turning that assumption on its head: societies and institutions think through us much more than the other way around.

Within a hierarchical culture the world is seen as controllable so long as the right structures and rules are in place. Most governments tend towards hierarchy. It is the natural world-view of civil servants, political leaders and most of the consultants working in and around big business and governments. To every problem there is a solution – so long as it is firmly enough implemented by a sufficiently powerful leader or elite team.

In an egalitarian world-view, the problems usually arise from too much hierarchy and inequality, and not enough bonding and solidarity. More discussion with more people is seen as an unmitigated good, and any measures which widen inequalities are to be resisted. In an individualistic world-view the answer to problems is more freedom – let people determine their own choices, and things will come right. Dissent is to be celebrated; rebels are heroes; and the world is made, and remade, by the imagination and energy of individuals. The fatalistic world-view is most common among people with little power and little experience of power.

What is striking about these four world-views is that they can be found at every level of human organisation – from families and streets to global companies and the United Nations (UN). They are constantly in tension with each other, merging and combining in new ways. Indeed, they need each other. Hierarchies need to re-energise themselves with the creativity of passionate individuals, and some egalitarianism, to reinforce their sense of common purpose. Egalitarian cultures need some hierarchy to resolve disputes and make decisions. Individualist cultures need some hierarchy to enforce the rules, and some egalitarianism to encourage people to care for each other. All, perhaps, need some fatalism to get by and to avoid a constant state of rebellion.

In their book applying Douglas's ideas to the world of public policy, *Clumsy Solutions for a Complex World*,[2] Michael Thompson and Marco Verweij use the example of climate change to show how these different perspectives can shape a strategic argument. For egalitarians, climate change is a consequence of the the profligacy of the rich North. A rapacious capitalist system has led to widening inequalities and the destruction of our shared environment. The flaws of big government and big business have wrecked the world. The solutions therefore lie in a return to smaller-scale institutions, which are closer to nature and free from gross inequalities, and a return to a simpler and more sustainable life-style.

From a hierarchical perspective climate change is a problem that can be solved only with a new hierarchy. Climate change is the result of millions of individual decisions that make sense in isolation but that together risk destroying a common resource. The world now needs strong rules and strong enforcement to cut CO_2 emissions. That will mean binding treaties that go well beyond Paris; new organisations – perhaps a World Environment Organisation – to enforce them; and equivalent laws and regulations across nations. Scientific knowledge, collected by the Intergovernmental Panel on Climate Change, has provided the world with an authoritative truth about the climate that now needs to be taken seriously.

From an individualist perspective, both of the other groups are scaremongers, using unproven science to impose unnecessary burdens on the world. Past experiences show that, given the freedom to do so, people and markets are sufficiently adaptive to avoid disaster. New technologies will arise from competition to cut emissions, if that is what is needed, and in any case the solutions proposed by others are likely to be worse than the problem they are seeking to address. For the fatalists, we are simply all doomed. All four stories are plausible; all are strongly held by different groups; and all are resistant to disproof by any new evidence.

The same patterns can be found in relation to migration. For individualists, immigration is a good thing: there should be as much mobility of labour as possible. Given the freedom to do so, migrants will contribute to their new society and overcome any barriers. For egalitarians too, migration can be a good thing, but needs to be supported by strong rules against discrimination. For hierarchists, however, migration is more likely to be seen as disruptive and needs to be accompanied by active social engineering to ensure that migrants are properly socialised and integrated.

Rationalists like to believe that policy battles end with one side winning. But in practice this rarely happens and, when it does, it causes more harm than good. Hubristic hierarchy – in the form of planning – was repeatedly discredited in the 20th century, just as hubristic neoliberal faith in markets has been discredited in more recent decades and extreme egalitarianism was undermined by the anarchic experiences of revolutions in full swing. Many of us learn in life that overly neat and rational solutions don't work in practice, and Douglas would argue that the best institutions and the best societies achieve a rough and ready balance between different cultures. Their inconsistency is what makes them work. This is perhaps not a new insight. But it is surprisingly rare to find it in any discussions of public policy, which tend to implicitly rely on one or other cultural lens.

Yet, as Michael Thompson and his collaborators have shown, the most successful policies and strategies tend to draw on many cultural models at the same time: they combine expert analysis and design with widespread deliberation and partnership between many players, along with markets and other arrangements that tap into individual motivations. The World Wide Web is an outstanding example which has fed off all of these, even if the internet was originally imagined as a decentralised complement to the command and control system for the US military. The Kyoto Protocol of 1997 was an example of relying on just the single top-down bureaucratic regulation of activities – but without much realistic prospect of implementation, let alone effective monitoring (the Paris Agreement of 2015 was subtler in its tools). In practice, combating climate change will depend on the interaction of many cultures; some regulations and penalties, combined with market forces, favouring energy efficiency and renewables; and egalitarian cultures driving people to adopt more sustainable life-styles and to take responsibility for the future of the group – in this case humanity.

How should we use these insights? They cannot be translated into a precise method, a reliable set of tools which can be applied to any situation. Indeed, these insights are warnings against using any one set of tools as the definitive answer to such complex things as human society. But they are very powerful tools for thinking about any strategy to change the world, and any attempt to achieve social change. Bluntly, if it doesn't contain some room for all of the cultural frames, then it will likely fail. So, for example, public service reforms based only on incentives are as doomed to failure as strategies to cut antisocial behaviour that rely only on coercion. The purist visions of wholly egalitarian structures using the blockchain, or platform cooperatives, are as unlikely to thrive as their purely authoritarian equivalents.

Douglas's work is a healthy antidote to the simplistic versions of 'solutionism' which promise to rain down solutions onto grateful populations. It's also a healthy reminder that meanings and feelings matter as much as rational analysis and evidence: how people make sense of an idea may be as important as the idea itself.[3]

Perhaps more troubling, however, are the implications of her work for the future. In more fractured societies, with weaker families and hierarchies, there are bound to be more isolates, more people detached from groups and hierarchies, who will be seeking meaning in enclaves. Some may be content to take refuge behind a wall of virtue. But others will take up arms.

Mary Douglas's biggest insight is perhaps a warning against depending too much on rational argument. How we see the world depends as much on where we sit as on what we think, and human beings in whatever stage of development can often be understood better through their rituals and behaviours than through their doctrines and beliefs.

11

A theory of belonging: How do we feel at home?

Introduction

The French writer Albert Camus once called it the most painful question of our time: 'Where can I be at home?' The question has less to do with geography than with intangibles like identity, comfort and the strength of the networks linking us to other people. But the idea of being 'at home' – or belonging – is a powerful lens through which to make sense of some of the troubles of our era: why countries struggle to integrate large numbers of migrants and refugees, and why so many have seen backlashes, including the rise of nationalist populist parties and movements like Alternativ für Deutschland in Germany or Lega Nord in Italy.

Here I set out an approach to social belonging that seeks to explain what makes people belong in a community and how they might belong more. The pioneers of social innovation are often instinctive advocates of diversity and pluralism, and of a more open and connected world. Yet millions of their fellow citizens are uncomfortable with this cosmopolitan perspective, which they fear threatens their identity, their borders and their security. The tension between the rooted and the mobile, the local and the global, has become one of the crucial challenges of developed societies. Eagerly exploited by figures like Donald Trump and Marine Le Pen, it has also become one of the biggest threats to social innovation.

The central premise of my argument is simple: people are keenly attuned to reading feedback from social environments as to whether they belong. These feedback systems – which range from informal networks to politics – explain much about why some very diverse communities feel a strong sense of belonging while other, fairly homogeneous ones do not, including groups with a long history in the same place.

The argument challenges the widespread assumption that structural forces make new kinds of social conflict inevitable. Instead, it argues that the details are all-important. Otherwise people in similar places can experience belonging in very different ways.

The framework therefore aims to serve as a practical tool to help shape community engagement and involvement in Europe and beyond. It offers an alternative perspective to the theory of 'thick multiculturalism', which portrays modern societies as made up of distinct communities, each with its own strong identity and sense of belonging. It also differs from research on social capital (defined as value created through human relationships or networks) that has struggled with the incompatibility of diversity and strong attachment to a larger community. Its thesis is that, when people feel threatened and lack positive feedback, they seek to return to primordial sources of belonging, and that, the more related these are to protection, the more attractive they will be: family, nation-states, authoritarian leaders and so on.

Background: Snapshots from London

For settled communities in stable times, the question of belonging is straightforward. People grow up knowing their neighbours and instinctively feeling at home in their village or city neighbourhood. But in unstable times with high levels of migration and high turnover in urban neighbourhoods, many people, not just new migrants arriving in bustling and alien cities but also long-standing residents who see their localities transformed around them, are likely to feel they do not belong. Indeed, this may be the explicit or implicit message they receive from the labour market, landlords and public authorities.

In London, for example, by the early 21st century nearly half of the workforce was foreign born, there were over 30 communities of foreign nationals with more than 10,000 members each and London's schoolchildren could speak over 300 languages. Similar patterns could be found in many big cities – from Berlin to Paris to Malmö. The speed of these changes has been extraordinary, and perhaps even more so in port cities such as Hamburg, Marseilles or Rotterdam.

Such diverse, fast-changing places look very different from the same cities a couple of generations earlier. In the 1950s, Michael Young and Peter Willmott's study[1] of neighbourhood and community relations found a world where residents of the east London neighbourhood of Bethnal Green were not lonely: wherever they went, they knew the faces in the crowd. The study analysed the social relations underpinning this web of mutual recognition, support and interaction. Long-standing residency across generations, reinforced by overlapping ties of extended family and friendship, had fostered a strong sense of ultra-local identity. Bethnal Green was a socially homogeneous place – white and working class – with the men employed mostly in the docks, as artisans or as manual labourers.

Formal female employment in Bethnal Green was low. Grandparents living nearby helped to raise grandchildren. Private space offered few amenities and was reserved for the immediate family, but front doors were unlocked and the street was a playground not yet overtaken by cars.

A follow-up study published in 2006 found a very different picture. The Bangladeshi families who now lived in many of the same streets in the London neighbourhood of Tower Hamlets had similarly strong kinship networks. But east London's white working-class population felt alienated from its own neighbourhoods. They saw the allocation of resources (particularly housing) as unfair, even though allocation was mainly determined by objective need and took no account of family links or roots.

The white working class saw their culture and traditions disrespected in public celebrations – which were more likely to mark Eid, an Islamic holiday at the end of Ramadan, or Diwali, the Hindu festival of lights – as well as in the mass media, which portrayed them in an unflattering light as 'chavs' and 'yobs' (British slang for working-class youth who are typically white, wear branded clothing and are seen as poorly educated and aggressive).

A similar pattern was found in research I was involved in at the Young Foundation in the late 2000s in the working-class communities of Barking, Stoke-on-Trent and other places struggling with the aftershocks of deindustrialisation.[2] In these places, a culture and economy based on full-time male breadwinners working in manufacturing has disappeared without a viable successor. High levels of worklessness have persisted, and most available jobs are relatively insecure ones in services and distribution. These areas showed significant support for the far-right, anti-immigrant British National Party, and marked alienation from the mainstream political parties. They were also among the most likely to vote for UKIP, and then for Brexit in the 2016 referendum, which was seen as a chance to 'shake things up' and get their own back on an establishment which had done nothing for them.

Meanwhile, other new groups in areas of east London – including a 30,000-strong Somali community in Tower Hamlets – also doubt whether they belong. They suffer very high levels of unemployment (over 90%, according to official statistics) and disengagement from mainstream public services and politics. For them, the challenges are different: being portrayed as alien, suspected of sympathy for al-Qaeda or ISIS, and having strong ties within the community that are not matched by the weak ties outside it.

Reading our surroundings

So, how should we make sense of these patterns, versions of which can be found in so many cities around the world? How is it both newcomers *and* long-standing residents can feel that they don't belong?

My framework for making sense of these patterns starts from the simple observation that human beings evolved to be able to read their surrounding physical and social environments because this was essential to their prospects for survival. It is in our nature to be able to analyse whether a group still has a place for us, whether we are likely to be cared for and protected in a particular place or whether we risk being ostracised and rejected. Nothing mattered more for much of our history.

These deep-rooted survival sensitivities can be seen at work among small children in school playgrounds, teenagers on the street and employees in workplaces. In each case we can see people trying to read the messages, trying to be accepted, valued and recognised and fearing rejection.

But the systems we need to read have changed, and the sheer range of people and institutions we have to interpret and negotiate with are of an order greater than ever before, not least with ubiquitous social media that can, at the extreme, turn someone from unknown to pariah within a few hours.

People belong when the most important systems around them send signals that confirm and recognise their value. These are the systems that provide the essentials of life: nourishment, care, protection and prosperity. It shouldn't be surprising that their messages matter.

The framework: Feedback circuits

There are least ten key feedback circuits from which people receive these crucial messages about belonging.

1. The first are informal but strong ties of family and friendship. People feel that they belong when they have ready access to others who know them well and care for them, including family and close friends. The importance of these ties explains why first-generation migrants cluster in the same localities and why, even today, a third of British citizens live within five miles of their birthplace. Such ties explain why some communities can thrive with little support from the state.

2. Second are ties of association. Churches, clubs and voluntary organisations bind people who find connection and common purpose. There is a growing body of evidence (notably in the work of social psychologist Miles Hewstone[3]) on the importance of contact in shaping community dynamics:

where people see their peers engaging with people from other communities (as friends, co-workers or spouses), they are more likely to feel a sense of common cause and less likely to feel enmity. To a lesser extent, we belong as we become used to the same people in local streets and parks – the people whom psychologist Stanley Milgram in 1972 called 'familiar strangers'.[4]

3. The economy is the third source of feedback. Positive messages from the economy include the availability of entry-level jobs as well as opportunities for advancement. Negative messages include overt discrimination or the sense that the local economy has no interest in a significant part of the population. This may be particularly important for university graduates who do not see job opportunities that match their skills and education.

4. Next come power and politics. A political system in which key roles are filled by people who look like you and share your values will encourage feelings of belonging. So too will leaders who give shape to a community, articulating common aspirations. Europe's cities vary greatly in this respect. In some, such as Paris, large minorities were for long effectively disenfranchised, while in others, such as Bradford, the governing elites are more broadly representative. Leaders can also either transcend or accentuate community divisions.

5. Then there is public culture. Whether in the form of billboard advertisements, media representations or festivals, all can reinforce a sense either of belonging or of alienation. Extensive historical evidence shows the impact of shared symbols and mythologies and of activities (like choirs or dancing) where people 'keep together in time', in historian William McNeil's words.[5] Formal rituals like citizenship ceremonies can play a part in reinforcing belonging, as can histories that newcomers can opt into (such as those emphasising past migration). Many local areas are now trying to construct more inclusive local histories and myths.

6. Safety is even more basic. It is hard to belong if you and your family feel physically at risk on the streets. Levels of violent crime and antisocial behaviour strongly influence feelings of belonging. In one UK government survey, 83%

of people who felt they belonged to the neighbourhood thought people would intervene if children were spray-painting graffiti, compared to 67% of people who did not feel they belonged to the neighbourhood. Black Lives Matter in the US was a response to policing policies in many cities that made black communities feel threatened rather than protected.

7. Physical environments play their part in reinforcing a sense of security. Attractive buildings, trees, green spaces and public squares can make people feel at home – and a lack of them can amplify feelings of dispossession. Much is now known about which designs do most to encourage neighbourliness (through appropriate scale, lines of sight and building density). Recognisable boundaries that give shape to a community can also reinforce belonging, so long as those living there receive other positive messages.

8. Everyday public services that are of the people as well as for the people can also influence belonging. In rural societies, police officers, health professionals and teachers live in the same communities they serve. The patterns in cities are less clear cut, and the mismatch between public services and communities creates tensions, such as the continuing battles over Muslim schools, or healthcare that is attuned to Koranic teachings.

9. It's hard to feel at home if you can't find a home. If people like you, your family and your friends can afford housing in the community (to rent or to buy), and the owners or landlords are willing to rent or sell to you and those like you, then you are receiving a positive message. Public housing policy also matters. Many researchers have shown the damaging effects of UK public housing policies that separated families in an effort to allocate strictly according to need. Although classic social policy norms justify this type of rationing, such policies essentially told local people they had no claim on their locality.

10. Finally, there is law and its enforcement, which shapes the mood of a place. The legitimacy of law – that it reflects the community's values and protects its interests – is critical to belonging. In many places, new negotiations are needed

over non-negotiable rules (for example, on the place of forced marriage). The law can also foster belonging when it enables legitimate 'asymmetric deals', or special rights for certain communities, such as UK laws exempting Sikhs from wearing a helmet while riding a motorcycle. Other examples include special provisions for halal foods or special housing provisions for Hasidic families. Equally important is how laws are enforced. Policing strategies that appear discriminatory have fuelled community conflict in many cities.

Undoubtedly, many other feedback circuits are at work. This list is only a provisional one. But it should already be apparent that it is possible to roughly map out the messages different groups receive about whether they do or do not fit in, and, in light of this, to shape strategies that address the biggest barriers to belonging.

In many traditional UK working-class communities (such as in Barking and Dagenham in London), and in many former industrial regions across Europe and the US, every one of these ten feedback circuits, with the partial exception of the first, sent negative belonging messages to significant groups of citizens. They were not recognised by the economy, political power or visible culture, and they felt unsafe.

By contrast, in many highly diverse but more affluent communities, such as Margaret Thatcher's former parliamentary constituency of Finchley in London, the feedback systems send positive messages about everything, from the economic value of newcomers to appreciation of their cultures.

Belonging and social innovation

If this analysis is right, it has obvious implications for the practice of social innovation. In many urban contexts the renewal of positive feedback circuits should be a top priority, as much for grassroots innovators as for public authorities.

What kinds of public culture, for example, do the most to encourage belonging? Some places have experimented with communities cooking big meals for others as a symbol of mutual recognition. How can entry-level jobs be organised to ensure that every community can see a line of sight to opportunity for their children? How can police forces reflect the communities they're meant to serve?

A few years ago I was part of a network of hyper-diverse cities that tried to share their experiences, linking Toronto and parts of London, Marseilles and Malmö. We were interested in formal structures and rights, but it soon became clear that the details were all-important: how local media operated; how gossip flowed; and how everyday interactions on the street took place. So, programmes that helped people know, even very superficially, neighbours from other communities turned out to have a big impact on belonging. Being able to greet others on the street makes a big difference to feelings of belonging. So, if an elderly man or woman sees a group of teenagers from a different ethnic background on a street corner and knows the name of one of them, and so can say hello, the dynamic is quite different than if they default to seeing them as a nameless mob. As I show in the next chapter, the details of how recruitment for jobs takes place, or how political leaders behave, matter more than underlying structural factors. To this extent the casual analyses of many commentators who ascribe conflicts to clashes of civilisation, or as the inevitable results of high unemployment, are just wrong.

Questions raised by the feedback–circuit framework

This sketch throws up many questions. First, *what is the right level of belonging?* In relation to each of these feedback systems, the maximum is not necessarily the optimum. Hostility to others can accompany an overly strong sense of belonging. Similarly, too much attachment to family and friends may militate against taking up opportunities, while too much deference to political leaders may permit corruption. What communities generally need is enough belonging, but not too much. Indeed, many individuals find some security in the relative anonymity of big cities.

The most dangerous groups may be the ones that switch from very weak feelings of belonging to very strong ones. As the anthropologist Mary Douglas suggested in her 'grid and group' theory, people who experience little belonging (the isolates) are the most likely targets of extremist political entrepreneurs, who then try to bring them into what Douglas calls 'enclaves', with a high degree of belonging and a very black-and-white vision of the world.

A second question concerns *which feedback systems matter most*. Is there a hierarchy of importance? This may in part depend on the values of the wider society. In capitalistic societies the economy may be paramount as the symbol of belonging; in others, recognition of religions or access to power channels like the military may be more important.

A third question concerns *the importance of geography*. It is feasible to feel a strong sense of belonging without living in a particular place. Increasingly, immigrant diasporas are held together by media, the internet, greater levels of transnational ownership (for example, a home in the country of origin), cheap air travel and remittances. Interestingly, migrants who feel that they belong to a diaspora do not automatically feel out of place in the country where they live. As sociologists such as Peggy Levitt have shown, you can feel 'at home' in two or more places.

Equally, many educated 'elites' have a very strong sense of belonging to the world, held together by their employers, networks of university alumni and the ubiquitous smartphone (though again this does not always mean they are detached from where they live).

For others, particularly young families and the elderly, geography is paramount, and neighbourliness is particularly important to wellbeing. The tension between groups who see a locality more like a hotel than a home is already acute in some inner urban areas, such as Westminster in London, or Manhattan in New York City.

A final question concerns the role of structure or choices. The social scientist Charles Tilly (covered in the next chapter) explained better than anyone why, in some contexts, feelings of alienation fester and explode, while in others they are contained, even though the objective conditions may appear very similar. Underlying social and economic conditions may create the breeding ground for conflict. But the actions of community leaders, police and politicians – and whether political entrepreneurs inflame tensions or heal them – are often decisive, whether in explaining communal violence in India or community divisions in cities like Antwerp and Brussels. In other words, it is misleading to assume that conflict automatically results from particular patterns of ethnicity or religion. With the right cultures of leadership, places can get by successfully with very high levels of diversity and difference.

Recognition

The underlying assumptions of this argument are not new. Hegel argued that one becomes an individual subject only by recognising, and being recognised by, another subject. Much of the feedback-circuit framework is essentially about recognition or its absence. Another, more recent philosopher, Charles Taylor, wrote that 'our identity is partly shaped by recognition or its absence, often by the misrecognition of others – and so a person or group of people can suffer real damage, real distortion, if the people or society around them mirror back to them a confining or demeaning or contemptible picture of themselves'.[6]

My claim is that we can analyse in more detail what these mirrors are and so avoid the assumption of recent political theories of recognition that claim defined group identities as all-important.

Cultures are neither very coherent nor bounded. As the philosopher Kenneth Appiah wrote, cultural purity is an oxymoron.[7] Belonging is made up of many strands that are constantly being woven and also unravelled. The ability of communities to understand and shape these processes may be the key to achieving greater wellbeing in growing, diverse and fluid cities in the years ahead.[8] Belonging can be shaped and made; indeed, it always has been.

12

The interpretation
of social change

Why are women paid less than men? Why were there riots in some north-western English cities in 2000, but not in London? What is the significance of bloggers or of the World Social Forum?[1]

One of the strange features of our times is that well-educated people can get by with very little idea of how to answer questions like these. Many people rely on very simple interpretive frameworks to make sense of what they see around them or on the evening news. So, for example, conflicts between Muslims and Christians are ascribed to culture or history. Gender pay gaps are interpreted as the result of misogyny. The internet is ascribed with magical powers to turn the tables on multinational corporations or governments.

Anyone involved in social innovation needs better ways of thinking, both to grasp the possibilities and the barriers and to understand why apparently better ideas may not spread and scale.

Charles Tilly's work was probably the outstanding contemporary example of an engaged but theoretically rigorous sociology. It is a symptom of sociology's relative detachment that he remained largely unknown outside academic circles, even though he was one of the most fertile thinkers in US social sciences, combining a rare sharpness and a breadth of interest, covering diverse topics ranging from the rise of the state in 18th-century Europe to racial inequality, and from political violence to the conditions for democracy in central Asia. In some ways he was old fashioned – he offered explanations and showed how some things cause other things to happen. His accounts have real people, history and drama, and have consequences for how change might be achieved more successfully. They are thus very different from the sweeping generalisations, usually detached from any detailed analysis, of some of the most fashionable social theorists.

Like all of the best sociologists, Tilly started with close observation. Pay inequality is a good example, which Tilly investigated along with many other kinds of inequality in his book *Durable Inequality*.[2] Economists have found it hard to explain why gender pay gaps are so persistent, since in a properly functioning labour market employers should have incentives to reward women as much as men for their skills and their work. Tilly points out that any detailed observation of how pay and jobs work in the real world soon shows that the most important determinant of pay is which jobs people go into: 'Since compensation varies systematically by job more than it varies by gender within jobs, the big question we have to ask is not "how come individual bosses discriminate against women" but: "what is the process by which women stream into some occupations and men into others?"'[3]

The answers lie in processes of self-reproduction. Jobs are mainly allocated by people who are themselves already in jobs, and, whether consciously or not, they tend to favour people like themselves, sometimes because they feel more comfortable with them, sometimes as a favour. None of this need be consciously discriminatory. But, wherever there is a dividing line between an 'us' and a 'them' (like men and women, whites and non-whites), people tend to erect further barriers. Some of these may be occupational boundary lines, like those between doctors and nurses, which have enabled professional men to hoard opportunities for themselves. Some may be cultural boundaries, like the familiarity with opera or the classics that have been requirements for advancement in parts of the civil service. But the net effect is that many inequalities are, as Tilly puts it, 'durable': they survive over long periods of time and run along simple us/them boundary lines.

In the case of hiring, Tilly argues, 'the mechanism by which people get jobs almost guarantees that whatever inequalities exist outside the plant reappear inside. We try to patch it up, as Michael Young pointed out, by creating meritocracies and school screening, but it doesn't by any means compensate. Within any organisation the people with power will reproduce whatever it is that gives them the advantages they have.'

What can be done? Laws banning discrimination are necessary but far from sufficient conditions for change. 'If you want to change the balance of opportunity you have to plug disadvantaged groups into self-reproducing structures. So, if a new plant is set up you ensure there is a nucleus of that group amongst the original hires.' Alternatively, you deliberately break down some of the barriers to mobility – like professional demarcations that traditionally made it hard for nurses to take on more senior roles. And if you want to improve the relative position of an ethnic minority, like the Mexicans from Pueblo in New York City, you direct job opportunities to the 'dense networks of communication and the churches, increasingly protestant not catholic, that have become Mexican headquarters in New York. The general point is that very large-scale policies on discrimination and minorities miss the level at which the crucial processes are occurring.'

These processes of hoarding explain some of the dynamics of social mobility, including the data suggesting that it is has been static or declining in the UK and US since the 1980s.[4] The well-off have become better at hoarding opportunities, using private schools, tutors and cultural capital to outwit policies designed to promote meritocracy. Within societies the result may be a dramatic shift in the structure of opportunity which is invisible if you only look at economic data such as the distribution of income.

> Recent studies of Brazil, for example, show that it has a class structure like an hour glass with a very large bottom. In the lower part you have a system in which over the last couple of generations people have moved out of agriculture into low level service and manufacturing and there is plenty of mobility. Then there's a bottleneck, much narrower than in the past, and above that there's another circulation of the educated elite, again with plenty of mobility. Below the bottleneck you have almost all the black

African ancestor population. Overall social mobility hasn't changed much, but the possibility of moving from the agrarian sector into the elite has diminished drastically.

A very different example of a complex social phenomenon that is commonly misunderstood is rioting. Much of Tilly's later work was on collective violence (notably in his book *The Politics of Collective Violence*[5]), examining the patterns that connect communal violence in South India, gangs in London and genocide in Rwanda. Careful observation soon puts paid to most of the conventional accounts. For example, until partition the majority of Muslims and Hindus in India had long coexisted peaceably, disproving any claim that there is a fundamental cultural incompatibility between the two religions. Nor does history work as an explanation. In India, as elsewhere, there are plenty of examples of deep historical enmities that have disappeared, or lost their potency (there are, for example, few Scottish nationalists threatening to set off bombs in London).

Instead, the study of conflict shows that, although historical memories play a part, as does the struggle to secure scarce resources like land or housing, these are not enough to explain worsening conflicts. Instead, the crucial factor is that leaders, or what Tilly calls 'political entrepreneurs', see it as in their interests to accentuate divides, to seize on incidents and make them symbols of a larger conflict – like India's Narendra Modi, who as Chief Minister of Gujarat did so much to stir up hatred between the Hindu and Muslim communities. This is more likely if community organisations – and political parties – don't cut across communal boundaries. But even this doesn't make violence inevitable, unless leaders choose to encourage it and third parties, like the national government, do not act to dampen it down. The general point is that bigger factors are insufficient to explain why conflict happens; instead, it is in the interplay of small actions and decisions that tiny incidents either turn into conflagrations or are quietly forgotten.

For many European countries with large, and increasingly alienated, Muslim populations an accurate understanding of these dynamics matters intensely. If you believe in an unavoidable war of civilisations the outlook is bleak. However, Tilly's analysis suggests that this viewpoint not only is analytically flawed but also risks encouraging the very problems it warns against. A subtler approach is to look at the dynamics of the situation.

> Once you have a significant Muslim population in a European city you are likely to see the creation of political entrepreneurship and the reinforcement of us/them boundaries. So, people come to be defined as Muslim rather than, say Bangladeshi. For governments and mainstream political parties that raises the question of whether it is possible to compete with the power of those who are benefiting most from the erection of the Muslim/non-Muslim boundary by giving them stronger incentives to gain power and prestige in other ways, for example through a major political party, or through being involved in the allocation of regeneration funds.

'Canada offers a telling example', Tilly goes on to say:

> If you draw the map of French speakers in Canada you see a big mass in Quebec and a couple of adjacent provinces and then a string of Francophone settlements in every province westwards. In every other province, from Ontario to Manitoba and British Columbia the Francophones have made their peace with the Anglophones. There is nothing inherent in the Francophone/Anglophone relationship which breeds conflict. What made the difference was the incentives for politicians and their organisations to accentuate divides.

These examples – inequality and conflict – illustrate Tilly's distinctive method, which is concerned above all with relationships between people and how people are changed by their relationships and their interactions. He argues that 20th-century social thought has suffered from two common flaws.

The first has been to see things too readily as systems, as in the now largely forgotten work of figures like Talcott Parsons:

> We talk about society and community as if they are real things, but they are words rather than things. To judge whether something really is a system you have to look for some attributes – such as homeostasis and coordination – which are generally there in organisations (and governments) but which exist only to a limited degree in national societies. Jumping too quickly to abstract words like 'society' takes attention away from the many networks and relationships which make up the reality of social life, and which often cut across national boundaries.

The other flaw has been to focus too much on individual intentions and consciousness, as economics has been particularly prone to do with a whole edifice of assumptions about individual motivation. The limits of a social science based too narrowly on individual intentions can be seen in the example of the ultimatum game, where the experimenter gives someone $100 and then lets them offer someone else a share of the pot. If agreement isn't reached, neither gets anything.

> According to orthodox economics if I get $100 and give you even $1 you should be satisfied since you are better off. But the fact is that neither participant in such an experiment in any country accepts a small offer. The offers are usually in the range of 60 to 40. Sometimes they're 50/50. To understand this, it is not enough just to ask how individuals process experiences as individuals; you have to see the relationships between people and why they matter.

The work on happiness by many economists illustrates the same point.[6] This concern with human wellbeing is a very welcome widening of the horizons of economics. Unfortunately for the economists, the available evidence shows that relationships – marriage, friendship and belonging – are critically important to making people happy, and that these relationships all change who we are. Yet individualist economics has no robust concepts for understanding how people compare themselves against others, or why people form relationships (the best that economics has done to understand children has been to analyse them as equivalents to consumer durables, like refrigerators).

The virtue of looking in detail at the dynamics of relationships is that it throws light on otherwise intractable issues. A good example that Tilly cites is Peter Bearman's work on American schools.[7]

> Bearman shows that in US high schools there is a hierarchy of cliques, usually with the varsity athletic teams as the central cluster. The best athletes get the chance to dispense the most valued goods, including buildings, parties and prizes. Second it shows that schools vary – in most sports is most respected, but in some academic achievement is central to the hierarchy of respect. And third, everyone's school performance depends on what the central clusters are. Kids do better academically in schools in which the central clusters are the eggheads and so on. So, a lot of creative policy may come from analysing what are the clique structures of these schools and what kinds of alternative rewards might there be for teenagers to win respect. In particular, how can the most disaffected teenagers be given access to resources that would win them prestige amongst their peers, as an alternative to dealing drugs or stealing cars.

Bearman's work on teenagers pledging to remain virgins until marriage has given similar insights into teenage sex. If there are no pledgers in a student's community, pledging has little effect on sexual behaviour. If there are too many pledgers in a student's community (more than 30%) pledging also provides little benefit for the teenager. Pledging works only when it gives teenagers a sense of unique identity with a group of their peers, and it certainly does not work when it's a national policy that everybody follows.

In his book *Social Movements, 1768–2004*[8] Tilly returned to a topic he had worked on in the 1980s: the rise and role of social movements. The book offers a synthetic history from 1768, the time of John Wilkes, to the era of Greenpeace and Jubilee 2000. Within a few decades around the turn of the 19th century, the British campaigns against slavery and for Catholic emancipation invented many of the methods of campaigning that have since become commonplace, from demonstrations and petitions to mass-membership organisations. Since then there have been a growing number of social movements, all trying to proclaim their 'worthiness, unity, numbers and commitment' through marches and fasts, and more recently through mega concerts and text messaging.

One of the many unanswered questions about social movements is how much they have been transformed by the internet. There is no doubt that the internet has made it easier to organise large numbers of individuals and small organisations in what Howard Rheingold called 'smart mobs'.[9] A few moments in the past saw ideas spread almost like a virus across national boundaries – for example, in the pan-European revolution of 1848, or the student protests of 1968 or the fall of communism in 1989. But this sort of global coordination has become far simpler and far more common – as in the global demonstrations in February 2003 against the US intervention in Iraq, or the big demonstrations against Donald Trump.

But it would be wrong to conclude that the internet has irreversibly weakened the power of governments or big corporations. For a start, internet access remains in global terms confined, with a significant proportion of the world's population not connected. It speeds up communication among elites, including NGO elites; but, according to Tilly, it may lead to less communication with the disenfranchised.[10] It may also reinforce the tendency of many modern NGOs to pursue visibility and media coverage as an alternative to their main objective – a common trap, since coverage gives the appearance of success.

Just as importantly, the internet has not altered the basic feature of social movements, which is that they rarely have influence except where elites are divided. Anti-globalisation demonstrations in Seattle in the early 2000s, for example, worked to the extent that they did only because they strengthened the hand of the people within the World Bank or national governments who already wanted a greater focus on poverty, governance and civil society. 'Any time a mass representation of demands has had a response there's almost always someone in the establishment who is already sympathetic.'[11]

Economic change and innovation are another example of a topic that cannot be properly understood without sociology. Tilly cites a classic study of innovation carried out by Johann Peter Murmann, one of his students.[12]

> The invention of synthetic dies for the textile industry occurred in Britain in the 19th century. But by 1914 Germany had 95% of the market even though Britain continued to be the home of the world's largest textile industry. So, Britain went from being the fountainhead of innovation to being the consumer of German technology. What Murmann points out is that the separation between firms and government and universities impeded any kind of collaboration and created mutual suspicion. Whereas in Germany they colluded with each other and scientists made the circuit, going from buyer to university to government and so forth, cross-fertilising and helping the system as a whole to adapt.

Can sociology help us to think about politics and the big strategic choices that society faces? Tilly argued that here, too, greater sociological literacy could at least clarify the nature of ideological choices. He cited the work of Robert Goodin and collaborators (*The Real Worlds of Welfare Capitalism*[13]), who analysed how different kinds of system – conservative, liberal and social democratic – performed in delivering results to their citizens. The work drew on long-time series data from the US, Germany and the Netherlands, tracking people's fates year after year between the late 1970s and early 1990s. To avoid ideological bias, the study took as its starting point the criteria which the advocates of each system deemed to be the most important, and then observed what actually happened, for example to the relationship between security and competitive enterprise. The conclusions of the research were pretty clear: social democracy scored better on all of the morally desirable outcomes of welfare systems than the other two. But the key point is that this is an example of a creative use of social research to address big questions.

One of Tilly's last books was called *Why?*.[14] It was concerned with how we explain events such as 9/11, the democratic revolutions in Kiev, or medical malpractice – an issue that particularly interested Tilly as he underwent treatment for a very serious cancer. Social science generally looks for causal links, or correlations. Medical malpractice inquiries, like parliamentary inquiries or judicial inquiries, generally investigate whether the rules were followed, not whether what was done was right or wrong. But most of the public use stories to understand things. Rationalist academics and policy makers disdain stories, yet by better understanding how people frame stories and then share them we may get a much better grasp of how nations hold together or why some campaigns succeed and others fail.

Part IV
Good and bad social innovation

13

Know your impact (and in praise of better borrowing)

This chapter is about evidence and whether we can, or should, know our impact, the effect we have in the world. It addresses the difficulties as well as the possibilities of evidence for innovators and politicians, civil servants and head teachers, charities and doctors. I also touch on the question at the level of daily life, the moral question of whether we help those around us to be healthier, happier and more prosperous. Knowing our own impacts is, I argue, as much a moral prerogative as the traditional philosophical injunction of knowing ourselves.

The enlightenment story

Many of us imbibed from an early age what can be called the enlightenment story. In this story new knowledge is steadily accumulated, mainly in universities and from academic journals. Theories are invented, tested, refuted and then improved. Scepticism helps to refine them and, as Wittgenstein wrote, the child first learns belief and only then learns doubt.[1] You could say that at school we learn knowledge, and then at university we learn to question that knowledge.

Belief is strengthened precisely because it has already been knocked down. And so, accumulating knowledge shows that this medicine, that economic policy or this teaching method works and many others don't. The successful method then spreads, because when you design a better mousetrap the world beats a path to your door.[2] It spreads because people are rational and want to do better and are persuaded by evidence. And so, the world progresses. Light replaces darkness. Effective solutions displace failed ones.

It's easy to mock the enlightenment story. The sociologists of science have shown a much messier pattern of change – full of barriers, wilful resistance and peer pressure. But the old enlightenment story contains a good deal of truth and is preferable to the alternatives. Because of intense pressures to act on evidence, and habits of doubt among maintenance staff and engineers, aircraft do not drop out of the sky. Smoking made the slow progress from evidence of harm, through taxes and warnings to full-scale bans, and millions of lives were saved.

Experimental methods have been used for many decades. In the US, for example, the Manhattan Bail Bond Experiment in the early 1960s randomly required low-income defendants to post bail or not, and found that requiring bail didn't affect the rate at which they appeared for trials. Welfare experiments in the 1970s showed that guaranteeing incomes for the poor led to only a small disincentive for men to work. In the 1980s a big randomised study found that requiring people to pay a small amount for doctor visits led them to use the health service less but didn't affect their health.[3]

The enlightenment model isn't impossible in government and public power. When I worked for the UK prime minister at 10 Downing Street, I encouraged policy reviews to begin with a public survey of what's known, and this was done for the Social Exclusion Unit and the Strategy Unit without much resistance. There are plenty of policy fields that have been rich in evidence. The Cochrane Collaboration stands out as a model of structured collation of evidence that mutually reinforces the work of the National Institute for Health and Care Excellence (NICE), which gives the NHS detailed analyses of the effectiveness and cost-effectiveness of treatments. We also have decades of examples of evidence challenging political assumptions – showing that classroom numbers really don't make much difference in schools and that police on the beat don't do much to reduce crime, or that investment in early childhood pays back more than investment in universities.

We also have many examples of counter-intuitive findings, such as that tax incentives for savings did little for overall savings (savings fell as incentives rose – the opposite of what was expected). One of the most glaring examples is the One Laptop Per Child initiative. It was much hyped, and very popular with the information technology industry and some politicians in the 1990s and 2000s, but it was badly managed and clearly ineffective in delivering good educational outcomes.[4] It also constituted a fairly scandalous diversion in countries where the annual education budget is a matter of a few dollars. In all of these cases knowledge exists that couldn't be gained except through painstaking, careful research that is then used for the public benefit.

Timothy Wilson's book *Redirect*[5] is a particularly readable account of many well-designed, well-intentioned and highly scaled programmes in the US focusing on such goals as the reduction of teenage pregnancy and crime, which on close examination turned out to have either no effect or a harmful effect.

What's difficult?

So, what's the problem? Why not just celebrate a steady expansion of evidence and say a little prayer of thanks each time we use Google to help us find it?

The first problems quickly become apparent if you reflect on your own life. How much do you really base your daily life on evidence? We know lots about diet, smoking, drinking and relationships and how these affect our health and happiness. But many very well-informed people appear quite capable of ignoring it (including me). We rationalise our reluctance to follow evidence by doubting its status, or just compartmentalising it so that desire and habit override reason. So, if it's hard for us to always act on the evidence, why should we be surprised that it's hard for institutions or politicians, who generally reflect the public rather more than we would like to believe?

Then there is the problem that evidence doesn't always speak in a clear voice. In many, if not most, of the big issues of public policy and social action there are genuinely held beliefs that are at odds with each other. The evidence may also be slow to emerge. The Head Start early years experience is an important example.[6]

A series of active early intervention models drew on theories and evidence and went on to generate a strong consensus behind preventive spending. But what's less often remembered is the uncomfortable fact that early evidence was negative or mixed. Many programmes take time to work. Often the best ideas don't do well in early trials. Indeed, most good ideas would have been killed off by very rigorous early assessment. The earliest cars, for example, were very inefficient when competing with horses: they broke down more often and cost more.

So, it turns out, we need subtle craft knowledge and experience to make judgements about new ideas, and can't usually rely on purely quantitative evidence to guide us. When models are mature, then we can evaluate them using empirical methods. But early on they are more like children, liable to confound the tester.

It's been said that all theories are born refuted[7] – they are usually inferior to the prevailing theories, but then become refined, knocked about until they explain things better.

Then, too, we can't discount the difficult relationship between knowledge and action. Terry Eagleton put it well: 'to act at all means to repress or suspend … to suffer a certain self-induced amnesia or denial'.[8] Since there is so rarely enough knowledge to be certain of any action, whether it's a government passing a new law or an individual embarking on a new relationship, action involves risk. To attempt to be aware of every possibility or nuance may be disabling and so, in practice, decision makers scan and scour for inputs, but then, having made a decision, put doubt to one side.

All the time they have to ask: how much knowledge do you need before you can act? The answer depends on the costs of inaction. The penalties for omission are less than those for commission, but it can be just as irresponsible not to act on the basis of partial knowledge. Clearly, the costs and risks matter too: the greater these are, the more knowledge is needed. Equally, the more irreversible the action, the more needs to be known. But sometimes the only way to gain knowledge is to act tentatively, and see what happens. In any case, certainty will always be elusive.

Supply and demand

If these are some of the reasons why it's harder than it appears at first glance to know your impact, and to act on that knowledge, what else can we learn from the evidence about evidence? Evidence-based policy, practice and management are not new ideas. They have been with us for two centuries.

So, there is plenty of evidence about evidence. Some of the lessons come from the many studies and RCTs conducted by people like Jeremy Wyatt on the use of evidence.[9] These show that the take-up of evidence depends greatly on who it comes from, who endorses it and how it's then communicated. A new idea with evidence behind it is more likely to spread if it comes from peers, if it's embedded in training and if it's repeatedly reinforced.[10]

The evidence on evidence also shows that you can't easily predict who will use knowledge. Just as freedom of information laws have ended up being used by big firms and rich newspapers more than by pressure groups, so too open data will have surprising end uses. Who, for example, benefits most from more publicly available data on burglary patterns? Is it more likely to be used by the homeowner who is burgled once a decade or by the criminal who commits burglaries every day?

But the bigger lesson from the evidence about evidence is one that is continually ignored. This is the lesson that supply does not create demand. The world doesn't automatically beat a path to the door of the inventor of a better mousetrap.

Again, some of the reasons were set out by Thomas Kuhn, who showed the sociological nature of scientific knowledge and why it's so often necessary for models and paradigms to fail, and their guardians to move on, before space is made for the new.[11] But, despite this understanding, there is still a gross imbalance between the amounts of money, time and attention devoted to the supply of evidence and those devoted to demand. It's still the case that evidence is provided as if that's the end of the story and not just the beginning, with complaints that if only the foolish people were brainy enough to use our evidence all would be fine. There's no shortage of websites, best practice databases and repositories, even though we know that repositories are usually places where things are gathered and then forgotten, and that observatories observe but, sadly, not many people observe them. The result is a strategic problem of the underuse of knowledge and evidence. There are only very weak incentives in place for academics to review the evidence to make it useful. There are better rewards for creation than for digestion. Simple principles, like Michael Young's suggestion that statistics travel best accompanied by stories and vice versa, are routinely ignored.

All of this in turn derives, in part, from a misleading mental model of knowledge which sees it as essentially linear in nature, emanating from research and then passing via various intermediaries into practice. Yet, as a brilliant book by Jon Agar[12] shows, even the physical sciences developed in the 20th century more through interaction with the working world of real-life problems than they did as a result of pure abstract reasoning.

Epistemology

The knowledge that resulted – for example, from Einstein's work in the US Patent Office – was useful to the world, but also universal. All disciplines aspire for their knowledge to be consistent across time and space – and the power of the laws of relativity, and the beauty of mathematics, lie, in part, in the permanence and universality of their abstractions. But how many other fields can claim the same? Economics almost certainly can't, and is better understood as mapping various regularities in particular historical periods.

The same is true of all social knowledge – it is often contextual and contingent, and one of the most interesting aspects of dealing with any kind of evidence is working out just how much it can be taken out of context. Does a well-designed programme to reduce childhood obesity, or to get welfare claimants into jobs, work in Italy as well as in Estonia, let alone in India?

This is obviously a very important issue for the fashion for RCTs in development. These are a useful corrective to the often negligent attitudes to evidence, but have to be treated with caution. Only when many RCTs in many different contexts show similar results should we be confident that they're on to something. Just as nearly half of all evidence in medical journals is later overturned, so is it unwise to jump to conclusions in social policy. It's also a very important issue for behavioural economics, much of which is based on small experiments with undergraduates in US universities. It may turn out that they precisely mirror much older, poorer populations, but this isn't likely. The question of universality also takes us to issues of segmentation – many interventions may work well for some but not for others. It's the same problem with medicines that are very uneven in their efficacy. So, aggregate experiments are bound to be misleading, often understating the effectiveness of interventions that do actually work well for, say, 20% of the population but have no effect at all for the other 80%.

We need subtlety in the use of evidence, but also to recognise that some of the crucial knowledge will be context bound, often more a practical, craft knowledge than a science.

Some of this thinking guided the creation of what we called an Alliance for Useful Evidence at Nesta in 2012. We chose these words deliberately and with care. It was an Alliance – because it had to be a broad coalition, engaged in a campaign to change minds and change behaviours; it had to be Useful – because we saw the problem as a lack of usefulness and usability from providers of evidence, and a lack of use on the part of the people who needed it; and it focused on Evidence – because of a commitment to drawing out conclusions from what is seen rather than from deduction or ideology.

A practical goal was to help the many practitioners on both the supply and the demand sides to be better at generating and using evidence, knowing when you should randomise and what may be the uses of data matching and mining – or how to think about evidence from other countries.

Several thousand people who work with evidence joined the Alliance, which also ran training sessions for civil servants and politicians. During the 2010s a dozen What Works Centres were set up in the UK, covering fields that ranged from policing to children in care, from education to wellbeing, and many others sprang up around the world.

The aim was to promote sophistication in the use of evidence – rather than a binary choice between a slavish use of evidence and ignoring it entirely. We want to have precision where we can. As Don Berwick, President Obama's health adviser, put it: 'Some is not a number. Soon is not a time.'[13] But we also wanted judgement, and to cultivate managers and leaders who see it as part of their job to leave behind more evidence than they inherit. This meant focusing not just on a binary question of 'what works' but also branching out to a series of other 'w' questions: where does it work (we shouldn't assume that what works in Kansas will work in Karachi); when does it work (what works in stable times may not work in a recession or famine); who is needed to make it work (the calibre of people responsible for implementation may be all-important); and so on.

For the Alliance there was also an implicit moral goal of encouraging those with power to realise their impact and to be called to account more regularly on how they understand the knowledge they use.

This task of making evidence more used and useful involves sophistication, but also simplification. The widespread use of quality-adjusted life years (QALYs) and disability-adjusted life years (DALYs) has undoubtedly helped the use of evidence in health. In education, the moves to assess a wide range of interventions through the metric of their contribution to a typical term's improvement is another promising example. Simplification makes it much more likely that evidence will be used. This was also why we promoted a common framework of standards of evidence – a series of steps that could be used to assess any programme, ascending from whether it had a clear logic model to confirmatory data, through evidence from a control group to replication.

But there was still the job of persuasion, of encouraging policy makers to believe that their chances of success will improve if they make more use of evidence. Despite the impressive strength of many researchers and research teams in government, their work is often underused. Politicians are right to be sceptical of evidence. I'd be worried if any minister believed that the evidence would tell them exactly what to do. But we shouldn't have any sympathy for ministers who believe that their instincts are so superior to any evidence that they don't need to bother. Rather, what we need is a healthy, robust interaction with evidence: understanding it and understanding its limits, rather than simply seeing it as typical civil service obfuscation – Sir Humphrey with a PhD.

Figure 13.1: The Nesta standards of evidence framework

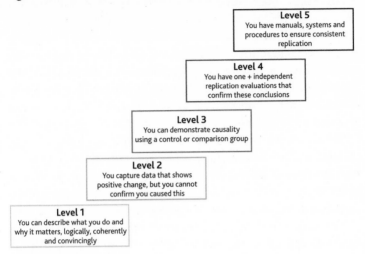

Level 5
You have manuals, systems and procedures to ensure consistent replication

Level 4
You have one + independent replication evaluations that confirm these conclusions

Level 3
You can demonstrate causality using a control or comparison group

Level 2
You capture data that shows positive change, but you cannot confirm you caused this

Level 1
You can describe what you do and why it matters, logically, coherently and convincingly

Optimism for the future

It's easy to feel pessimistic about the state of evidence and truth when some politicians appear to thrive without any regard for facts, and some crucial decisions appear to be made without any attention to evidence. Anti-evidence politicians can thrive all too well. But, seen in the longer view, a more positive counter trend is also apparent.

In the everyday work of policy makers and professionals, evidence is more visible and more used than ever before. That's true of doctors, teachers, police officers and social workers. They don't always follow it; but it's more pervasive than ever before.

Many other countries have also developed similar bodies to reinforce attention to evidence – the US now has the What Works Cities network[14] funded by Bloomberg; Canada is setting up its own centre; and countries from France to Japan are developing their own initiatives to embed evidence, drawing on the UK experience.

It should still be an option to ignore evidence – that's an essential part of democracy, just as we as individuals are free to ignore lots of evidence about how we should live. Parliament is sovereign, not professors. But politicians should have to say why they ignore the evidence. So, a police commissioner may choose to have more police on general patrols – ignoring evidence that this may have little effect – but should identify why they are doing so, or why they are not targeting hotspots. Politicians should be able to follow their values, for example, not funding contraception in development, regardless of the evidence on HIV or prosperity – but they should have to explain their rationale. Decision makers are entitled to ignore evidence; they are not entitled to be ignorant of it.

Whatever we do, and whoever we are, the odds are that someone else has come up with a better idea than the one we can dream up. Indeed, that was of course the Enlightenment ideal, that all could benefit from the collective intelligence of the republic of letters, the work of scientists and the pursuit of reason.

Yet social action and policy are very far from the Enlightenment ideal. David Olds, the creator of 'family nurse partnerships', points out that after 30 years, including innumerable studies and many RCTs, barely 5% of children who would benefit in the US actually do so.[15]

John Hattie's work of distilling thousands of studies on schools is remarkable, at least in part, for being so little known by policy makers, head teachers and columnists pontificating about schools.[16] Restorative justice is a great example of a promising idea that was then tested, adjusted, improved and shown to work – but has hardly been scaled to any degree. Even in health, which has a more developed infrastructure for adoption than any other field, it takes nearly 20 years for research to change clinical practice, and nearly a decade for NICE guidelines to become everyday practice.

The barriers to adoption are legion. There's the syndrome of 'not invented here' which leads people to ignore ideas that aren't theirs. Creativity and originality are often valued more than results, while everyday laziness and inertia stop people from taking the trouble to learn from others. All are compounded by the fact that those responsible for public services are rarely held to account for poor adoption, which is not covered in audit reports. But, for our evidence system to work, this is the vital missing part. We need super-adopters, master borrowers, if we're to have intelligent services that both know their impact and work hard to improve it.

For anyone in doubt about this, just look at a surprising icon for adoption: Steve Jobs, that great designer and entrepreneur who is sometimes regarded almost as a prophetic figure. What's less often talked about is his skill as a borrower. Bill Gates spoke about how they had both drawn on the inventions of Xerox: 'We both had this rich neighbour called Xerox and I broke into his house to steal the TV set and found out that you had already stolen it.'[17] Jobs also borrowed from Fraunhofer, Napster and many others, and brilliantly synthesised their ideas into coherent designs that worked. But he achieved far more as an adapter than as an inventor – very few of his ideas were original. Perhaps what we really need are prizes for the best users of others' successes, the best plagiarists and best digesters.

In the 2010s Samsung was locked in a ferocious legal battle with Apple over smartphones. Certainly Samsung was very energetic in learning from Apple and trying to outdo them. The courts around the world are still judging how much of that was creative adaptation and how much it was theft of intellectual property. But for me the most striking thing about this example is that it has no counterpart in fields like health, education or welfare. It's very rare to hear of big charities, governments, local authorities or hospitals going all out to copy the best from someone else. But that is partly why we have such speed of development and improvement in mobile phones, and so much less in other areas of life that arguably matter more. And remember, even if you want to invent, and many of us do, the best way to invent is, first, to learn how to copy the best, as the greatest artists always did.

The moral argument

I've tried to make the moral case – that you should know your impact – and the practical argument that if you take this seriously your best action may be not to invent but to copy. I've argued that evidence is not eternal and that we should think of it not in terms of the linear flow from pure knowledge to practice but, rather, as a circle of questioning, discovering and experimenting, generating new questions and hypotheses as well as knowledge – not in a court of law, where a dispute is either proved or not proved or where someone is guilty or innocent but, rather, in a world where everything is on probation.

I hope that we can make evidence more ubiquitous, more part of the daily life of everyone with power. Because it helps to make power a better servant. And because it embeds a moral duty of accountability – a principle of knowing your impact – that is, arguably, a fundamental pillar of democracy.

14

The evolution of measures that matter: How do we know if social innovation is working?

> In the kingdom of ends everything has either a price or a dignity. What has a price can be replaced by something else as its equivalent; what on the other hand is raised above all price and therefore admits of no equivalent has a dignity.[1]

One of the fascinating features of the history of science is how often new ways of seeing preceded new insights. The achromatic-lens microscope in the early 19th century paved the way for germ theory, and X-ray crystallography in the early 20th century played a vital role in the later discovery of the structure of DNA. In the same way flows of data – for example, about how people move around a city, or how blood cells change – can prompt new insights.

But how important is measurement to social change? Many people are attracted to metrics and indices of all kinds. But, as my colleague Mark Moore used to warn, 'do you really think the leaders of the Civil Rights Movement were counting the placards or measuring the decibels of their cries for human rights?'[2] In social change, as in our own daily lives, measurement often feels inappropriate for the things that matter most.

This chapter examines some of the history of social observation as a tool for public policy, social innovation and social change, and I suggest where it might lead in the future. Without some means of measurement, it can be hard to know if a social innovation is good. It may feel good to the beneficiaries – but still be less effective than an alternative. Or it may work well for one group but not another. And, even if it may not be appropriate to measure the passions of movements, once these ideas become part of the mainstream, and are transformed into the cool logic of laws, regulations and programmes, measurements do start to matter a lot, as the Civil Rights Movement discovered.

A short history of measurement

For centuries, governments have sought to map and measure social phenomena in order to better exercise control over them. In the modern era these attempts can be traced back to figures like Sir William Petty in England and the cameralists in Prussia. Many censuses and surveys were motivated by the need to raise taxes – and there were many clashes between central authorities wanting to impose standardised measures, and local interests trying to resist them. In Weberian bureaucracies standard measurements are vital to the exercise of hierarchical power, and generally the standardisers won.

Standardisation is now promoted as a tool for democracy and accountability. It ensures that tax burdens are fair. It allows citizens to compare policies over space and time and hold individual units of government to account. The more objective and consistent the data, the greater the level of accountability. For these reasons campaigners have argued for standardised measures of such things as child poverty and nutrition, wellbeing and unemployment, while cynical governments have often done their best to adjust the numbers and obscure the results.

But the democratisation of data and statistics has a long way to go. As Dudley Seers wrote:

> There are virtually no statistics anywhere on most of the aspects of life that really matter – the average distance people have to carry water and food; the numbers without shoes; the extent of overcrowding, the prevalence of violence; how many are unable to multiply one number by another, or summarise their own country's history. Naturally, there are no official

data anywhere on the number tortured or killed by the police, or how many are in prison for political reasons. Many of the more important social factors are inherently unquantifiable: how safe it is to criticise the government publicly, or the chance of an objective trial, or how corruption affects policy decisions.[3]

Why measure? And why too much measurement is harmful

Better metrics do not of themselves deliver better outcomes. You can't fatten a pig by weighing it. But if you don't have some means of weighing it you may find yourself unable to persuade others that it's as fat as you believe. Many methods try to put a price on value. The idea that the value to be gained from a new training programme can be directly compared with the value from a health screening programme or water conservation is immediately appealing to busy bureaucrats and ministers.

I first became interested in the idea of public value when I read a remarkable book called *Relevance Lost*.[4] A history of management accounting is not likely to be a gripping read. But this book tells in a lively way the story of how, over two centuries, successive generations of business leaders, technicians and management accountants devised new ways to track value in everything from railways and steel to aerospace and software. It reveals that value is rarely easy to grasp and is never an objective fact. The economists' accounts of managers equating marginal costs and marginal returns turn out to be fanciful. Instead, even within firms, value is constantly being re-estimated and reallocated in the light of changing priorities and changing production technologies.

It is quite wrong to say that what can't be measured can't be managed (a moment's reflection should show that). But having agreed measures can make it a lot easier to manage things. These are necessary but not sufficient conditions for success, though. Many organisations have gone too far – turning measurement into an end rather than a means – from banks to government departments and philanthropic foundations. The measurements that are a vital contribution to judgement all too often become a substitute for judgement, an obsession with what can be counted, rather than what counts, which squeezes out creativity and discretion. As with so many things in life, balance is all-important, which is why I focus equally on the virtues of measurement and on their vices.

From things to people, from state to society

Looking back at the history of measurements, a series of long-term evolutionary trends over the last two centuries have changed what we observe. These are some of the main shifts:

- from taxable things (buildings, animals, people) by which government measures society, to measures by which society judges itself and what government is doing (such as the OECD's PISA scores for school exam results, or the measures designed by Transparency International, an NGO which ranks countries according to their perceived levels of corruption);
- from physical objects (steel production and so on) through aggregate concepts (like GDP and gross national product) to intangibles (such as innovation indices or measures of the value of creative industries);
- from single measures to indices, like the UN Human Development Index or Indices of Civic Health;
- from activities to outputs to outcomes (such as QALYs and DALYs in health, or carbon reduction measures and so on);
- from objective facts to subjective measures (such as fear of crime and patient satisfaction).

During this evolution measurement has moved from being *primarily* a source for policy makers and the state to being also a source for the public, informed citizens, activists and the media to assess the progress being made by their societies and the contribution made by their governments.

The growing role of measurements in public policy

Standardised measures were once primarily used as a tool for taxation or for military conscription. Now they are integral to public policy in many fields, as well as to philanthropy. Examples include:

- the use of formal quantitative targets in strategic plans (in US and Australian states, and for a time in the UK government), which helps to sharpen up policy, strategy and accountability for results – in some of these cases, like the Oregon Benchmarks programme[5] and equivalents, the public were involved in setting quantitative goals for governments, and then reviewing them over time;
- open coordination methods of the kinds used by the European Union – within the EU, the system of open coordination (and the Lisbon Treaty commitments) relies on common metrics to allow countries to benchmark each other's performance and to manage public finances and other aggregates within agreed parameters;
- performance management methods used by higher tiers of government to monitor lower ones (for example, the use of GDP as a performance target within the Chinese government structure);
- metrics used to support quasi-markets (for example, enabling incentives for outcomes in welfare or crime reduction);
- standardised metrics as part of international treaties and international governance (for example, the 1997 Kyoto Agreement led to widespread use of new metrics for carbon emissions and their abatement); and
- standard frameworks for measurement in fields like impact investment, promoted by umbrella bodies such as the Global Impact Investing Network.

Measurement and action

The growing importance of metrics of all kinds looks unlikely to abate. Politics is helping to drive this trend. Political leaders have an ambiguous relationship with standardised measures. On the one hand, many wish to set formal targets, both as a signal of intent and determination to the public and as a lever to galvanise their own bureaucracies and public services. On the other hand, politicians run the risk of becoming victims of their own promises or of being held to account for movements in indicators that they cannot realistically control. Some politicians eagerly embrace measures as a way to amplify their influence on the system; others do the opposite, preferring to take refuge in sweeping promises or taking on enemies.

The more ambitious methods try to be inclusive and exhaustive, capturing every direct and indirect impact of an intervention. In principle, they and their equivalents can justify actions now that will save money in the future, showing how helping ex-offenders into work, investing in young children or promoting health will lead in the long run to higher tax revenues or lower prison bills. Detailed methods have been used to estimate the direct costs of an action (for example, a drug treatment programme), the probability of its working and the likely impact on future crime rates, hospital admissions or welfare payments. Analysis of this kind can be very powerful. In the US, for example, researchers identified what they called 'million-dollar blocks', where the costs associated with criminals topped the million-dollar mark. In principle, good preventive actions targeted at the people living in these blocks might save far more than they cost if they diverted some people from a life of crime. In the UK, analysis of the Sure Start programme for young children showed that it caused big reductions in children's hospital admissions in poor areas, again justifying investment in prevention.[6]

Many funders have tried to integrate evidence into decision making. Nesta, for example, required recipients of grants and investment to track their impacts and to ensure that they were rising up the hierarchy of standards of evidence so that they could be more confident that they really were doing good.

Challenges

With more widespread use of metrics, however, the problems of standardisation have also become more apparent. Here are just a few:

- *Excess simplicity*: Single measures always risk encouraging excessive focus, and excessively simple responses to complex problems. The pendulum swing against the 'new public management' in the 1990s and 2000s was in part explained by the costly unintended consequences of excessive focus, which at its worst led some agencies to dump problems on other agencies. Not all simple measures have to be simplistic. Some simple measures work well because they capture a wide range of factors. For example, it is very hard to target child mortality levels in ways that do not bring benefit to whole populations. By contrast, targeting measures of household burglary may divert resources from other, equally important crimes.

- *Distortions to behaviour*: There is a very large literature on the many ways in which bureaucracies and professions respond to standardised targets, particularly where money or other rewards are involved. Some of these responses were prominent in the planned economies of the communist bloc: keeping performance down for fear that improvements would be used as baselines for impossible targets; or 'storming', bringing in extra resources during periods of intense scrutiny. There are also the common risks of 'threshold effects' – excessive attention to groups on either side of targets – and the tendency to 'hit the target and miss the point'. In theory, measures which are more about outcomes than outputs are less vulnerable to these distortions.

- *Diminishing utility*: Standardised measures may decline in utility over time. This is a familiar pattern in monetary policy: according to Goodhart's Law, as soon as any measure of money supply becomes an official target it becomes less useful as a target (because of the behaviours of markets trying to second-guess movements in the indicator). The example of school tests is also a good one. Standardised tests and international benchmarking have been powerful tools to drive up standards. They have sometimes challenged complacency in national systems and also directed attention to new places to learn from. But they have also diverted attention away from equally important but less measurable aspects of learning (such as character, emotional intelligence, abilities to collaborate and so on). And just as within national systems it's clear that schools can learn to 'teach to the test' (rather than necessarily improving pupils' genuine understanding), so too can whole systems be taught how to improve their performance to some extent, in cross-national tests.

- *Obsolescence*: Some standardised measures reflect society or the economy at a particular point and become less useful over time. This has been a major issue, for example, with measures of inflation, which need not only to be updated in line with changing patterns of consumer spending (based on baskets of goods and services). They may sometimes have to be reformed in more radical ways, such as to take into account fundamental shifts in spending (for example, mortgage repayments or user fees that have replaced tax-funded public services). Another example is measures of R&D spending. These evolved at a time when investment in technological R&D was becoming increasingly important to national economies. However, these measures do not encompass equivalents to R&D in much of the service sector, as well as in fields like design, rendering them less useful for temporal or cross-national comparisons. Although changing indicators may run counter to the goal of having consistent time series, the utility for policy makers of evolving indicators may outweigh the utility of consistency.
- *Limited relevance*: Most standardised measurements reflect the views of officials, experts and professionals. But their views of what matters may be very different from those of the public. A good example is the measurement of quality in health services. Official statistics tend to measure such things as waiting times, efficacy of operations and mortality. Yet, when asked, the public often describe much more everyday issues, such as service styles, as being more important.

Disaggregation and aggregation

Measurements have always been concerned both with averages and aggregates and with differences. GDP measures, for example, are primarily meaningful as aggregates. John Hicks's economic models, which subsequently became the standard in the post-Second World War era, turned GDP measurements into the foundation for a science of macroeconomics and a practice of macroeconomic management. The causal relationships were often counter-intuitive, as well as directly challenging the previous orthodoxy. They brought a systemic perspective into economics by modelling how various aggregates interacted (and required careful measurement and consistency across time in order to be useful).

But in many fields the priority has shifted: the greatest value of measurement comes from revealing differences and surprising imbalances. More unequal societies and economies are ill-suited to aggregates. Social clusters and cultural patterns are not easily captured by overall poverty measures; instead, often the greatest insights come from spotting patterns of relationships or spatial concentrations. Understanding behaviour also depends on segmenting the public: what works for one group may not for another.

The virtues of disaggregation are particularly acute in relation to wellbeing. Many countries now measure wellbeing systematically; for example, the UK began doing so in the early 2010s. But the most interesting insights from these measures are not the aggregate figures that tell us that the overall happiness of the population increased from 7.1 to 7.2. Instead, the insights come from finding differences: between places, social groups or age groups. The same is likely be to true of measures of social connectedness.

There are many long-standing measures of social need, ranging from nutritional requirements and minimum incomes to housing. However, these largely material measures are increasingly being supplemented by measures of psychological need and wellbeing, including both single measures and composite ones (for example, analysing who feels appreciated, who has people to rely on, who feels optimistic). Using this data creatively opens up important new avenues, for example, in the design of welfare supports. Moreover, it chimes with public perceptions: recent data in Europe shows that the public now see material and psychological needs as being on an equal footing.

Loneliness is a good example, which can be measured with some confidence and has been turned into a field for public policy and civic action. But these measures are not as well established as the material measures and are not surveyed as regularly or integrated into policy analysis. Indicators of this kind are needed to guide changing approaches to social policy and welfare, including greater interest in such issues as how to cultivate personal resilience or help-seeking behaviour, or how to measure and mobilise social networks of support.

Where next?

I've described some of the many advantages of standardisation, and the growing demand for standardised indicators across many domains to support public accountability, as well as policy learning.

I've shown that this growth forms part of the broader shift towards humanising and democratising data, making it fit better with lived experiences and the concerns of the public, including greater use of subjective measures. I've also suggested some of the risks which come from linking indicators too closely to policy decisions. And I've suggested some of the tensions between social science's need for consistent and comparable time series data and the sometimes more variable needs of the business of government.

Looking to the future, we can expect the practice of measurement to change dramatically, mainly because of the vast growth in the collection of social data of different kinds. Much of this is currently harvested by social media companies, which are tracking who links to whom and how different behaviours correlate, or analysing moods (anger, joy, resentment) through semantic analysis. Who controls this data is set to be a fierce battleground.

My hope is that we will see much more precise common measures emerge, particularly for global commons and public goods, and for such things as literacy and public health. These will make it easier to justify higher levels of investment, and help in a small way to counter the extraordinary skew of global capital which flows away from the very things most of us most value.

But, at the same time, I hope that we will also see a further shift to a more human way of looking, subjective as well as objective; attending to relationships as well as things; to the intangible as well as the tangible; and, above all, to a focus on disaggregation and difference rather than averages.

15

Good and bad innovation: What theory and practice do we need to distinguish them?

Technology is the answer, but what was the question?[1]

Introduction

Many firms, charities and governments are in favour of more innovation, and like to side with the new against the old. But should they? A moment's reflection shows that it's not altogether coherent (whether intellectually, ethically or in terms of policy) to simply be in favour of innovation, whether that innovation is a product, a service or a social idea. Some innovations are unambiguously good (like penicillin or the telephone). Others are unambiguously bad (like concentration camps or nerve gas). Many are ambiguous. Pesticides kill parasites but also pollute the water supply. New surveillance technologies may increase workplace productivity but leave workers more stressed and unhappy. Smart missiles may be good for the nations deploying them and terrible for the ones on the receiving end.

In finance, Paul Volcker, former head of the US Federal Reserve, said that the only good financial innovation he could think of was the automated teller machine. That was an exaggeration. But there is no doubt that many financial innovations destroyed more value than they created, even as they enriched their providers, and that regulators and policy makers failed to distinguish the good from the bad, with very costly results. In technology, too, a similar scepticism had emerged by the late 2010s,[2] with digital social media described as the 'new tobacco', associated with harm rather than good, with addiction rather than help. Or, to take another example: when the US Central Intelligence Agency's venture capital arm, In-Q-Tel, invested heavily in firms like Palantir, which then became contractors for the intelligence and military (a prime example of the 'entrepreneurial state'), it was far from obvious how much this was good or bad for the world.

The traditional justification for a capitalist market economy is that the net effects of market-led innovation leave behind far more winners than losers, and that markets are better able to pick technologies than bureaucracies or committees. But even if, overall, the patterns of change generate more winners than losers, there are likely to be some, perhaps many, cases where the opposite happens. It would be useful to know.

But how should we judge? And what actions might flow from a more balanced assessment of innovations and new technologies? No society delegates all decisions to markets. Instead, they tend to be highly regulated and constrained – whether to ensure that cars are not unnecessarily dangerous or that foods don't contain excessive quantities of salt or sugar. We can argue about whether regulation is excessive or inadequate. But laissez-faire has not worked in any known society. Given that that is the case, anyone in charge of directing public money to R&D or other innovation activities should want to ensure that more good rather than bad things are likely to result. The public, too, take a discriminating view of innovation. In countries like the UK, most people are open to new ideas. But they want to know what outcomes these will achieve, and are sceptical of anyone who says that new things are inherently better, or that global competition is a sufficient justification for developing a particular new technology.

So, what methods should be used to distinguish good from bad? There is no shortage of approaches, and there are some very impressive academic experts and some excellent overviews of the field, mainly focused on responsiveness and more open processes.

But the methods proposed are often hard to put into effect. This chapter suggests a framework that complements these methods. It recognises the inherent difficulties involved in assessing future possibilities, while arguing that intelligent judgements can guide allocations of money and the design of policies and regulations.

The challenges of assessment

How should a new field of technological or social advance be assessed – whether it's a new material like graphene or new methods in a field like medical robotics or a new way of organising microfinance? Some have tried to find answers. The European Commission, for example, promised to back 'responsible innovation', which is defined as an 'approach that anticipates and assesses potential implications and societal expectations ... with the aim to foster the design of inclusive and sustainable research and innovation'.[3] That's a worthy aim. But the definition is close to being tautologous, defining responsible innovation as innovation that takes account of its possible effects, without showing how this is to be done.

Part of the reason is that the disciplines that could have provided a more rigorous and useful approach have largely failed to do so. Economics has developed few coherent or comprehensive methods for analysing which kinds of innovation are good and which are bad. It can see when consumers do or don't want to buy something new, and the analysis of externalities can show in retrospect which innovations generate 'bads' (like pollution) as well as benefits (such as cheaper products). But economics offers no ways of doing so ex ante, beyond traditional cost–benefit analysis. Economists from Marx to Erik Brynjolfsson have written about the distributional impact of technology, but on the whole it has been a minority interest, and anyway more concerned with technologies in general, such as automation, than with specific innovations.

Another potential source of methods is technology assessment (TA), which became widespread in some places in the 1970s and 1980s through formalised offices linked to governments or parliaments, and active networks of TA institutions. There are methods for constructive technology assessment, anticipatory assessment, real-time technology assessment, value-sensitive design and others. But it's not clear how much influence these now have on key decisions – whether from public or private funding bodies. Much work has also been done on how individual scientists should think about their own responsibility, and there are some strong examples of institutions working to establish a balanced approach to complex areas of science, such as the Nuffield Bioethics Council and the Ada Lovelace Institute for AI ethics.

As I show later, however, any attempts to assess technologies are fraught with difficulty, since we cannot know with much certainty how they may develop, let alone what effects they may have. As a result, most innovation agencies primarily use assessment tools designed to measure how well an innovation is progressing towards commercial viability (for example through surveying the perceptions of investors or communities). Some use very rough and ready cost benefit analyses, but very few use more comprehensive forms of TA.

Grounds for scepticism

There are at least four grounds for scepticism about any systematic attempts to assess emerging technologies or innovations of any kind.

The first is that no one can predict how they will evolve. Conference speakers love recounting the many examples of people closely involved in key technology sectors, from computing and transport to energy, who dramatically misread how their field would develop. Being an expert is no guarantee of being able to make accurate predictions.

The second is that, even if you can predict how a technology will evolve, it's very hard to predict who will benefit or suffer from it. In 1867, Marx wrote that the self-acting mule was threatening cotton spinners (a skilled job) and replacing them with unskilled children. Serious industrial experts like Dr Ure agreed with him. In fact, the mule spinners weren't put out of jobs; changes in the way factories were managed meant that these skilled cotton workers kept their highly paid jobs well into the 20th century. Forecasts of the effects of technology on jobs since the 1960s have been equally inaccurate; indeed, futurology has consistently exaggerated and misinterpreted the effects of automation on jobs.

The third reason for scepticism is that it's impossible to define what the counterfactual to any given innovation is. A coal mine despoils nature and emits lots of CO_2. But if the alternative is to chop down and burn a large forest, the mine might be better both for nature and the climate. This concern applies to other innovations too. If a nuclear war happens at some point, then we would probably be better off had nuclear weapons not been invented. But if you were considering whether to invent the atom bomb in Los Alamos in 1943, your choice wasn't between inventing nuclear weapons or nuclear weapons never existing, but between you inventing them then or someone else inventing them later and, in all likelihood, using them against you.

The fourth is a general problem of anything future oriented: the incumbents who may stand to lose most from an innovation are likely to be well organised and powerful, while potential future beneficiaries may be powerless and lack a voice.

These are all reasons for caution and humility. In any system it's useful to allow a fair degree of freedom either for inventors or for entrepreneurs. Excessive application of precautionary principles can inhibit very desirable progress.

But it's implausible to conclude that no scrutiny or debate is either useful or feasible. It's inherently unhealthy for any society to see technologies as things which emerge magically, and over which there is no possibility of control.

A framework for thought and action

So, what are reasonable ways of assessing and then supporting innovations at different stages of their life cycle that avoid these pitfalls? Here I suggest what's needed.

A staged approach to knowledge, risk and uncertainty

It's very hard to know early on what innovations will turn into. This is the justification for some exploratory innovation relatively untrammelled by too many controls. Over time, however, the likely impacts become clearer. But this poses a big challenge. When a technology is young, it's hard to assess; when it's mature, it may be too late to reshape it.

So, a rough compromise aims early on to explore possibilities and potential threats, and to identify potential triggers or irreversible steps which could warrant more intensive scrutiny. For almost any technology, the moment of coming near to market, or of being purchased for use by a government, should be a trigger. But for others – where the potential risks are particularly large – the critical moment may be an important technical breakthrough (AI falls into this category). A lot of work is underway on the governance of these kinds of risks. The key is to keep choices open, not to close them off. Many of the methods being suggested to support responsible innovation offer stage-gate models that ask what kinds of information are needed at each stage.

Distinguish different types of good, and guide innovation to the ones with the greatest potential benefit

The value of innovation will depend on the kind of good or service that it leads to. There are at least five very different kinds of goods (though these are sometimes confused or conflated in economics), and policy should be designed to distinguish them.

The first category includes goods with network effects or positive externalities that become more valuable if others are also consuming them – like telephones and other network technologies. Public health would also fall into this category. Because of their positive externalities, there is a case for judging growth in consumption of these as more valuable to an economy than growth of other kinds of consumption. For similar reasons, innovation that contributes to goods of this kind should be a higher priority for any society.

A second category encompasses more normal commodities, like clothing or tins of baked beans. Whether or not I consume these doesn't have much impact for better or worse on other people. These are the types of good around which most economics is shaped. Their profitability can be improved by reducing inputs or increasing the extent to which they are reused or recycled. But their external effects are modest.

The third category contains goods that destroy value for some while creating it for others. These include cars (which create pollution, noise and dislocation for those who don't own them), airlines (which disproportionately worsen climate change) and many other industries. Economics recognises that they produce 'negative externalities'. It measures these when doing exercises in cost–benefit analysis, and policy makers try to internalise them through taxes or regulations. But only the most obvious and material externalities are recognised in economics; and even the ones that are recognised aren't measured in terms of GDP or company accounts. Later on, I look in more detail at these distributional questions.

Fourth, there are what the economist Fred Hirsch called 'positional goods', whose value comes from their exclusivity. Stately homes and tropical islands developed for luxury tourism are classic examples, as is getting on the guest list for the best parties or membership of the most exclusive golf clubs. Their scarcity can be physical, meaning that a good is scarce in some absolute or socially imposed sense (such as land used for pleasure and personal enjoyment); or the scarcity can be social, meaning that it can be subject to congestion or crowding through more extensive use (as in the case of a privileged education). It's hard to see why innovation policy should ever prioritise goods of this kind – though the Concorde aeroplane, the flagship of UK and French innovation policy in the 1960s, was arguably as much about positional value as absolute value.

Finally, there are goods whose very value comes from the negative externalities created for others. At the extreme are weapons: teenagers buy knives and nations build nuclear missiles to frighten others. Their negative impact on lived value is not an unfortunate by-product but, rather, integral to them. Roughly half of all direct public spending on innovation in the US, Russia, the UK, France and other countries goes on military technologies.

It should be obvious that innovation spending should treat these goods very differently. Yet most funding rules make no distinction between them, and this is particularly a flaw of tools such as R&D tax credits.

Consider distributional effects, even though these are hard to predict

In retrospect, it should be fairly straightforward to look in a rounded way at the distributional effects of new technologies, even if this is very difficult to do in advance. You would expect to look at the following categories:

- gains to consumers (who presumably won't buy the new thing unless they see gains, though in the longer term they may suffer losses, for example if a new kind of food harms their health);
- gains (and sometimes losses) to investors;
- gains to some workers who get better jobs;
- losses to other workers who lose their jobs or see a cut in pay;
- a mix of gains and losses to natural capital.

Such assessments can be comparative, static or dynamic: for example, will this cluster of technologies create new jobs and business clusters or have knock-on effects on many other sectors in the manner of some general-purpose technologies? They're rarely easy because of the sheer number of possible factors involved. But they can at least in principle be reasonably objective and avoid cultural judgements (such as 'smartphones/satellite TV/Snapchat will destroy our culture …'). They can also be done in real time, tracking the actual effects of technologies (for example, what effects are different national choices between nuclear and solar power having distributionally?).

Assess ethically and apply the Golden Rule test

The ethical assessment of innovations is more complex. A useful starting point is to look for compatibility with the Golden Rule: do unto others what you would have them do unto you. Good innovations are ones that we would want for ourselves and those we love. Bad ones (like many of the financial innovations of the 1990s and 2000s) clearly breach the Golden Rule in that the providers would not want themselves to be consumers.

Taking a broad look at technology, some innovations are clearly compatible with the Golden Rule, while others support predation, making it easier for governments, armies or businesses to control, exploit or conquer. Technologies for war, or for surveillance, are by their very nature contrary to the spirit of the Golden Rule. There is no missile system or directed energy weapon for which it makes sense for others to do unto you as you would do unto them. Computer viruses are very obvious predators, secretly stealing your credit card details, often to support organised-crime syndicates.

New fields of technology bring new patterns of predation as well as empowerment. The internet of things, with its arrays of sensors, is a good example. There are great potential advantages to the efficiency of transport, energy and security. But almost any action may now be generating data to be matched, mined and commercialised without your knowledge or consent. You may not mind, since there is no immediate harm to you. But something of you is being taken without your permission and without any reciprocal benefit to you.

Other technologies are more obviously compatible with the Golden Rule – like mobile phones (which become valuable only if others have them), oral rehydration therapy, yellow fever vaccines or new crops enriched with vitamins. Others sit in between, like cars that simultaneously provide value to their owners but also take away clean air, space and peace from people who don't have them. An interesting case study was the attempt by Facebook to introduce free internet access[4] in India, which showed just how different perceptions of value can be.

Then, too, there are technologies of predation that benefit people but leave nature worse off. How you view these depends on just how human-centric your world-view is. In the eyes of some, large-scale mining, whether of the land or the oceans, is by its very nature predatory (even when it doesn't come with the messy combination of displacement, abuse and occasional windfall pay-offs to indigenous communities). To others, it's just the good fortune that humans enjoy, thanks to their evolutionary superiority.

Agency and assessment

Who might make these assessments? And who might act on them? Interest in this field is currently limited to a few big funders (like the European Commission and research councils). But there are many other potential users/creators of more systematic assessments of innovations at different stages of development:

- governments, innovation agencies and with them regulators and policymakers, at national or transnational levels – most TA is attached to governments or parliaments;
- businesses and investors, including ones committed to corporate reporting on environmental, social and governance issues, or employee organisations – this is a very underdeveloped field;
- universities and research centres, which have more capabilities, and the whole panoply of science and technology studies to draw on;
- citizens, NGOs, social movements and the media, aiming to represent a civic interest, though these usually campaign for or against technologies rather than playing an overt role in assessment.

Each of these may judge innovations in different ways. But there would be benefit in common frameworks, language and analytical technique, for example around descriptions of risk and opportunity, or design of experiments to improve knowledge about these. And there should be great advantages in more truly society-wide processes that debate in a rounded way the possibilities and threats of emerging technologies.

Outcomes and actions

What effect should an assessment regime seek to have? How might it be acted on? Such methods are only worthwhile if they lead to action:

- to *encourage* – where a major potential is diagnosed but without adequate economic or other support to drive its development (drugs for rare or poor country diseases are a good example);
- to *block* – where the harms are serious and the priority is to slow down, redirect or stop R&D and technology development;
- to *redirect* – where they may aim to guide R&D or commercial investment (for example, drones for social good) or regulation.

This obviously raises the question of how the arbiters of spending in fields like R&D could be more systematically held to account for their use of assessment tools to guide decisions. This would be a useful outcome from any work in this field – a more systematic combination of Golden Rule-based evaluations and natural capital evaluations.

This chapter has aimed to contribute to the conversation about how we fill the space between two undesirable and intellectually incoherent poles: on the one hand, a hard precautionary principle which tries to stop any discovery or invention that might bring with it risks and losses; on the other hand, the view that, because any assessment is difficult, we should just let technologies develop according to the push from scientists and inventors and the pull from markets.

Neither position adds up. But finding a sensible path between these extremes is complex, even though it's clearly important for innovation ministries, agencies and funders. It matters because in the end governments have to act, spending our money to promote novel solutions. Without more intellectual rigour we end up backing the bad or the indifferent, or simply succumbing to the influence of the well-connected.

Part V
Social innovation and the future

By the late 2010s significant majorities in rich countries expected their children to be worse off than themselves. The future had ceased to be a place of hope. Instead it became as much a place of fear, where jobs would be destroyed by robots, our minds would be enslaved by machines and power would drift out of people's direct control.

The most important task of social innovation is to rekindle a sense of power, a sense that we are able to shape and create a future in which we would want to live. That in turn depends on the ability to see and imagine alternative possible futures that can guide us to action. In this part I look at how this is to be done, starting with the future of social innovation itself before turning to how we should think about the future in a much broader sense.

16

Social innovation in the 2020s

In November 2018, Carlos Moedas, who was then the EU's commissioner in charge of research, science and technology, gave a fulsome endorsement of social innovation: 'In the European Union', he said, 'we are going to put more money into social innovation, not because it's trendy, but because we believe that the future of innovation is about social innovation.'[1]

His words signalled an important shift. Social innovation is not a new concept or practice, but it has become increasingly part of the mainstream. There are now hundreds of social innovation centres, funds, courses and incubators of all kinds, most of which didn't exist in the 2000s. Here I attempt an overview of what was achieved during the 2010s, what's missing and what might be priorities for the 2020s, in what, despite Moedas's comments, could be a much less favourable political climate in many countries.

In the mid-2000s I co-wrote a report, titled *Social Silicon Valleys*, which tried to set out a roadmap for social innovation. At the time I was part of a group trying to build on what had been achieved in supporting social entrepreneurship and social enterprise, using a more systematic approach to social change that didn't over-fetishise the heroic individual entrepreneur and that recognised the role that governments could play.[2] The report made a series of recommendations, calling for:

- new sources of finance, including public and philanthropic investment in high-risk R&D, targeted at the areas of greatest need and greatest potential;

- more open markets for social solutions, including public funding and services directed more to outcomes and opened up to social enterprises and user groups as well as private business;
- new kinds of incubator for promising models, and 'accelerators' to advance innovation in areas such as chronic disease or the cultivation of non-cognitive skills;
- new ways of empowering users to drive innovation themselves – with tools, incentives, recognition and access to funding for ideas that work;
- new institutions to orchestrate more systemic change in fields like climate change or welfare – linking small-scale social enterprises and projects to big institutions, laws and regulations;
- new institutions focused on adapting new technologies for their social potential – such as AI – as well as more extensive, rigorous, imaginative and historically aware research on how social innovation happens and how it can be helped.

We weren't hopeful that much would happen. Yet a surprising amount of what was recommended subsequently happened in the dozen years after the report was published, even if the implementation of these ideas was often messy and fragmented. National cultures remain very diverse – and what social innovation means in Bangladesh (home of some of the strongest institutions for social innovation, like BRAC and Grameen) or Kenya (home of Ushahidi and some of the most dynamic digital innovation) is very different from what it means in a US city or a European nation. But there are some common patterns.

One is the spread of social innovation centres and labs – dedicated physical spaces and organisations aiming to promote social innovation in the round, with prominent examples in Quebec, Adelaide, Amsterdam, Beijing, Delhi, Lisbon, Rio, Tilburg, the Basque Country and many others. Some are based on foundations (like the Lien Centre in Singapore or the Bertha Centre in Cape Town), others on buildings (such as the Centre for Social Innovation in Toronto), while others originated as offshoots of government (like the Australian Centre for Social Innovation and Nesta in the UK).

There's been a big expansion of social investment funds (although only a small minority of these focus on innovation, these provide a new route to help innovations grow to scale) and of new funding tools that can support social innovation, such as crowdfunding platforms. Many governments have created social innovation funds (from Hong Kong and Australia to France and the US), and fairly comprehensive national policy programmes have been introduced in a few countries, from Malaysia to Canada.

The European Commission incorporated social innovation into many of its programmes, including the European Social Fund and the Horizon 2020 science and research funding. The United Arab Emirates now commits 1% of public spending to public innovation – a rare example of shifting towards more serious allocations. There are dozens of university research centres (from Dortmund, Waterloo, Stanford and Northampton to Glasgow Caledonian, Vienna and Barcelona) and courses for undergraduates and mature students. International NGOs – such as Oxfam, Mercy Corps and the Red Cross – are taking innovation much more seriously as a way of responding to new technological opportunities and challenges, as are many UN agencies, notably UNICEF and the UN Development Programme.

Many big firms have announced initiatives using the social innovation label, including tech firms like Hitachi and Dell and consultancies like McKinsey and KPMG, even if many of these are little more than cosmetic. The long-run shift to more detailed reporting of social and environmental impacts is beginning to influence investment (even if much that uses the label 'impact investment' falls a very long way short of serious social innovation). Social innovation skills are becoming much more widely accessible – for example, through the Nesta DIY Toolkit used by well over 1 million people worldwide, and through content provided by organisations like IDEO.[3]

Digital social innovation (DSI) has taken off – over 2,000 organisations were mapped by DSI Europe in 2018,[4] and there are thousands of others around the world, sometimes described with the 'civic tech' label. There are hundreds of social innovation incubators and accelerators of all kinds, and transnational networks of social incubators such as Global Social Entrepreneurship Network (GSEN), Impact Hub and makesense.[5] A few mayors have defined themselves by their commitment to social innovation (such as Won Soon Park in Seoul and Virginio Merola in Bologna). There are social innovation prizes in the US, Europe, China and elsewhere, new tools such as social impact bonds (over 100 now, globally), and new legal forms – like community interest companies and B Corporations.

There are new campaigning tools – like Avaaz and Change.org – and new kinds of social movement pioneering social innovation in fields like disability, refugee rights and the environment. There are social innovation media – such as the *Stanford Social Innovation Review*, *Apolitical* or the *Good Magazine*. And there have been some significant surveys of the global social innovation landscape, including from the Economist Intelligence Unit, and regional surveys in Latin America, East Asia and Europe.

On the boundaries of these there are also new hybrids. The Standby Task Force is a good example of a growing field, as a digital volunteer organisation for collaborative, crowdsourced crisis mapping. In response to crises, it puts together specialist teams for *media monitoring* (searching Twitter, news feeds and other social media for relevant crisis events and filtering irrelevant reports), *geolocation* (finding physical locations of reported crisis events) and *verification* (checking the quality and correctness of mapped events).

Finally, there has been at least some progress in clarifying boundaries and definitions. It's now better understood that social innovation is not the same as social entrepreneurship, or enterprise, or creativity, or investment, though these all overlap.

False starts?

Not everything succeeded. President Obama's Office for Social Innovation in the White House did good work but did not survive the change of president. The UK's Big Society programme likewise didn't survive a change of political leadership. There have also been some uneasy transitions. Traditional innovation agencies have adopted some of the language of social innovation, but with uneven results (although Sweden's Vinnova, Finland's Sitra, Canada's MaRS and Malaysia's AIM have all done well in complementing technology support with a new focus on social innovation, most have not).

Organisations associated with the earlier wave of programmes devoted to social entrepreneurship have sometimes struggled to achieve a better balance between support for individuals and the broader needs of innovation (given that the model of a single individual developing an innovation, or venture, and then growing it, remains very rare).

The field of social innovation also has its share of risks. One is the risk of fetishising innovation as an end in itself rather than as a means to other ends. For most organisations for much of the time, innovation may be less important than the effective implementation of existing ideas or the adoption of ideas from elsewhere (I used to advocate that governments should spend around 1% of their budgets on their own innovation, but that the majority of time, money and effort should go into good implementation). Innovation can often seem exciting and sexy, while implementation and adoption are dull. But innovation without a wider system for implementation and adoption risks being pointless, and funders would often do better to prioritise adoption and adaptation of ideas rather than novelty.

Another risk has been excessive managerialism. A few US consultancies had a big influence, promoting a thinned-down version of social innovation, shorn of its politics and passions. This risk overlaps with that of 'solutionism': the belief, often promoted by Silicon Valley entrepreneurs and philanthropists, that for every problem there is a solution that can be rationally discovered and then scaled up. The attention of mainstream business gurus was also a mixed blessing. For example, the Harvard Business School professor Michael Porter had long been a fierce critic of social action but then switched 180 degrees to promote the concept of 'shared value'. For some this was a welcome conversion; for others, it was shameless hypocrisy.

A very different risk can be seen in the new tools for advocacy. Anger and expression are vital fuels for social change, but they can become addictive, especially when amplified by social media, with expression becoming an alternative to the hard graft of achieving change. The internet has become a powerful tool for mobilising people, but it is much less effective at channelling that mobilisation into sustained change. The failure of the Arab Spring of 2010–11 was a very visible example of this pattern.

In general, social innovators have steered clear of the traps and successfully made the transition from being a marginal idea to one that is more mainstream, and healthily focused on practice. Yet the scale of activity is still small relative to the scale of needs. The projects and initiatives listed are modest, and most of the organisations mentioned are fragile. In some fields, hype has greatly exceeded reality (including, at times, impact investment). Meanwhile, vastly more innovation funding still goes to the military than to society, and the world's brainpower is still directed far more to the needs of the wealthy and of warfare than it is to social priorities.

More worrying is the shift in climate. Relatively centrist, pragmatic governments of both left and right were sympathetic to some of the arguments for social innovation. By contrast, authoritarian leaders – from Bolsonaro in Brazil to Duterte in the Philippines, from Trump in the US to Erdogan in Turkey – tend to be hostile, suspicious of civil society and activism of any kind, and much more favourable to innovation that's linked to either the military or big business.

So, what could be achieved in the 2020s, in what may be a less favourable climate? What could organisations with power and influence do to strengthen the most useful forces for change?

Social innovation: Ten possible priorities (2020–30)

Here I suggest ten challenges and priorities that could define whether social innovation becomes a recognised part of the mainstream or remains more marginal.

Tackle big issues and at the right level of granularity

The most important challenge is to achieve, and demonstrate, big inroads on the major issues of our time, such as ageing, unemployment, stagnant democracy or climate change. This will require moving on from the units of analysis and action of previous eras. Much past activity focused on the individual (social entrepreneurs and innovators), the individual venture or the individual innovation, while at the other end of the spectrum, macro initiatives tried to change the behaviour of all businesses, or all charities, or to promote systems change at a global level. I expect that most impact will come from tackling issues at a middle level – specific sectors in specific places. So, addressing the most complex challenges may be much more practical at the level of systems, or of industries in particular places, for example, how to sharply improve the performance of the housing sector, childcare or training in a city or region.

Grow funding at serious scale

A significant proportion of R&D spending, both public and private, needs to be directed to innovations that are social in both their ends and their means. That funding needs to grow steadily in order to ensure that there is capacity to use money well. It also needs to be plural, including grant funds, investment through loans and equity, convertible funding, matched crowdfunding as well as public procurement, and outcomes-based funding and bonds, as well as participatory budgeting.

Link action to evidence of impact

Every aspect of social innovation needs to be attuned to evidence and a willingness to find out what achieves most impact. This doesn't mean making a fetish of RCTs or costly evaluations. But it does require doing more to embed analysis into the everyday work of organisations, where possible testing alternative models, adopting common standards of evidence and promoting a sophisticated understanding of how to discover what works, where and when.

Connect into movements, activism and democracy

Social innovation in many countries will need to become more, not less, political, and to be willing to campaign on many fronts. That means going far beyond 'clicktivism', including direct action in countries where the political climate is hostile to social and civic action. It means linking individual social innovations to broader programmes for change, while also tapping into the emotions that so often drive social change. Politics, and being active in democracy, are vital for social innovations to thrive.

Make the most of digital

There's been an extraordinary flowering of DSI and civic tech, particularly around open data, open knowledge, the maker movement and citizen science. But these haven't yet made strong links to previous generations of civil society organisations and charities, and many have struggled to achieve large scale. Civic tech and DSI need better routes to scale, which depends on the right kinds of finance, incubation and links into procurement.

Shape the next-generation internet

The biggest challenge will be to design the next-generation internet on principles closer to those of social innovation, and indeed to the founding spirit of the internet and World Wide Web, with open source, open data, net neutrality and citizen control. There are some promising projects underway – such as Tim Berners Lee's Solid and Indie,[6] and Nesta's projects on data commons[7] and the Next Generation Internet across Europe.[8] But the search for an internet which is not dominated either by American corporations or by the Chinese and Russian states will be a major struggle requiring fresh thinking.

Broader and deeper social innovation skills

Social innovation depends on certain capabilities: knowledge about how to generate ideas, develop them and scale them. Those skills are scarce and sometimes as much undermined as helped by fashions. We need much more widespread support for practical skills in design, prototyping, pilots, experiments, social investment, evaluation and iteration. These need to include online tools and MOOCs (massive open online courses), mobilising existing universities and colleges and creating more grassroots academies.

Better adoption

It's often assumed that social innovation is all about radical new ideas and out-of-the-box thinking. But most innovation in most fields is much more about adoption and incremental adaptation. The first question for any innovator should be: what can I borrow or adapt? And funders should give more weight to smart adoption rather than originality.

Mature policy debate

We're just beginning to see serious national policies around social innovation. To help these evolve, we'll need better comparative analysis of multiple national strategies – and, ideally, competition – as well as reflection on how the goals of innovation policy and social innovation policy might be better aligned, so that policies around funding, new legal forms, tax incentives, procurement and commissioning can work better.

Continually reaching out

The risk for a field like social innovation is that it becomes inward looking or an echo chamber. Many in the field are urban, well educated and young. But the most useful innovation comes from diversity and from encounters of people from different backgrounds. So, the very tendencies that give the field some of its coherence can also become a trap. This becomes particularly obvious where social innovation is engaging with seriously divided societies. The ability to empathise, to understand symbols and to heal scars turns out in some contexts to be as important as rationalistic analysis and action.

Achieving these ten priorities doesn't require a top-down plan, even if one were possible. But they do require rapid global awareness, fast learning and a willingness to cut through hype.[9] During the 2020s we will need more, not less, energetic cross-pollination. It continues to be true that practice is ahead of theory, but also that practice is held back by weak institutions and uncertain methods, which means that there is far too much unnecessary reinvention. As we face a potentially more hostile climate there'll be even more need for alliances between practitioners and interpreters who can spot the kernel of new ideas and show their broader transformative potential.

17

Thinking about the future

> The world of the future will be an even more demanding struggle against the limitations of our intelligence ... not a comfortable hammock in which we can lie down to be served by our robot slaves.[1]

What of the longer-term future? How can we make sense of it? There are many futurists, and all too many people with views about what the future will bring. But there are no experts on the future. It's not possible to be an expert on something that hasn't yet happened, and most experts perform poorly as predictors.[2]

Some of the reasons are obvious: their models are too simple to cope with complexity, or work only in stable periods but not in periods of turbulence. But we have no choice but to attempt some view of what lies ahead, and social change depends on some degree of optimism that what should happen will happen. Our era looks ahead to distant horizons. The ancient Greeks imagined us looking backwards in time, which meant that the past was ahead of us, the future always behind us, which made it oddly more frightening because it was unseen.

Expertise and humility

Futurism is by any standards an odd activity. The more publicly visible a futurist is, the more likely they are to be wrong. The media reward exaggeration in a reinforcing feedback loop that turns otherwise sensible people into quite silly ones (you could cheekily call it the TED paradox: the more coherent and articulate the picture of future possibilities, the more misleading it probably is). Another lesson is that the more you hold on to a single dominant explanation for change, the more likely you are to be wrong – whether it's the inevitability of democratisation, technology's power to liberate humanity or the eternal nature of ethnic conflict. The world obeys many laws, not just one, and trends produce counter-trends. That's why technological determinism – the assumption that new technologies will diffuse into a grateful world and drive change in a linear way – so often misleads, even though it's as popular as ever.

Serious analysis and thought do confer some advantages in understanding how patterns evolve – but only if leavened with a good deal of humility. Otherwise, expertise breeds overconfidence and thus a tendency to make mistakes. As Helen Keller is reputed to have said, 'To be blind is bad, but worse is to have eyes and not see!'

What should we be seeing?

In any era, there are conventional views of the future. Today they focus on driverless cars, 3D printers, the Internet of Things – most already real and growing fast, and so fair bets. There are others which are provocative and may be right – the shift to new foodstuffs like locusts, learning in teacherless classrooms, living in self-managing buildings, using digital memories to supplant our own or moving in a world where virtual beings and real ones intermingle without clear boundaries.

There are other conventional futures which are probably wrong. Since the 1960s most futurists have predicted the end of work or permanent jobs and a move to project-based work. The management guru Peter Drucker reflected futurists' conventional wisdom when he predicted that by the early 21st century universities would have disappeared, replaced in their entirety by online courses.[3] Read quite a few futurists today, and their forecasts are identical to the ones made a generation ago, suggesting that some futurists are remarkably conformist.

Yet, in the OECD economies job tenure hasn't fallen at all, and employment levels have generally gone up. Across the world universities are booming, and building new campuses and facilities at an unprecedented rate. So, it's right to be sceptical

– particularly of conventional wisdoms. Here I suggest some complementary ways of thinking about the future which provide a partial protection against the pitfalls.

The shape of the future

The first is to create your own composite map of the future by engaging with the trends. There are many methods available for mapping the future – from Foresight and Scenario Planning to the Delphi method.[4] Behind all are views about the shapes of change. Any quantitative exploration of the future uses a common language of patterns, for example these, which summarise the shape of trends: / \ – U or J. Some things will go up, some go down, some change suddenly and some not change at all. All of us have implicit or explicit assumptions about these. But it's rare to interrogate them systematically and to test whether our assumptions about what fits in which category are right.

Let's start with the J-shaped curves. Many of the long-term trends around physical phenomena look J-curved: rising carbon emissions, water usage and energy consumption have been exponential in shape over the centuries. As we know, physical constraints mean that these simply can't go on – the J curves have to become S shaped sooner or later, or else crash. That is the ecological challenge of the 21st century.

New revolutions

But there are other J curves, particularly the ones associated with digital technology. Moore's Law and Metcalfe's Law describe the dramatically expanding processing power of chips, and the growing connectedness of the world. Some hope that the sheer pace of technological progress will somehow solve the ecological challenges. That hope has more to do with culture than evidence. But these J curves are much faster than the physical ones – any factor that doubles every 18 months achieves stupendous rates of change over decades.

That's why we can be pretty confident that digital technologies will continue to throw up new revolutions – whether around the Internet of Things, the quantified self, machine learning, robots, mass surveillance or new kinds of social movement. But what form these will take is much harder to predict, and most digital prediction has been unreliable – we have YouTube but not the interactive TV many predicted (when did you last vote on how a drama should end?); relatively simple SMS and Twitter have spread much more than ISDN (Integrated Services Digital Network) or fibre to the home. And plausible ideas like the long tail theory – which predicted that, thanks to the web, millions of people would make a living by selling small quantities of books or music – turned out to be largely wrong.

If the J curves are dramatic but unusual, much more of the world is shaped by straight-line trends – like ageing, or the rising price of disease that some predict will take the costs of healthcare up towards 40% or 50% of GDP by late in the 21st century, or incremental advances in fuel efficiency, or the likely relative growth of the Chinese economy.

Also important are the flat straight lines – the things that probably won't change in the next decade or two: nation-states not unlike those of the 19th century are likely to continue to exist; air travel will continue to make use of 50-year-old technologies; and schools will not be so different from those in the 19th century.

Great imponderables

If the J curves are the most challenging trends, the most interesting ones are the U-shaped curves – the examples of trends bending – like crime, which went up for a century and then fell sharply in many countries in the 1990s and 2000s; or world population, which has been going up but could start going down in the later part of this century; or divorce rates, which seem to have plateaued; or the Chinese labour supply, which is forecast to turn down in the 2020s.

No one knows if the apparently remorseless upward trends of obesity and depression will turn downwards. No one knows if the next generation in the West will be poorer than their parents. And no one knows if democratic politics will reinvent itself and restore trust. In every case, much depends on what we do. None of these trends is a fact of nature or an act of God.

That's one reason why it's good to immerse yourself in these trends and interrogate what shape they really are. Out of that interrogation we can build rough mental models and generate our own hypotheses – ones not based on the latest fashion or bestseller but, hopefully, on a sense of what the data show and, in particular, what's happening to the deltas – the current rates of change of different phenomena.

Stories

Most people find stories much easier to grasp than numbers, trends or models. Our brains are just wired that way. So, it's not surprising that history has often been shaped by compelling stories of the future. Some were the stories of threats and dangers – warning of invasion or plague, punishment by a cruel God or the decline of civilisation. Others were stories of hope that promised the City on the Hill, the coming of the Messiah or the arrival of communism.

Modern politics is also saturated with simple stories about the future that are used to justify or block reforms. Albert Hirschman called the latter 'rhetorics of reaction' – stories which warn of futility (nothing will work), perversity (reforms will have unintended negative consequences) and jeopardy (reforms will threaten things we care about).[5] Their mirrors are the rhetorics of progress, which argue that reforms are needed to build on past reforms, to right past wrongs and to achieve a future golden age.

Stories are, by their nature, neither logical nor analytic. But they do help to make sense of confusing information and, as the futurist Gaston Berger put it, some future stories usefully 'disturb the present'. That's the case with a lot of science fiction – from Margaret Atwood and Ursula Le Guin to Charles Stross.

So, apart from reading a lot of science fiction, how can we use stories to think about the future? Here I look at different types of story that can help us peer into the crystal ball.

Scenarios and scenario planning

Many futurists advocate scenarios – plausible but coherent accounts of what might happen – in the form of scenario planning, made famous by the global oil company Shell and others. They're helpful at getting rigid organisations to think more flexibly; they acclimatise participants to potential surprises; and, in theory, they help organisations to recognise whether their current strategies are robust against different possible futures.

Unfortunately, they also have a few weaknesses. Many scenarios (particularly the ones used in big businesses and governments) are dull as stories – too blandly broad-brush to excite. It's very hard to get them owned by a lot of people, but that's the only way they're useful. And too often the process gets in the way of the really tough issues, rather than illuminating them.

'What if ...' stories

Another approach to stories is deliberately more provocative than scenarios: the idea is to pursue 'what ifs', thinking through a possible trend or taking an idea that exists in embryo and thinking through what would happen if it was generalised. So, in the first category we can ask: what if growth went into reverse for a generation or globalisation was stalled by pandemics and cyber disasters? What if technology and medicine continue to drive up life expectancy but make no progress in improving morbidity, leaving hundreds of millions with chronic conditions like untreatable dementia? These are good mental workouts, but they can also be taken further.

Most of the really interesting shifts in history are shifts in categories as well as quantities, and radical change nearly always involves changes in how things are seen or defined. Yet, for that very reason, these are the hardest changes to predict.

So, another kind of 'what if' story looks at ideas as well as trends. A good example is the sharing economy and collaborative consumption, which is growing all over the world, but remains rather baffling to conventional economics and is largely invisible in policy discussions. So, we can ask what might happen if people shared their cars, homes, tools and even their time, using online platforms. This might greatly reduce the demand for goods, raising usage rates instead. What if this grew to 30% or 50% of GDP? What diversity of business and organisational models would appear? Would tax systems be adapted to promote it (perhaps rewarding leasing over purchasing commodities, incentivising multiple uses of things, for example, through discounts on vehicle tax for people who put them in sharing schemes)? What would happen to jobs? Or trade?

New hybrids

It's then possible to construct narratives which imagine the dynamics, for example, the battles which would be fought with existing industries (like the car industry) and how the politics would play out. We can also try to imagine the unforeseen effects on careers, financial returns or urban planning. Another example would be to imagine what if all schools were replaced with online learning – so that school buildings were turned into flats and children spent their days doing Khan Academy-type lessons, attending MOOC-like universities and absorbing personalised feedback from smart algorithms.

Thinking this through quickly reveals that much of what schools do isn't easily replicated in the virtual world – it's more about socialisation and signalling, or even just providing children somewhere to be while their parents are at work.

So, even if digital education worked brilliantly for maths and science, some other institutions would need to fill in the gaps. The pressures to get results would soon force educators to act on the evidence that most successful digital tools work only when they are combined with offline elements – so new hybrids would emerge.

The technological singularity – promoted by Ray Kurzweil – is, or at least should be, another good 'what if' story. What if automated intelligence outpaced and took over from human intelligence? Thinking through the dynamics can be invigorating, though unfortunately it's often used (particularly in Kurzweil's own writings) as a linear, rather mindless story that ignores much that's known about how technologies and societies interact.

These are scenarios, but very different from the ones found in scenario planning. They aren't well suited to guiding a big organisation into uncertain waters. Instead, they can be interrogated, deconstructed and played with as prompts.

Backwards stories

Another kind of story looks backwards. Leadership training programmes sometimes ask their participants to write their own obituaries. It's a morbid thing to do – but its virtue is that it makes you think about what really matters to you. It prompts a conversation with an imagined version of yourself in a few decades' time. What would your future self wish you had done today? A similar device works for nations. Imagine if our politicians could meet their counterparts in the year 2043 – what would they wish they had or hadn't done? The challenge then is to write a story you might be proud of, which describes what you did and why it worked.

This can be embarrassing. But it brings to the surface the emotional aspects of the future that otherwise get ignored – the role of love, pride, glory and care. And it can show you just how much your life is diverted to what's urgent rather than what's important. Pre-mortems are a similar idea: before a big project, conduct a serious assessment of why it went wrong.

In these stories we work out how to be a hero in our own lives. The collective versions make the community a hero in its own history, something which happens quite often in wartime, but too rarely in peace.

Compensating our story biases

We are well designed to listen to the stories. We also respond better to certain kinds of story – ones with drama, conflict, big personalities and sudden twists. You can see this clearly in relation to threats. The threats we respond to best are fast and visible (like a car coming towards us). They may involve people (because we are highly attuned to social feedback) and have a moral component (because we are good at taking moral offence).

So, child abuse, climate change and the threat of terrorist gangs with nuclear weapons all generate big responses – the effect of humans having evolved in highly social environments full of physical threats. If you wanted to kill humanity, you would design threats which were the opposite. Invisible, slow moving, detached from human agency and any visible moral calculus.

Perhaps a slow disease or, even better, a self-inflicted one would do the trick. Climate change fits the bill rather too perfectly.

The implication is that it's useful to learn how to spot the threats and issues that we are most likely otherwise to ignore – the weak signals, the slow burn trends, the issues without moral colour.

Stories that ask why and offer answers

As I showed in Chapter 12, the American historian and sociologist Charles Tilly wrote brilliantly on the role of stories in social science (in particular in his book *Stories, Identities, and Political Change*[6]). He saw that coherent, compelling and detailed stories of how things change could connect the rigorous work of social science to a public audience. Stories always simplify and 'omit a large number of likely causes, necessary conditions, and especially, competing explanations of whatever happened ... and particularly omit direct, incremental, interactive, unintended, [and] collective' factors. But their virtue is that we can distinguish more or less convincing stories of how change happens – the best ones are clear but also rich, nuanced, attuned to sequencing or the interaction of interests, cultures and beliefs.

The same is true of possible futures – we shouldn't be afraid of stories but should demand better ones. So, if we're told that robots will destroy millions of jobs, we should ask in detail about causal patterns and dialectics. For example, about potential political responses and productivity effects or why past forecasts of this kind were so wrong. Tilly was an unusually engaging academic because he repeatedly asked why: why did inequality persist? Why did events like 9/11 happen? It's not a bad strategy to adopt when faced with stories of the future – whether Pollyanna-ish promises that technology will solve everything, or apocalyptic predictions that we're all doomed. Just keep asking why. From the pieces that are left, we can try to construct stories that do a better job.

Action

It's sometimes glibly claimed that the best way to predict the future is to invent it. That's easier said than done. But it does contain a grain of truth. So, another approach to understanding the future that I want to cover is the combination of thought and action – what's sometimes called praxis.

Here the idea is that you best understand how change happens not just by reading books (even this one!) but also by direct engagement in transforming the world. Change is not purely cognitive – it's more like a craft, a mix of hand and brain, requiring us to push, prod and tinker with the world to get a grasp on its dynamics.

Perhaps one of the reasons why so much futurology is uninspiring and predictable is that it's done too much as a cognitive exercise – the futurists read each other's books and write their own, rather than getting their hands dirty in the grit of real change.

The alternative is the mindset of the entrepreneur or social innovator. They rarely jump in one go to a neat new solution that is proved to work. Instead, they constantly adapt in response to the resistance of things on the road to success. It's also the mindset of the inventor and, in a very different way, of the activist – arguing, cajoling and mobilising to find the weak chinks in power structures.

A brilliant book which links the theory and practice of, well, linking theory and practice, is *Disclosing New Worlds: Entrepreneurship, Democratic Action and the Cultivation of Solidarity* by Charles Spinosa, Fernando Flores (the computing specialist and one-time minister) and the philosopher Herbert Dreyfus.[7] With compelling stories and some serious theory, they show how active engagement in shaping the world is one of the ways we become fully human.

Prefiguring the future

The prototypes that designers and engineers build help them to see and think. Fast, real-life trials with rough models may tell you more than detailed work on paper. The related idea in politics was that activists would create 'prefigurative' projects or organisations that would, at a small scale, anticipate a future society. They would try to demonstrate different values or organising principles and encourage people's confidence that apparently utopian ideas might work after all. As I show in my book *The Locust and the Bee*,[8] a surprising proportion of 19th-century utopians were also involved in practical projects. William Morris's written accounts of the future might have been far fetched, but he was successful as a producer of textiles and wallpapers (even working on commission to Queen Victoria).

The garden city movement is another fascinating example of prefiguring a possible future in the present. Inspired by a utopian novel[9] and founded by Ebenezer Howard, the garden cities were imagined as self-contained communities of around 30,000 people, mixing homes, workshops, and agriculture in the surrounding fields.

Two were built during Howard's lifetime: Letchworth Garden City and Welwyn Garden City, both in Hertfordshire, England. His ideas proved very influential across the US, from Woodbourn in Boston to Jackson Heights in Queens, as well as further afield, from Argentina's Ciudad Jardín Lomas del Palomar to Colonel Light Gardens in Adelaide, South Australia.

William Gibson's comment that 'The future is already here – it's just not evenly distributed' is often quoted.[10] It's true that the embryos of the future are bound to exist in the present, but they won't be the same when they grow up and become mainstream. Computers now are not just a widely distributed version of computers from the early 1980s, nor are urban farming projects and organic food supply chains, hackathons or cheap airlines. That's why more biological metaphors may be better than the distribution metaphor that Gibson used: the future is already here; it's just unevenly seeded.

There are plenty of things around us that could prefigure the future – from political parties like the Pirate Party to electric car clubs, to chatbots acting as doctors. But in their mature forms they'll be radically different from their forms today. So, it's right that we should want to engage with these seeds of the future, but we shouldn't be surprised that, when they grow big, they'll no longer be quite what we had in mind.

Fast and slow

It's a cliché of the modern world that change is happening at an unprecedented pace, and it's easy to see why. We are surrounded by an exponential rise of knowledge and floods of technologies. That leads many to assume that if change can't be achieved quickly you may as well give up.

A clearer view of the present shows just how much doesn't change. Most of us in countries like the UK live in quite old houses, do quite old jobs and work for organisations that existed in some recognisable form a generation or two ago. Half the people in your train carriage or workplace will still be around in 40 years' time, as will many of the institutions you deal with and most of the buildings you visit.

Some industries move incredibly fast – and the usual metric to show this is how quickly a new technology reaches its first 100 million users. But these measures ignore the fact that most of the fast technologies rest on infrastructures that took much longer to create – like the internet. And they ignore the fact that in some industries the pace of change has slowed – in pharmaceuticals and aerospace, for example.

Historians argue that previous periods, particularly the 19th century, were much more disruptive. The generations who witnessed the arrival of the railway and the telegraph, or later the arrival of electricity and cars, arguably experienced a much faster pace of change than we do today – not to mention periods of revolution, civil war and world war.

By most standards we live in relatively stable times – so incredibly stable that it makes sense for someone in their twenties to save for a pension they may draw in 50 years' time (my hunch is that the current fashion for using the word 'disruptive' could take hold only among people living in very secure environments).

One implication is that if you want to understand the future by changing it, you should calibrate your feel for the pace of change. Some things do change very fast, especially where digital technologies are involved. But many fundamental changes still take decades to work their way through – from low-carbon industries and life-styles to global justice and bodily implants. Anything that requires fundamental changes in behaviours and cultures will almost certainly take a long time. So, if you're serious, don't rush it, and don't be disheartened if the world doesn't immediately respond to your prods and pushes.

Embedding the future into government

Other examples of praxis put a future-thinking capacity into the heart of governments and parliaments. I wrote about some of these in my book *The Art of Public Strategy*.[11] Finland has a Committee of the Future, set up in 1992; Hungary had a Parliamentary Commissioner for Future Generations, and Israel's Knesset a Commission for Future Generations. The closest Britain had was the Sustainable Development Commission, abolished in 2011, though Wales in 2015 passed a Well-Being of Future Generations Act and created a new post of Future Generations Commissioner.[12] In the past I've advocated a party of the future. At the very least we need some institutions to speak up for future generations. Without them, the interests of the future are bound to be silenced by the din of the present.

Among the Canadian First Nations there is the notion that when the elders of all the tribes gathered to deliberate, someone had to represent the seventh generation into the future and speak on their behalf. We're grasping for something equivalent.

We also need more mundane ways of institutionalising attention to the future. It's common in futures work to emphasise that any comments on the future are not predictions. They aim to enlighten or to provoke. The future is too uncertain to predict. There's a lot of sense in that. But there is a remarkable virtue in more precise prediction, however difficult it is to do well. In many fields of human life, trying to predict the results of your actions and then learning from what actually happens is the root of intelligence. It's how we learn to drive a car, play a musical instrument or shoot a bow and arrow.

The spread of predictive algorithms has made prediction more precise. Healthcare has been using algorithms for decades, as have the police and criminal justice systems. Often, they have found that the algorithms are better predictors than the average professional. In a very different field, Philip Tetlock's work on expert political judgement was damning of the experts' ability to predict.[13]

My proposal would be not to eliminate prediction but to make it much more explicit, and to make it part of how professions and experts learn and are held to account. This is beginning to happen as teachers predict children's exam grades. Doctors can predict the risk of patients needing to return to hospital. Governments can offer predictions of the impacts of their policies at the same time as they get laws passed and budgets agreed. Business leaders can predict how well their new strategy will go. Journalists can predict what they think will happen in forthcoming elections.

Learning as the crucial missing element

The aim should not be to encourage a culture of blame. The world will never follow predictions precisely. But being held accountable for what you have learned about why your prediction didn't come true contributes to much more intelligent debate and more intelligent systems. The key is to have systematic processes of reflection on what actually happens. This learning is the missing element. Journalists are the obvious example of this, but there are many others.

Many of the best minds have got things badly wrong. The journalist Anatole Kaletsky authoritatively told the world in 2007/08 that the financial crisis would be short and mild. The Nobel Prize-winning economist Paul Krugman said that the internet would be no more important for economies than the fax machine. The futurist Peter Schwartz boldly predicted, just ahead of the financial crash, that the world was on the verge of an unprecedented period of faster growth that would last for several decades. Ray Kurzweil is notorious for having got many predictions wildly wrong, alongside some accurate ones. My friend Will Hutton forecast in the mid-1990s that the UK economy was going down the tube, just as it began the longest period of growth in its history. John Gray repeatedly predicts disasters, while others, like Matt Ridley, repeatedly predict triumphs, neither much bothered by inconvenient reality, and both confident that at least some of the time they will appear extraordinarily wise and prescient. I've lost count of the number of writers who have predicted China's imminent collapse since 2000 (though very few then explained why they had been wrong).

I've made my fair share of mistakes too. I predicted that there would be a revolution in Saudi Arabia in the early 1980s; that every UK household would have a fibre connection by 2000; and that the Conservatives would win a big majority in the 2010 election. I over-estimated the margin of victory of the Brexit camp in the UK referendum in 2016. In the mid-2000s, I thought that both Ireland and Iceland would be models for the world, rather than exemplars of hubris and disaster, and I've repeatedly over-estimated the pace of change. But I would like to think that, when my predictions didn't materialise, I changed my mental models of how the world works and made them more accurate.

Reducing the stupidity of public life

So, I would like a world where many more people in positions of prestige are encouraged to make specific predictions, and then given visible opportunities to comment on what they've learned when the world moves in surprising ways. No one should be taken seriously who doesn't do this. Various people at different times have proposed repositories of forecasts to encourage this. The idea can also be built into the normal work of professions, with requirements to make regular and explicit predictions. It would be extremely uncomfortable for the powerful and influential. But it would also be immensely useful, a great leveller and possibly the single most important step in reducing the stupidity of public life.

Escaping from prose

In the last decades of the 20th century futures studies became highly academic. Its outputs were texts: thick scenario documents; academic peer-reviewed journals; texts littered with references to other texts. This was the price the field paid for being taken seriously. And sometimes the format of prose really is a good way to explore complex trends, especially when peppered with graphs and forecasts.

But this is not the only way to think about the future, and not necessarily the best. An opposite view sees futures revealed through practice rather than representation, what people do rather than what they write. In this view the best way to understand the future is to seek out the places or people who seem to be shaping it and make sense of what they do and how they think. If the future is reluctant to give up knowledge of itself too easily, then perhaps you have to become part of the phenomenon to grasp it, and work to shape it rather than being a detached observer – a version of the insights of anthropology which argued that you had to be inside a phenomenon to grasp its logic. By contrast, too much detachment may condemn you to believing too strongly in the conventional wisdoms of your own society.

Philosophically, this is the spirit of 19th-century pragmatism rather than 20th-century analytics – of William James, John Dewey and Charles Peirce, and more recently the spirit of the philosopher Roberto Mangabeira Unger. The world is made through the trial and error of practical people, shaping tools that are useful to them. Abstracting too much misses the crucial issues. We become more fully human by realising our potential in tension with the world as it is, bending it to better alternatives. In this view the study of the future should be a close ally of activism, and of all attempts to shape, or guide, the direction of social, technological and economic change. It should be explicitly linked to emotion, to what we want and what we care about, and shouldn't be embarrassed about taking a stand, having hope that one future may defeat others. An apparently remorseless trend becomes something to challenge or shift rather than something to rationalise. The activists who are reshaping political parties, or inventing new digital monies, or reimagining food, are part of this tradition. No text-based analysis can tell us whether they are right or wrong; only history will. This pragmatic view of the future may be fatal to any attempt to turn futures into a discipline, a self-referential field of journals, conferences and professorships. But it might in the end be more useful.

In 1937, a few years after the Great Depression, an extraordinary movement emerged in Britain. It was called Mass Observation. Its idea was to mobilise thousands of people in the systematic observation of their fellow citizens – to describe how people lived, how they talked and how they ate. Its founder was an anthropologist called Tom Harrison, whose career ranged through ornithology to fighting as a guerrilla. The movement pulled in filmmakers, poets and writers of all kinds, and hundreds of volunteer researchers, and inspired people to look at the world around them with fresh eyes. Mass Observation petered out in the 1960s. But we may now need something equivalent, though oriented to the future as well as the present. After all, the world of futures has become very much an elite activity – with specialist think-tanks working for the biggest firms and the richest governments. Futurism today tends to be an insider's game, for Silicon Valley billionnaires at the Singularity University, or Davos conferences, and reflects their values, myopias and hopes.

It wasn't always like this. In the early 19th century there were movements of the people concerned with the future, and a belief that the world was theirs to shape. Utopias were to be found on the streets as well as in the top strata of society. One example of many was the movement prompted by Étienne Cabet's writings on the utopia of Icaria.[14] His utopia promised absolute cleanliness and absolute symmetry, helped by laws to specify everything from food to dress, and with all citizens engaged in government (as well as voting), supported by a Department of Statistics to provide them with the facts they needed. This may sound like a rather weird vision of the perfect future. But Icarian societies spread in working-class communities all over France, and then in the US, where communes were set up in Texas, Louisiana, Illinois, Missouri, Iowa and California.

That was a time when much of the elite clung desperately to the past, fearful that their world was soon to be swept away – a diametrically opposite sentiment to the swaggering confidence of today's club-class elites.

Mass Observation was built around methods. So, what might the methods of mass futurism be? Perhaps they would observe the things around us that might portend possible future worlds: new ways of talking; new ways of thinking or dreaming; new styles of interior decoration; or new ways of cooking and loving. Some of the really interesting examples will be somewhat invisible, woven into the texture of life. But perhaps that's what will make them most interesting – how a family thinks about their diet, or their links to relatives spread across the world, for example. We might then map aetiologies, the journeys made by these novelties as they weave their way into the mainstream. Some of this would precisely mirror Mass Observation, which mapped the new behaviours and vernaculars as they emerged. But it would also prompt us to ask how the best emerging futures could be spread more quickly. Doing some mass futurism might be fun. And it may be a healthy expression of a self-aware democracy that refuses to submit to fatalism.

Part VI
Fresh thinking

This final part brings together shorter pieces as prompts for fresh thinking about the future. It's to be dipped into, rather than read in one go. But the pieces cover some of the most important current debates and issues in the practice of social innovation, in an unashamedly opinionated way.

18

Sparks, ideas and comments

The case for DIY societies

The more we know, the more we realise the near-infinite variety of galaxies around us. They are vastly greater in number than anyone imagined a century or more ago. Something comparable has happened in the social realm. We have slowly come to appreciate the vast variety of possible societies and social arrangements. There are many common elements – families, hierarchies, states – and some convergent trends. But for every generalisation there is an exception, and one of the virtues of anthropology is to make us see our own normal social arrangements as strange, the result of random luck rather than nature.

If we imagine social evolution as a branching tree of possibilities, then only a tiny fraction of those possibilities have ever been travelled. We catch glimpses of what might be possible when we visit another country or city, or look at cults and communes, or read science fiction, but they're only glimpses.

In the conservative view, what is is, because nothing else can be. It's a view asserted forcefully, until what was impossible happens and becomes everyday, and the lines are redrawn.

Most possible social arrangements wouldn't work, or last: brittle, intolerant hierarchies; anarchic egalitarianism; pure market capitalism. All of these turn out to be unstable. But there is still a vast possible social space full of options that could be viable.

We can explore some of this range of possible social arrangements at the macro level through imagining utopias and political programmes, and at the micro level with ideas about a new park, a housing estate, a way of curing or teaching.

But social imagination of this kind has been constricted and constrained. Until recently only a tiny minority believed that they had any right to design and imagine how a society could be organised: for the vast majority social arrangements were a given. In any case, you need skills and resources to imagine, design and then implement something radically new, which is why many of the 19th century's most influential imaginers were aristocrats (like Kropotkin or Tolstoy), or benefited from a patron (like Marx).

One group who did have the licence, and the time, to imagine were the social scientists. Nineteenth-century social science was full of optimistic designs for the future. But 20th-century social science, by contrast, became backward looking and sceptical. The price for seeing itself as a science was to focus on the evidence, which by definition meant sticking to things that had already happened, and explaining why they were as they were rather than how they might have been different.

Some groups, by contrast, are happy to explore and imagine, and are rich in resources to do so: around technology business there are numerous think-tanks, foundations and conferences, funded to let their imaginations roam. Their view of the world, and the future, which is usually male, technologically determinist and slightly bullying in tone, asserts itself confidently and visibly on the world. By contrast, the imaginary of other groups – poorer, female, Southern, rural – is less visible, and more tentative, for the simple reason that they have fewer resources to play with.

I'm convinced that we see only a fraction of the potential social imagination around us and are all worse off because of this. I like to think of the analogy with homes. In the past most people built homes just like everyone else, without space, literally or metaphorically, for much variation. A tiny handful with great wealth were given the freedom to design their own palaces and gardens, and in some cases could let their imaginations run riot.

In the recent past, however, millions of people have started exercising a similar muscle to the aristocrats and princes of the past: adapting, changing and recreating their homes and their decorations. This army of amateur architects and designers and DIY enthusiasts know when to use professionals – for the electricity or plumbing. But they see it as entirely natural that they should constantly adjust and improve the environment they live in.

This would have surprised the forward-looking architects of a century ago, who imagined future citizens living happily in the neat boxes and blocks they had designed, but never guessed how actively they would want to shape their spaces.

I see a precise analogy with societies at every level. We are slowly coming to see our own social world as a home which we are entitled and able to remake and reshape to suit us. This requires some skills, sometimes professional help, and some experience. But a hot, activist society with a similar spirit to DIY in homes is likely to be a better one. And it will be one in which we are less likely to feel alienated and more likely to feel at home.

A representational theory of social innovation

Every social innovation begins its life inchoate as a hunch, living inside only a few minds. Then, through discussion, action and more discussion, often over long periods, it comes to be named, represented and codified.

Only then can it be communicated, spread and taken up by others. In other words, representation plays a decisive role in social innovation, which is also why many innovators work hard to create a propagating network to 'spread the word': ambassadors, conferences, case studies and associations all provide a human reinforcement for the ideas. This work is hard, and involves cul-de-sacs and crossed wires. It's often said that the single biggest problem in communication is the illusion that it has taken place.

This has many consequences. Since there are now digital traces of so many activities, even in a world where only half the population has internet access, we can track and map social innovations, or will be able to soon, showing how and where they spread. It will also be possible to track how stable and sticky these representations are. A fair bet is that the more stable they are, the more likely they are to last. We will also be able to see how much the representations become embedded in things like training manuals, formal codes or policies, which again will make them more likely to last. Before long, serious research will be done to map and make sense of these patterns, and to understand why some spread and others don't.

As that happens, it should be possible to develop more rigorous hypotheses. We'll be able to explore the claim that it's not the quality of the idea that counts, but who it comes from or how it's framed. I expect that part of the explanation for which ideas spread and which don't is likely to be the density of relationships between ideas. No ideas spread in a simple way just because they are appealing or useful. Instead they are more likely to spread if they fit into already widely held bodies of knowledge and practice. They are helped, in other words, by supporting frameworks, grammars, ethics and aesthetics, and indeed by having some of the properties of a movement.

Green innovations are a good example. They are helped to spread by many factors: they draw on a widely shared ethic (that we should live, produce and consume responsibly, within planetary boundaries); they have an aesthetic (for example, organic, natural colours, curves, rough, matt); and they have structures of thought (like the idea of a circular or zero-carbon economy, as well as more conventional ideas about resource efficiency and cutting waste). Together these create a receptive environment for new green innovations (from household recycling to green roofs).

Seeing social innovation through this lens of representation may also make it easier to understand how some things are lost in translation: the representation may miss some crucial elements. Perhaps some pre-existing norms, or trust, or history turn out to explain why an innovation succeeded in one context but not in another. Rather as invisible dark matter helps to explain the movements of stars and planets, perhaps there is an equivalent social 'dark matter' that explains why, for example, microcredit, M-Pesa mobile monies and Alcoholics Anonymous spread, and failed to spread, in ways that surprised their advocates.

What of the future? At the moment we lack any sophisticated and standardised means of representation for social innovation, and indeed for many other kinds of public policy. Anything new has to be described from scratch. This is not true in other fields. Compare music, which has a hugely developed means of representing notes and their qualities, and a hugely intensive infrastructure for training, so that a pianist playing a Beethoven sonata is likely to be faithful to the composer's intent (and if they are not, it will be a choice). Engineering and medicine also have well-developed and highly standardised means of representation, which makes it much easier for people to work in other countries and to collaborate.

It's possible that in the future comparable systems of representation will develop for social organisation. There have been attempts in neighbouring fields – like Christopher Alexander's attempts at a pattern language for architecture (which had a big influence in software).[1]

A crucial lesson of collective intelligence is that the more standardised the language, the easier it is for systems to work – barcodes, URLs and medical terminologies are examples. They all show that the right taxonomies and representations don't have to crush rich complexity and variety but, as in music, can support it.

Imagine if, when you arrive in a strange city, you could interpret transparently the social nature of this hotel, that restaurant or housing estate through standardised representations of their organisational logic and form, ownership, ethics and so on. Or imagine if, where a company was trying to take over yours, you could, again, draw on a common language to describe it. The job of creating such a representational language – a comprehensive social semiotics – looks to me like a viable project, albeit a difficult one. It could be helped by the use of large data sets to discover commonalities or where different words are used to describe similar things (and vice versa). It would help us to build tools for active social design – so that someone contemplating creating a new social enterprise, or a new method for reducing plastic waste, could visualise the different options and components and use this to discuss them with others.

For now, even our own neighbourhoods are largely illegible in social terms. No wonder we feel alienated.

Why? Or do you really need a theory of change?

I've long been interested in social change, and how to understand what causes what in the myriad of causes and effects that make up a society. The phrase 'theory of change' is bandied around throughout the world of social action. When I first arrived at Nesta I tried to discourage my colleagues from using the phrase and circulated a critique. That had no effect at all, and we continue to use it and to encourage the organisations we fund to have one. But I remain sceptical of how the idea is presented, even though I'm wholly supportive of the underlying notion.

First, the positive. It must be good for any organisation to have a coherent account of why the things it does might have the effects it wants. In Nesta's standards of evidence framework we call this level 1: a logic model that plausibly links actions to results (the higher levels add in data, evidence of causation and so on). A surprising proportion of projects and programmes struggle to get to this first level.

The problems come with the phrase 'theory of change'. Each of the words is somewhat misplaced and doesn't stand up to scrutiny. A theory is generally taken to mean an idea, principle or law that is separate from, and more general than, the thing being explained. So, a theory of change should be general – like the theory claiming that higher income in a country tends to lead to more democracy, or that higher levels of education for girls will tend to lead to a lower birth rate, or that sending criminals into classrooms will dissuade teenagers from becoming criminals themselves. The advocates of theories of change use the word 'theory' in an opposite sense to describe a specific explanation of a specific example (albeit one that should then have predictive power), but never explain why they do so.

The next problem is the use of the word 'theory' in the singular form, not plural. Any serious explanation of anything in the social world should be suspect if it uses only one theory – for example, a theory of financial incentives, or peer influences. All successful models are assemblies of multiple elements and theories. Again, I've no idea why the advocates chose to do this. They might benefit from reading Scott Page's rather wonderful book *Model Thinker*,[2] which encourages the use of models to understand social phenomena but points out that all complex phenomena require multiple models to make sense of them: the task for anyone wanting to understand is to help their models to interact with and interrogate each other.

Even the word 'of' is misplaced. The purpose of theories of change is to guide action. They are in this sense theories *for* change, rather than *of* change. A theory of change is a backward-looking theory in the classic social science sense. I have less of a problem with the word 'change', but it too is misleading. What we want an explanation for is an effect, an impact or an outcome, not the change process itself.

I admit that these comments are pedantic and that most of the time the ways in which the idea of a theory of change is used are helpful. But it's good to be careful with language, and sloppy use of words encourages sloppy thinking.

Unfortunately, the problems go further. The typical theory of change, as set out in many accounts, risks being misleading in two rather important ways. One is that it tends to be far too linear, assuming that inputs lead to outputs and that outputs lead to outcomes. This sometimes happens. But anyone familiar with systems thinking will be wary of linear explanations, especially where complex social phenomena like homelessness, poverty or isolation are concerned. I used to advocate mapping systems to show all the links between different causes, and then to be precise about the strength of knowledge about each of those links, and about who had the power to influence them. These types of system maps provide a useful starting point for then thinking about how a particular organisation or intervention can work within a system, but there isn't anything quite comparable in the theory of change literature. Social phenomena often involve interdependence and reciprocity rather than linear causation. Indeed, much of the most important social change is more like a metamorphosis of mutual influence than a physics-like chain of causes.

The second, related problem is that theories of change risk squeezing out the space for learning. The advantage of the kind of systems map I have just described is that they are explicit about the limits of knowledge and where, through action, you might want to generate better knowledge about what works and what affects what. Our own use of the phrase at Nesta makes this explicit as we encourage organisations to move up the ladder of evidence, generating additional knowledge about what works and why.

So, the motives for wanting a theory of change are entirely healthy, and for any organisation which hasn't thought rigorously about what it does, and what effects it has, the process of working out a theory of change is useful. But these are just starting points.

Let me now go a step deeper. Clever people always want an explanation of why things happen. We should always want to encourage curiosity about how the world works: why the sun shines, why plants grow, or why brains produce thought. That hunger drives knowledge.

But knowing why or how something works isn't always necessary for effectiveness. This is one of the odder features of knowledge, and it's counter-intuitive. But it's true in many domains.

Psychology is one of the most striking. Over the last century it has discovered many treatments that work. But almost without exception these treat symptoms rather than being based on any reliable understanding of causal mechanisms. It would be preferable if there were some stronger theory to underpin a discipline that has only ever replicated 1% of its trials. But the field gets by all the same.

In our own daily lives we are not too troubled by a parallel situation. We find a spouse or partner or buy a house without much in the way of theory to guide us (and if we do find a theory it's as likely to mislead us as to help us). Does it matter? Probably not.

Drugs like penicillin were discovered and manufactured long before there was a detailed understanding of how they worked at a cellular level. Again, it mattered more that they worked than that we knew how they worked.

In computing, many theories have grown up to justify machine-learning methods that are satisfactory – sufficiently generalisable – but don't attempt to construct comprehensive causal models. Examples include Lesley Valiant's 'probably approximately correct' algorithms, which aim to be adaptive mechanisms that try to do better than the alternatives.[3]

Milton Friedman was a strong advocate for parsimonious but strongly predictive models in economics. The models didn't need to be plausible as explanations as to why the economy works the way it does, but were nevertheless useful.

What is the implication? It's helpful to have logic models, and theories of change. But it's best not to fetishise explanations or to expect too much of them. Much of life is about trial and error, incremental improvement and adaptation. Given the choice, it's better to have a rough but effective approach than a beautifully comprehensive theory that can't be acted on.

Governance sinkholes: How shifting tectonic plates create the need for new institutions

Governance sinkholes appear when shifts in technology, society and economy throw up the need for new arrangements. Each industrial revolution has created many such sinkholes – and prompted furious innovation to fill them. The fourth industrial revolution will be no different. But too many of our governments are too distracted to think about what to do, let alone to act.

As the earth moves and water erodes layers of rock, sinkholes appear, fissures open in up in the earth and volcanos erupt. Something similar happens in societies and economies. As currents of change erode old structures, and as tectonic plates shift, new holes and gaps appear.

These are the places where new rules, and new kinds of organisation, are needed but are missing. Over the last two centuries the process has played itself out repeatedly. Technological change usually prompts a responsive social change – because without it so many people lose out.

In the 19th and 20th centuries rapid urbanisation and industrialisation initially had disastrous results for millions as they moved to cities blighted by pollution, high crime and disease. In response, societies created a plethora of new institutions – from police to public health, from universal education to inspectorates, from trade unions to microcredit, from welfare states to regulators. Their job was to fill the holes which otherwise too many people fell into. The 'big stink' of 1858, which led London to create institutions for public health and a network of public sewers – still in place 160 years later – is a good example.

The fairy-tale stories of technological change in which technologies simply rain down onto a grateful population omit this. So do the dominant stories in economics. These at least recognise that institutions play a role in letting markets work, but they typically ignore everything else. Equally misleading is the simplistic view that less regulation is always better than more. (If you're in any doubt, just do a thought experiment of a world where there are no rules for cars: no driving tests, vehicle safety tests, road markings, speed limits, drink–drive rules, emission standards and so on.)

The fourth industrial revolution is not so different from the previous ones in this respect. As technologies are deployed they create, and reveal, gaping holes in the landscape – sinkholes which people and places fall into. These become visible in the form of crises: crises of privacy, lost data, corporate misbehaviour or ethical infraction.

Indeed, if you look at these in detail you soon get a map of the fissures and gaps – where governance is needed but is missing. There are all too many of these now. Here are a few examples. One is long-term care, which currently lacks adequate financing, regulation, information and navigation tools, despite its huge and growing significance. The obvious contrast is with acute healthcare, which, for all its problems, is rich in institutions and governance.

A second example is lifelong learning and training. Again, there is a striking absence of effective institutions to provide funding, navigation, policy and problem solving, and again, the contrast with the institution–rich fields of primary, secondary and tertiary education is striking. The position on welfare is not so different, as is the absence of institutions fit for purpose in supporting people in precarious work.

I'm particularly interested in another kind of sinkhole: the absence of the right institutions to handle data and knowledge, at global, national and local levels, now that these dominate the economy and much of daily life. In field after field there are huge potential benefits to linking data sets and connecting artificial and human intelligence to spot patterns or prevent problems. But we lack any institutions with either the skills or the authority to do this well, and in particular to think through the trade-offs between the potential benefits and the potential risks.

Healthcare is a glaring example. There are obvious benefits to linking data sets to better target action on diabetes or cancer, and it's even better if these can pull together people's own experiences and insights, as well as those that the system generates. But who should do this? Who is credible? How should they be accountable? The NHS starts with a good base of trust, but it lacks any institutions to play this role, and so bumps into repeated problems.

Very similar issues arise in policing. We're beginning to see the emergence of new platforms that link together policing data and citizen-generated data, to observe crime and to act jointly to deal with it or to prevent it. But again, who should take responsibility for this? Whom can we trust to handle the often complex judgements and trade-offs? Likewise, in the area of jobs, great gains could be achieved from linking up multiple data sets on jobs and skills, particularly at a local level, and achieving what I've called a 'Google Maps' for jobs and careers that can help anyone navigate from where they are to where they want to be. But nowhere in the world yet has the institutions to do this both competently and legitimately.

In each case the task is one of orchestration, curation and value generation – with sensitivity to ethics and legitimacy. Various proposals have been put forward for data trusts and data collaboratives. Private companies have tried their own stop-gaps – from Google Deepmind and Babylon Health in the UK to Sidewalk Labs in North America – but have usually discovered the limits of their legitimacy. There are many options for creating data trusts to fill this gap – some focused on research, some on transport and some on public–private partnerships.[4] The crucial consideration is that the way they are designed should help them to create trust.

At a global level the sinkholes are even more evident. We will soon need a raft of new institutions to handle everything from governance of the internet to transborder data flows and cybersecurity. The EU is setting the pace, partly because it is just about the only transnational institution with the cognitive capacity to think these things through. One of the many tragedies of the current reversion to nationalism is that it makes it much harder to put these institutions in place.

Even more important is the global governance of extreme risks – pandemics are partially covered by existing institutions, but we lack any credible governance to protect the world from new generations of destructive weapons, whether out-of-control biological weapons or killer drones.

While the current wave of populism is probably delaying this necessary task of reinvention, this is likely to be a crucial space for social innovation.

The grammar of good government, or why prepositions matter

How might governments meet the public's expectations? Or are they condemned to perpetual disappointment and distrust? How might they be experienced as working with the grain of society, rather than sitting above it or apart from it?

The answer lies in the importance of prepositions, which sounds odd, but bear with me. The crucial point is that there cannot be a single answer to the question of how to improve citizens' relationship with governments, any more than there can be a single answer to the question of how you can improve your relationship with your parents, children or partner. Instead, prepositions point us to the important distinctions.

In some cases governments act *for* the public. They try to provide clean air, fire services and defence, and do so with a mix of tools, from spending to regulation. In these cases, our relationship is indirect. We want quiet efficiency, order, predictability and reliability, and governments which are smart enough to cope with complex causes and solutions.

Then there are the things governments do *to* people. They tax us and provide us with licences or passports. Here again the ideal is not so hard to define. We generally want efficiency, minimum friction and speed, and often we crave an ideal of simplicity so that we don't have to think too much about these things.

Then there are the things governments have to do *with* us. They can't make us healthy, wealthy or wise. Instead, healthcare, economic growth and education have to be partnerships. Governments can provide some of the enabling conditions and tools, but we have to do much of the work. These relationships can be more intense, more intimate and more subtle, and are mediated by professionals who work on behalf of the state. Often, we want to be treated as individuals with distinct needs and capabilities, and often we want a say in how we're treated.

Finally there are the things which are done *by* the people, while still involving government. These can be decisions – like the shift to participatory budgeting, giving the people a say on how money is spent. They can involve time, like volunteering to support a school or hospital.[5]

Good governments become fluent in all of these and avoid the risk of a category error. Such errors are very common. It's still a very common category error to believe that everything can be done to and for the public. An overreliance on performance management methods, and methods adopted from mass-scale business services, turned a sensible insight into an error when it led governments (and bodies like the World Bank) to believe that everything could be delivered to a grateful public. It's equally a category error to take *with* too far, as if the public wants to be endlessly consulted about every detail of policy. Life's too short for that. Anarchism is the extreme of *by*, while traditional authoritarianism is the extreme of *for*.

Prepositions matter. Understanding their differences is the beginning of wisdom. Become good at all of these and adept at how to achieve government for, to, with and by the public you serve, and the relationship can be happy and full of delight. It can even lead, just occasionally, to that rarest of things, gratitude.

The missing habits of R&D

Over the years I've done a lot of work with agencies and councils that are charged with funding R&D in many countries. Most are enjoying a boom, with higher absolute spending and rising shares of GDP. For anyone who believes that civilisation is largely improved by the creation and use of new knowledge, this is a welcome trend. But I'm repeatedly struck by what's missing in their methods, their cultures and their approach. Here I highlight three 'missing habits' that, for now, are almost completely absent from the theory and practice that guides the spending of billions of dollars, euros and yuan.

The first missing habit is *listening*, and in particular listening to the people whose money is being spent – about their lives, their hopes and fears and where new knowledge could achieve the most for them. The planners of R&D are often good at listening to researchers themselves, and some of the time they're good at listening to big business. But remarkably little work is done to listen to the people who pay the bills, and that's reflected in the distortions of R&D spending – towards hardware, prestige projects and the interests of the well-connected.

Even the most basic survey methods are barely used to find out in which fields the public most wants innovation. In 2014 Nesta commissioned a study of public attitudes to innovation, which was ignored by the then ministers, even though (or perhaps because) it showed a big gulf between where the public thought public money should be spent and where funds were actually deployed.[6]

The second missing habit is, surprisingly, *experiment*. In many walks of life improvement comes from vigorous and continuous experimentation. Wherever possible the best scientists and business innovators try, iterate, learn and improve. But this is very much the exception when it comes to science and technology funding, which tends to follow well-worn paths, with little experiment let alone gathering of evidence to discover what might work better.

There are now many experimental labs within government. But, with the partial exception of the National Science Foundation in the US, I'm not aware of anything similar for R&D. This links to the broader oddity of science funding – the relatively small role played by evidence or data compared to connections and influence.

The third missing habit is *open harvesting* – the habit of always trying to tap the widest range of minds, organisations and data. Open innovation methods are now mainstream in many fields. They're used by public organisations like NASA and private ones like Facebook. Large communities of inventors are now curated by organisations like TopCoder or InnoCentive. These have repeatedly shown that seeking out a much wider source of ideas leads to more creative solutions. Nesta's Challenge Prize Centre is expert at finding a far wider community of people with relevant expertise for solving problems – from antibiotic resistance to alternatives to wheelchairs. But these methods are still largely absent from R&D funding, which defaults to using traditional means to finance traditional recipients and, as a result, is often a lot less efficient than it could be.

Why are these three habits so rare? Why are systems packed with very clever people so resistant to change? I suspect that at least part of the answer can be summed up in one word: status. All three of the missing habits either explicitly or implicitly challenge the status of key groups. The first challenges the presumption that they know which problems matter most; the second challenges the presumption that their initial plans are the best possible ones; and the third challenges the presumption that they, and their colleagues, have a monopoly of wisdom.

If they were really wise, they would appreciate that cultivating these missing habits could enhance their work. Those of us involved in the field shouldn't give up, however. I suspect that these three habits will slowly gain ground. They are certainly spreading in many other fields, including within governments. In the manner of scientific revolutions, they may at some point simply become common sense. I hope we don't have to wait too long.

Disrupters and cleaners

When I was a teenager, I worked every holiday for an agency that sent me to clean people's homes. The money wasn't great, but it was convenient, and the work was satisfying: a job where you can easily see that you've done well and how you've made a difference.

Later I did many other similar jobs – cleaning out sample dishes in a hospital, cleaning the kitchens of a big hotel in London's West End and cleaning factory floors. This work coloured my world-view more than I realised. For it sometimes made me see the world as divided into two groups: on the one side, the people who make mess, and, on the other, the people who clean it up.

The first group are predominantly wealthy and male. The second group are predominantly poorer and female. The first group are very visible, and often high-status. The second group tend to be invisible and low-status.

A huge amount of human activity is essentially about maintenance: keeping places clean and tidy; maintaining parks, forests and agricultural fields; maintaining human bodies, especially those of children and the elderly; and sometimes maintaining minds. This is always less respected work. It tends to be repetitive. Some of it can be automated, but surprisingly little has been so far. We all depend on it.

Why does this matter to me now? I work in the field of innovation. Creativity depends on making a mess, and sometimes disrupting things. It feeds off disorder and making lateral or random connections. That's why the conventional wisdoms about creativity are so at odds with what I had to do as a cleaner. They promote throwing things up in the air, hacking, messing, mashing up. In what's become a classic phrase for the digital economy, they encourage people to 'move fast and break things'.

If you live in overly ordered, hierarchical and predictable societies these ideas are exhilarating. But I sometimes wonder whether these cult phrases of modern tech are parodies of the world-view of people who have never cleaned up, the pampered elites of North America, Europe and Asia who always had someone else to clean up after them. They've happily disrupted dozens of industries and also inadvertently left behind a tsunami of thrown-away gadgets and an ocean of messed-up data (the dark side of Moore's Law is a disturbingly steady growth in e-waste that is simply buried in the ground as people discard last year's iPhone or laptop).

But just imagine for a moment that the whole tech industry had been dominated by people who hadn't had such upbringings and who longed for neatness. It's not so hard to imagine, because engineering and other fields are steadily embedding the very different idea of a circular economy that has become, perhaps, the natural home for people who clear up their own mess – the idea of an economy and society where everything is collected and reused (there are also plenty of people in the digital world who value elegance, economy and neat code).

These two ideas now sit in an interesting opposition. On the one hand, many idolise the digital disrupters, the people who mess things up. These (nearly all) men are now some of the world's richest people, the new aristocracy of the 21st century. On the other hand, many think the world has far too much disruption, mess and waste, and long for an economy that is aware of limits, and responsible for its own actions.

We probably need them both, and to be able to cultivate both mindsets simultaneously. Perhaps what we should be wary of are people who adhere to only one – the disrupters who see that as an adequate world-view, and people who cling too tightly to order over imagination.

I was once told that Ernst Schumacher, the author of *Small is Beautiful,* had commented that in a world dominated by small institutions he would have written a book called 'Big is Beautiful'. What mattered was to get the balance right. The same is true of disruption and order. But my guess is that the world would be a better place if its rulers, just occasionally, had to tidy up after themselves.

Thinking about economy: How to save money

During the severe austerity of the late 2000s I developed the '12 economies' framework as a way for the people involved in local public services to think through their options. We wanted to help them get beyond the usual ways of cutting things so as to encourage more creativity and innovation. I ran many workshops using this method – including with NGOs, which faced similar pressures to achieve results with much less money.

In some respects it's very simple. It lists a series of ways in which services can save money, and provides a prompt for services struggling to cope with cuts. But it also opens up some deeper questions, since it reveals that the standard theory and practice of public finance is seriously deficient. Most economists are fairly familiar with economies of scale and scope, but much less familiar with notions of relational economies, economies of flow or economies of penetration, which should be part of their armoury. The framework also points to much more lateral ways of saving money – for example, asking where new kinds of public commitment can be mobilised, or where transparency can reduce costs.

To make this practical, we found that the most useful approach encouraged small groups of front-line staff or managers to generate options under each of the 12 headings and then assess which ones were viable in the short, medium or long term. Most groups could quite quickly generate options for achieving 10%, 20% or 50% savings, including very radical ones. Sometimes we would start off by getting people familiar with the approach by taking a live example – such as rural bus services or nursery education – and showing the options under each heading. Then some shared grounding in current data (such as costs, unit costs and so on) would help to sharpen the discussion.

These are the 12 economies to consider:

1. pure economies – stopping doing things (such as fewer bin collections);
2. economies of trimming – freezes, efficiency savings (such as 5% cuts to pay or opening times);
3. economies of delay – to capital, pay rises, procurement, maintenance or improvements;
4. economies of scale (such as aggregating call centres, back-office functions);
5. economies of scope (such as combining multiple functions in one-stop shops, multi-purpose personal advisers);
6. economies of flow (such as hospitals specialising in a few operations, cutting bottlenecks);
7. economies of penetration (such as combined heat and power systems, street concierges);
8. economies of responsibility – passing responsibility on to citizens (such as for self-testing);
9. circuit economies – reducing failure demand (recidivism, repeated hospital readmissions) through tools like social impact bonds and so on;
10. economies of visibility – mobilising public eyes (such as publishing the details of politicians' expenses or public contracts) and the power of shame;

11. economies of doubling up – actions that address two problems/needs simultaneously (such as retrofit programmes for the young unemployed);
12. economies of commitment – shifting provision from low- to high-commitment people and organisations (such as tapping into volunteer labour and so on).

Necessity can be the mother of invention, and times of severe austerity and constraint can prompt imagination. Hopefully, this framework makes that a bit more likely.

The dialectics of revolution

Here is a summary of the political economy of revolution, prompted by the Arab Spring and the history of revolutionary moments, from Europe in 1848 and 1968 to Latin America in the 1960s and the Middle East today. It's relevant to anyone interested in change.

> Most revolutions are defeated by counter-revolutions in the short run. But the counter-revolutions often lead in time to the success of the revolution's ideas. However, the revolutionaries are the least likely to benefit from their own revolutions.

And here it is in a slightly longer form.

- Most revolutions spawn successful counter-revolutions which defeat them in the short term.
- Most counter-revolutions pave the way for the slow success of the ideas associated with the revolution.
- So revolutionaries very rarely benefit from revolutions, but lots of other people do, later (at least from the good ones).
- Massive external support can change the odds, but not often.

It's a surprisingly common pattern. The upsurge of the counterculture in the late 1960s US gave us President Nixon; the French revolution of 1968 gave President de Gaulle a landslide; the protests of Istanbul gave President Erdogan a majority (and the failed coup gave him even more power); Egypt's Tahrir Square gave us President Sisi. It's probably true in business and technology as well. From Xerox and Napster to Bitcoin, revolutionary ideas usually provoke powerful incumbents to make counter-moves, which succeed in the short term but not in the long term. Later entrants then implement the new ideas (none of the now dominant digital companies was a first mover).

The main exceptions in both politics and business happen when the revolutionaries have access to large-scale financial and other external support – as when the revolutionaries in Vietnam or Cuba could benefit from support from China or the USSR; or new business ideas can benefit from very large sums of venture capital investment to carry them through long periods of losses. Otherwise, this looks close to being a reliable law.

Radical social change

The winners in life are people who adapt to the world. The losers in life are the people who expect the world to adapt to them. Seen in the long view, most losers are only losers, but the saving of the world depends on the small minority of the losers who have the courage to imagine what appears impossible but turns out to be possible.

On technology

Technology first tries to make people fit it – to make them predictable, orderly and lined up straight. Then, over time, technology becomes ever more complex, to the point where no one understands it. As it becomes complex it becomes more like society: opaque, unpredictable, full of odd interactions, crashes and shutdowns. When this happens, we find we need new skills to make sense of it – an anthropology of technology, which explores motivations, combinations and how to unravel the mess.

On progress

The more we know, the safer we become: risks are managed, contained and controlled. The more we know, the more we understand the full extent of the remaining threats that could hurt us, and so the more insecure we feel. So, knowledge breeds anxiety; intelligence breeds fear.

Collaboration

Everyone favours collaboration in principle because everyone has a clear picture in their mind of other people collaborating with them to help them achieve their goals. For this reason, the great majority are always disappointed. A necessary stage of all collaborations is learning this and getting over it. If you don't start with a willingness to sacrifice and suspend your cherished idea, don't expect to collaborate. But after this sacrifice real collaboration, sometimes, begins. And later you may discover that someone else's idea was better than yours.

Speeches and the strange phenomenon of blowing bubbles

At big conferences – of which I've attended too many over the years – I've observed a rough rule of thumb. The higher the status of the speaker, the less true content there will be in their speech. They will speak and fill the allotted time, but we will learn nothing new. A panel of grandees is likely to be even worse. Put five of them together and, however smart they are as individuals, you can almost guarantee that none will say anything interesting.

This form of speech is akin to blowing bubbles, and professional politicians, business leaders and diplomats become very skilled at doing it. Events like Davos or the UN General Assembly confirm this rule. Often the fringe events are full of fascinating detail, as are the one-to-one conversations. But the keynotes and the plenaries tend to be deadly dull.

For a while I was intrigued by this phenomenon as an example of collective stupidity: how do you turn a group that is individually smart into something that is collectively dumb? This is a subset of a broader research programme that applies to nations, firms and other organisations. Some make average people collectively brilliant. And some do the opposite.

Yet I've realised that clearly this norm of bubble blowing performs a useful function, perhaps subliminally restoring our confidence that the world is predictable, legible and stable. The very dullness of the speeches may be precisely their point.

The interdependence of hot and cold

Social change begins hot. It draws its energy from anger, resentment and frustration. This is what drives people onto the streets, impels the activists to give up their lives to getting new projects off the ground. Movements have to move people.

Yet, to have lasting impact the movements have to become cool. They take the form of bureaucracies, organisations with rules and employees. Protests turn into new laws, enforced by courts and judges. Placards turn into new norms.

Navigating this transition is hugely difficult for most movements, and usually requires new people – the consolidators who are often resented by the pioneers. But they both need each other. One without the other is useless. Hot without cold just blows away. Cold without the injection of energy from the hot is lifeless.

Notes

Introduction

1   J. Helliwell, R. Layard and J. Sachs (2019) *World Happiness Report 2019*, New York: Sustainable Development Solutions Network, http://worldhappiness. report/ed/2019/.

Chapter 1

1   The origin of this quote is contested, but it has most often been attributed to Arthur Schopenhauer.

2   Some material in this chapter is taken from a previously published article by the author: G. Mulgan (2006) 'The process of social innovation', *Innovations: Technology, Governance, Globalisation*, MIT Press, Vol 1, Issue 2, Spring 2006, pp 145–162.

3   The origin of this quote is contested, but it has most often been attributed to Lenin.

4   Michael Young anticipated today's interest in social enterprise and the broader question of how societies innovate. See, for example, his book: M. Young (1983) *The Social Scientist as Innovator*, Cambridge, MA: Abt Books.

5   D. Bornstein (2004) *How to Change the World: Social Entrepreneurs and the Power of New Ideas*, Oxford: Oxford University Press.

6   J.M. Keynes (1936) *The General Theory of Employment, Interest, and Money*, London: Palgrave Macmillan, p 383.

7   For comparisons between business and the social sector in making organisations great, see Jim Collins at www.jimcollins.com.

8   J.L. Bradach (2003) 'Going to scale', *Stanford Social Innovation Review*, Spring, https://ssir.org/articles/entry/going_to_scale.

9   For more detail on the methods to be used at each stage of the spiral see Nesta (2019) *A Compendium of Innovation Methods*, London: Nesta, https:// www.nesta.org.uk/report/compendium-innovation-methods.

10 M.L. King (2010) *Where Do We Go from Here: Chaos or Community?* Boston: Beacon Press.

11 A.W. Bellringer and C.M. Jones (1988) *The Victorian Age in Prose*, Amsterdam: Rodopi.

12 For example, Parkinson's UK, https://www.parkinsons.org.uk.

13 See, for example, E. de Bono (1970) *Lateral Thinking – Creativity Step by Step*, London: Perennial Library.

14 There have been many repositories of promising ideas. For example, the Global Ideas Bank which provided one such collection from the 1990s onwards, has now mutated into https://www.ideabank.global/.

15 See G. Mulgan (2014) 'Design in public and social innovation', Nesta, https://www.nesta.org.uk/report/design-in-public-and-social-innovation and the DIY Toolkit (https://www.nesta.org.uk/toolkit/diy-toolkit) for more on how these can be used.

16 This is one of many examples given in Thomas Schelling's classic article, T. Schelling (1956) 'An essay on bargaining', *The American Economic Review*, Vol 46, No 3 (1956), pp 281–306.

17 Useful websites include Poverty Action Lab, https://www.povertyactionlab. org; Social Action Laboratory, https://psychologicalsciences.unimelb.edu. au/research/msps-research-groups/social-action-laboratory; Innovation Lab Copenhagen, https://innovationlab.net; Civic Innovation Lab, https:// civicilab.com; Eastman Innovation Lab, https://www.innovationlab. eastman.com; MIT Community Innovation Lab, https://www.colab.mit. edu/; ETSU Innovation Lab, https://www.etsu.edu/ilab.

18 In Francis Crick (1995) 'The impact of *Linus Pauling* on molecular biology', lecture at Ohio State University (28 February), http://scarc. library.oregonstate.edu/events/1995paulingconference/video-s1-2-crick. html.

19 M.J. Pucher (2011) 'The value of failure', blog, Welcome to the real world! (24 October), https://isismjpucher.wordpress.com/2011/10/24/the-value-of-failure/.

20 R.M. Kanter (2009) 'Change is hardest in the middle', *Harvard Business Review*, https://hbr.org/2009/08/change-is-hardest-in-the-middl.

21 G. Mulgan (2005) 'Government and knowledge', *Evidence and Policy*, Vol 1, No 2, pp 215–26.

22 The project did survive for several years in Milton Keynes in England, but it never took off.

23 S. Beckett (1989) *Nohow On*. London: Calder.

24 C. Markides and P. Geroski (2005) *Fast Second: How Smart Companies Bypass Radical Innovation to Enter and Dominate New Markets*, San Francisco: Jossey-Bass.

25 This is often attributed to Harry Truman, but was also said in various forms by others, dating back to the Jesuit priest Father Strickland in the early 1860s.

26 S. Goldsmith, G. Georges and T.G. Burke (2010) *The Power of Social Innovation: How Civic Entrepreneurs Ignite Community Networks for Good*, New York: John Wiley. Stephen Goldsmith has remained engaged in the field, promoting innovative uses of data in cities across the US, among many other activities.

27 R.B. Fuller (1981) *Critical Path*, New York: St. Martin's Press.

28 The Bahá'í Universal House of Justice states: 'Social change is not a project that one group of people carries out for the benefit of another.' The Universal House of Justice, message to the Bahá'ís of the World, April 2010, https://www.bahai.org/library/authoritative-texts/the-universal-house-of-justice/messages/20100421_001/1#178319844.

29 See D. Marcus (2012) 'The Horizontalists: intellectual origins of OWS', *Dissent*, Number 4, Fall 2012, pp 54–59, and D. Graeber (2016) *The Utopia of Rules: On Technology, Stupidity, and the Secret Joys of Bureaucracy*, New York: Melville House.

30 K.H. Wolff (ed) (1964) *The Sociology of Georg Simmel*, London: Free Press.

31 After a period when governments' role in promoting innovation was downplayed, the 2010s brought a return to the 20th-century norm of recognising the vital role of states in promoting R&D and directing it to national priorities and missions. Mariana Mazzucato has done more than anyone to revive what was once conventional wisdom. Mariana Mazzucato (2018) *The Entrepreneurial State*, Harmondsworth: Penguin.

32 In the UK, the 'In Control' pilots delivered under the government's policy Valuing People and now recommended for wider adoption are a good example of innovation in the a new relationship between user and suppliers. See Prime Minister's Strategy Unit (2005) *Improving the Life Chances of Disabled People*, p 93. See also Self-Directed Support in Scotland, http://www.selfdirectedsupport.org.

33 R. M. Unger, 'Conclusion: The task of the social innovation movement', in A.Nicholls and J. Simon (eds) (2015) *New Frontiers in Social Innovation Research*, Basingstoke: Palgrave Macmillan, p 237.

34 See, for example, E. Pol and S. Ville (2009) 'Social innovation: buzz word or enduring term?' *The Journal of Socio-Economics*, Vol 38, No 6, pp 878–85.

35 A recent overview is R.P. Van Der Have and L. Rubalcaba (2016) 'Social innovation research: an emerging area of innovation studies?' *Research Policy*, Vol 45, No 9, pp 1923–35. The authors argue that the social innovation field forms into four distinct intellectual communities: (1) community psychology; (2) creativity research; (3) social and societal challenges; (4) local development. Rare examples of significant pieces from before the recent wave of literature include T. Rickards (1985) *Stimulating Innovation: A Systems Approach*, London: Pinter; J. Gerhuny (1983) *Social Innovation and the Division of Labour*, Oxford: Oxford University Press; W. Kingston(1984) *The Political Economy of Innovation*, The Hague : Nijhoff.

36 A few recently published collections include T. Osburg and R. Schidpeter (eds) (2013) *Social Innovation: Solutions for a Sustainable Future*, Heidelberg: Springer (mainly focused on the links to corporate social responsibility); R. Murray, J. Caulier-Grice and G. Mulgan (2010) *The Open Book of Social Innovation*, London: Nesta/Young Foundation; A. Nicholls and A. Murdock (2011) *Social Innovation: Blurring Boundaries to Reconfigure Markets*, Basingstoke: Palgrave Macmillan; A. Nicholls and J. Simon (eds) (2015) *New Frontiers in Social Innovation Research*, Basingstoke: Palgrave Macmillan; F. Moulaert and D. MacCallum (2014) *The International Handbook on Social*

Innovation: Collective Action, Social Learning and Transdisciplinary Research, Cheltenham: Edward Elgar.

37 This tradition is particularly associated with Frank Moulaert: F. Moulaert (2013) *The International Handbook on Social Innovation: Collective Action, Social Learning and Transdisciplinary Research*, Cheltenham: Edward Elgar Publishing (2013).

38 There is also a strong and distinct academic research field in Germany: J. Howaldt and M. Schwarz (2010) *Soziale Innovation im Fokus. Skizze eines gesellschafts-theoretisch inspirierten Forschungskonzepts*, Bielefeld: Transcript Verlag, and J. Howaldt, C. Kaletka, A. Schröder and M. Zirngidbl (eds) (2018) *Atlas of Social Innovation – New Practices for a Better Future*, https://www.si-drive.eu/?p=3407.

39 Ezio Manzini, based in Milan, has been a particularly impressive advocate for design methods: E. Manzini (2018) *Design, When Everybody Designs: An Introduction to Design for Social Innovation*, Boston, MA: MIT Press.

40 F. Westley, B. Zimmerman and M. Patton (2009) *Getting to Maybe: How the World Is Changed*, New York: Vintage.

41 R.M. Walker, E. Jeanes, and R.O. Rowlands (2002) 'Measuring innovation – applying the literature-based innovation output indicator to public services', *Public Administration*, Vol 80, No 10, pp 201–14.

42 D. Albury and G. Mulgan (2003) *Innovation in the Public Sector*, London: Strategy Unit, Cabinet Office.

43 P. Aghion, S. Bechtold, L. Cassar and H. Herz (2014) 'The causal effects of competition on innovation: Experimental evidence', Working paper, Harvard University, February 20.

44 J.P. Murmann (2004) *Knowledge and Competitive Advantage: The Coevolution of Firms, Technology and National Institutions*, London: Cambridge University Press; E. von Hippel (2005) *Democratising Innovation*, Cambridge, MA: MIT Press; R. Baumol (2003) *The Free-Market Innovation Machine: Analyzing the Growth of Miracle Capitalism*, Princeton, NJ: Princeton University Press.

45 R. Lester and M. Piore (2004) *Innovation: The Missing Dimension*, Cambridge, MA: Harvard University Press.

46 E.M. Rogers (2003) *Diffusion of Innovation*, New York: Free Press.

47 G. Mulgan and T. Steinberg (2005) *Wide Open: The Potential of Open Source Methods*, London: Demos/Young Foundation.

Chapter 2

1 A. Camus (2010[1942]) *Notebooks 1935–1942*, London: Ivan R. Dee.

2 'Generativity' is a useful additional word, linking to the Latin *genus* and *genera* and referring to offspring. Here the interest is in ideas but, crucially, ideas that are not only conceived and born, but also grown to maturity.

3 B. Godin (2014) *Innovation Contested: The Idea of Innovation over the Centuries*, New York: Routledge.

4 B. Godin (2016) 'Making sense of innovation: from weapon to instrument to buzzword', *Quaderni*, Vol 2, pp 21–40.

5 This was, after all, the period when the very idea of a society was being born. The decades before and after the French Revolution gave shape to the idea of society as more than the *societas* of the king and court, or a particular association; it then led to the idea that social causes could explain outcomes (like disease) and different ways of viewing humans as inherently social creatures.

6 With only a few earlier examples, such as Thomas More's *Utopia* (1551).

7 R.M. Unger (2019) *The Knowledge Economy*, London: Verso.

8 The analysis links to, but is distinct from, related ideas which use some of the same language: the emphasis on individual social entrepreneurs as agents of change (while leaving fundamental structures untouched); the emphasis on social or impact investment as a way to solve social problems (again, usually assuming only marginal change to the ways capital is organised); and the promotion of technology as a *deus ex machina* to fix the world (the preferred default for Silicon Valley and its evangelists). Seen as parts of a much larger whole, each of these movements has its place. But, taken out of context, they are at best incoherent and partial and at worst problematic as answers.

9 J. Mokyr (2016) *A Culture of Growth: The Origins of the Modern Economy*, Princeton, NJ: Princeton University Press, p 17.

10 R. Rajan (2019) *The Third Pillar: How Markets and the State Leave the Community Behind*, New York: Collins.

11 R. Boyd and P.J. Richerson (1985) *Culture and the Evolutionary Process*, Chicago: University of Chicago Press, p 2.

12 D. Acemoglu and J.A. Robinson (2012) *Why Nations Fail: The Origins of Power, Prosperity and Poverty*, New York: Crown.

13 Mokyr (2016, p 5).

14 R. Wolin (1990) 'Carl Schmitt, political existentialism, and the total state', *Theory and Society*, Vol 19, No 4, pp 389–416.

15 C. Alexander (2002) *The Nature of Order: An Essay on the Art of Building and the Nature of the Universe*, Berkeley, CA: Center for Environmental Structure.

16 M. Weber ([1905] 1930) *The Protestant Ethic and the Spirit of Capitalism*, New York: Simon and Schuster, p 124.

17 *Alice Walker: Beauty in Truth* [film] (2013), dir. Pratibha Parmar, Kali Films.

18 A. Ehrenberg (1998) *The Fatigue of Being Oneself: Depression and Society*, Paris: Odile Jacob.

19 D. Bollier and S. Helfrich (eds) (2012) *The Wealth of the Commons: A World Beyond Market and Stage*, The Commons Strategies Group.

20 A. Toffler (1980) *The Third Wave*, London: Collins.

21 J. Maxmin and S. Zuboff (2004) *The Support Economy: Why Corporations Are Failing Individuals and the Next Episode of Capitalism*, New York: Penguin.

22 See M. Yunus (2008) *Creating a World Without Poverty: Social Business and the Future of Capitalism*, New York: Public Affairs Press.

23 I cover this at some length in G. Mulgan (2013) *The Locust and the Bee*, Princeton, NJ: Princeton University Press.

24 J. Salter (2007) *Light Years*, London: Penguin.

Chapter 3

1 F. Fukuyama (1992) *The End of History and the Last Man*, London: Penguin.
2 Some material in this chapter is taken from a previously published blog post by the author: https://www.nesta.org.uk/blog/thesis-antithesis-and-synthesis-a-constructive-direction-for-politics-and-policy-after-brexit-and-trump/.
3 A. Corlett (2016) *Examining an Elephant: Globalisation and the Lower Middle Class of the Rich World*, Resolution Foundation, https://www.resolutionfoundation.org/app/uploads/2016/09/Examining-an-elephant.pdf.
4 J. Bernstein, A.J. Levitin and S.M. Wachter (2015) *The Reconnection Agenda: Reuniting Growth and Prosperity*, North Charleston, SC: CreateSpace.
5 E. Alden (2016) 'Jeff Immelt of GE gives the most important foreign policy speech of the year', Council on Foreign Relations, https://www.cfr.org/blog/jeff-immelt-ge-gives-most-important-foreign-policy-speech-year.
6 A. Bernstein (2015) 'Eduardo Galeano: author who chronicled the West's plundering of Latin America', *The Independent* (14 April), https://www.independent.co.uk/news/people/eduardo-galeano-author-who-chronicled-the-west-s-plundering-of-latin-america-but-who-later-10176702.html.
7 2019 Edelman Trust Barometer, https://www.edelman.com/trust-barometer.
8 O. Komlik (2018) 'Nobel winner Paul Romer on the backwardness of economics and economists' misleading use of math', https://economicsociology.org/2018/10/08/nobel-winner-paul-romer-economists-use-math-to-mislead/.
9 Of the kind originally provided in the UK by Learndirect before its ill-fated privatisation, and more recently by FutureLearn.
10 See J. Wilsdon and R. Jones (2018) *The Biomedical Bubble*, London: Nesta.
11 A. Bell, R. Chetty, X. Jaravel, N. Petkova and J. Van Reenen (2018) 'Who becomes an inventor in America? The importance of exposure to innovation', http://www.equality-of-opportunity.org/assets/documents/inventors_paper.pdf.
12 H. Field (2018) '98 percent of VC funding goes to men. Can women entrepreneurs change a sexist system?' Entrepreneur, https://www.entrepreneur.com/article/315992.
13 Peerby, https://www.peerby.com/one; Streetbank, https://www.streetbank.com/splash?locale=en; Bologna Regulation for the Care and Regeneration of Urban Commons, http://wiki.p2pfoundation.net/Bologna_Regulation_for_the_Care_and_Regeneration_of_Urban_Commons.
14 GoodSAM, https://www.goodsamapp.org/.
15 CONSUL, http://consulproject.org/en/.

16 J. Simon, T. Bass, V. Boelman and G. Mulgan (2017) *Digital Democracy: The Tools Transforming Political Engagement*, London: Nesta, https://media. nesta.org.uk/documents/digital_democracy.pdf.

17 Better Reykjavík, https://reykjavik.is/en/better-reykjavik-0.

18 'Paris Participatory Budget: good practice summary', https://urbact.eu/ sites/default/files/490_Paris_GPsummary.pdf.

19 Apolitical (2016) 'Portugal has announced the world's first nationwide participatory budget', https://apolitical.co/solution_article/portugal-world-first-participatory-budget.

20 M. Basu (2018) 'Exclusive: How Taiwan is reinventing government', GovInsider, https://govinsider.asia/innovation/taiwan-pdis-shuyang-lin-audrey-tang.

21 See G. Mulgan and V. Straub (2019) *The New Ecosystem of Trust*, London: Nesta.

22 There is no firm evidence that he ever said this.

Chapter 4

1 Metropolitan Museum of Art, 'Cuneiform tablet: administrative account concerning the distribution of barley and emmer, c.a 3100–2900 BC', https://www.metmuseum.org/art/collection/search/327384.

2 S. Gruber, 'The useful emperor: Joseph II', *The World of the Habsburgs*, https://www.habsburger.net/en/chapter/useful-emperor-joseph-ii.

3 G. Mulgan (2009) *The Relational State*, London: Young Foundation.

4 Bookshare, https://www.bookshare.org/cms/about.

5 Institute of Social Currency, 'The WIR, the supplementary Swiss currency since 1934', https://www.theeconomyjournal.eu/texto-diario/ mostrar/758830/wir-moneda-complementaria-suiza-activo-desde-1934.

6 LETSLINK UK, https://www.letslinkuk.net.

7 CBS News (2017) 'Creating new wealth on Sardinia, without cash' (6 August), https://www.cbsnews.com/news/sardex-creating-new-wealth-on-sardinia-without-cash; Bristol Pound, https://bristolpound.org.

Chapter 5

1 This short chapter draws heavily on conversations with Professor Mark Moore at Harvard's Ash Center.

2 Nesta was an investor in this Reconnections project organised by Social Finance: https://www.socialfinance.org.uk/projects/reconnections.

Chapter 6

1 See various papers I've written, including G. Mulgan (2012) *Systemic Innovation* (London: Nesta) and my book *Big Mind: How Collective Intelligence Can Change Our World* (Princeton, NJ: Princeton University Press, 2017).

2 A particularly good account of the systems methods used in China is Y.Y. Ang (2016) *How China Escaped the Poverty Trap*, New York: Cornell University Press.

3   D. Hanson (2013) 'Assessing the Harlem Children's Zone', https://www.heritage.org/education/report/assessing-the-harlem-childrens-zone.

4   NBS (2010) 'Evaluation of the national strategy for neighbourhood renewal – final report', https://www.thenbs.com/PublicationIndex/documents/details?Pub=DCLG&DocID=293753.

5   See for example E. Bardach (1998) *Getting Agencies to Work Together: The Practice and Theory of Managerial Craftsmanship*, Washington, DC: Brookings Institution.

6   E. Ostrom (1990) *Governing the Commons*, Cambridge: Cambridge University Press.

7   S. Kohler, 'Case 75: Living cities', https://cspcs.sanford.duke.edu/sites/default/files/descriptive/national_community_development_initiative.pdf.

8   See G. Mulgan and C. Leadbeater (2013) *Systems Innovation* (London: Nesta) and a follow-up collection: *Systemic Innovation: A Discussion Series* (2013), London: Nesta, https://media.nesta.org.uk/documents/systemic_innovation.pdf.

9   For example, the excellent work of the Rapid Results Institute, https://www.rapidresults.org.

10 S. Gibbons, H. Overman and M. Sarvimäki (2017) *The Local Economic Impacts of Regeneration Projects: Evidence from UK's Single Regeneration Budget*, Spatial Economics Research Centre, http://eprints.lse.ac.uk/86566/1/sercdp0218.pdf.

11 E. Batty, C. Beatty, M. Foden, P. Lawless, S. Pearson and I. Wilson (2010) *The New Deal for Communities Experience: A Final Assessment*, London: Department for Communities and Local Government, https://extra.shu.ac.uk/ndc/downloads/general/A%20final%20assessment.pdf.

12 HM Treasury (2010) *Total Place: A Whole Area Approach to Public Services*, Richmond: Office of Public Sector Information, https://webarchive.nationalarchives.gov.uk/20130125093102/http://www.hm-treasury.gov.uk/d/total_place_report.pdf.

13 'Delivering Social Change – signature programmes', https://www.executiveoffice-ni.gov.uk/topics/good-relations-and-social-change/delivering-social-change-signature-programmes.

14 360Giving, http://www.threesixtygiving.org.

15 WASHfunders, https://washfunders.org.

16 We used these in the report: Nesta (2009) *Transformers*, https://media.nesta.org.uk/documents/transformers.pdf.

17 UpRising, https://www.uprising.org.uk/.

Chapter 7

1   This chapter contains content from a previously published chapter, with the permission of Palgrave Macmillan: G. Mulgan (2012) 'The theoretical foundations of social innovation', in A. Nicholls and A. Murdock (eds) *Social Innovation*, London: Palgrave Macmillan.

2   A.O. Hirschman (1991) *The Rhetoric of Reaction*, Cambridge, MA: Harvard University Press.

3   J.G. Dees and B.B. Anderson (2006) 'Framing a theory of social entrepreneurship: building on two schools of practice and thought', in R. Mosher-Williams (ed) *Research on Social Entrepreneurship: Understanding and Contributing to an Emerging Field*, ARNOVA Occasional Paper Series, Vol 1, No 3, Indianapolis: Association for Research on Nonprofit Organizations and Voluntary Action, pp 39–66. This provides one of the best synthetic overviews of the social entrepreneurship field.

4   A. Nicholls (ed) (2006) *Social Entrepreneurship: New Models of Sustainable Social Change*, Oxford: Oxford University Press.

5   The Young Foundation/SIX report for the Bureau of European Policy Advisers, published in early 2010, provides a comprehensive overview of current definitions. G. Mulgan, S. Simon and L. Pulford (2010) *Study on Social Innovation for the Bureau of European Policy Advisors*, London: Young Foundation, https://youngfoundation.org/publications/study-on-social-innovation-for-the-bureau-of-european-policy-advisors-March-2010.pdf.

6   This definition has emerged out of a series of research studies I've been involved in, including G. Mulgan (2006) *Social Innovation: What It Is, Why It Matters, How It Can Be Accelerated*, Basingstoke: Palgrave Macmillan; G. Mulgan (2007) *Ready or Not? Taking Innovation in the Public Sector Seriously*, Nesta Provocation 03, London: Nesta; G. Mulgan, R. Ali, R. Halkett and B. Sanders (2007) *In and Out of Sync: The Challenge of Growing Social Innovations*, Nesta research report, London: Nesta; N. Bacon, N. Faizullah, G. Mulgan and S. Woodcraft (2008) *Transformers: How Local Areas Innovate to Address Changing Social Needs*, Nesta research report, London: Nesta.

7   Hirschman (1991).

8   These rhetorics are described in my 2009 book G. Mulgan (2009) *The Art of Public Strategy*, Oxford: Oxford University Press.

9   R.M. Unger (2007) *The Self Awakened: Pragmatism Unbound*, Cambridge, MA: Harvard University Press.

10 Unger (2007), p 55.

11 Unger (2007), p 56.

12 D. Bell (1976) *The Cultural Contradictions of Capitalism*, New York: Basic Books.

13 See note 18 below.

14 B. Latour (2005) *Reassembling the Social: An Introduction to Actor-Network-Theory*, Oxford: Oxford University Press.

15 G. Simmel (2010) *The View of Life: Four Metaphysical Essays with Journal Aphorisms*, trans. J.A.Y. Andrews and D.N. Levine, Chicago: University of Chicago Press.

16 E. Hopper, R. Lipgar, M. Pines and J. Berke (2003) *The Large Group Re-Visited: The Herd, Primal Horde, Crowds and Masses*, London: Jessica Kingsley Publishers, p 92.

17 I. Nonaka and H. Takeuchi (2007) *The Knowledge-Creating Company: How Japanese Companies Create the Dynamics of Innovation*, Oxford: Oxford University Press.

18 G. Mulgan (2007) provides a theoretical framework for the analysis of how social innovations spread, scale and grow.

19 J. Jacobs (1970) *The Economy of Cities,* London: Cape; J. Jacobs (1992) *Systems of Survival*, New York: Random House.

20 See F. Westley, B. Zimmerman and M. Patton (2006) *Getting to Maybe: How the World Is Changed*, Toronto: Random House.

21 See, for example, B. Arthur (2009) *The Nature of Technology*, New York: Free Press.

22 B. Mandelbrot and R.L. Hudson (2004) *The (Mis)Behaviour of Markets: A Fractal View of Risk, Ruin and Reward*, New York: Basic Books.

23 A good review of the literature relevant to development is B. Ramalingam, H. Jones, T. Reba and J. Young (2008) *Exploring the Science of Complexity: Ideas and Implications for Development and Humanitarian Efforts*, Vol 285, London: Overseas Development Institute.

24 G. Morgan (1997) *Images of Organisation Executive*, Berlin: Edition Berrett-Koehler, p 222.

25 R.M. Solow (1956) 'Contribution to the Theory of Economic Growth', *The Quarterly Journal of Economics*, Vol 70, No 1, pp 65–94; P.M. Romer (1994) 'The origins of endogenous growth', *Journal of Economic Perspectives*, Vol 8, No 1, pp 3–22.

26 W.J. Baumol (2002) *The Free-Market Innovation Machine: Analyzing the Growth Miracle of Capitalism*, Princeton, NJ: Princeton University Press.

27 E.M. Rogers (2003) *Diffusion of Innovations*, New York: Free Press. Rogers defines an innovation as 'an idea, practice, or object that is perceived as new by an individual or other unit of adoption. It matters little, so far as human behaviour is concerned, whether or not an idea is objectively new as measured by the lapse of time since its first use or discovery. The perceived newness of the idea for the individual determines his or her reaction to it. If the idea seems new to the individual, it is an innovation' (Rogers, 2003, p 12).

28 P. Stoneman and P. Diederen (1994) 'Technology diffusion and public policy', *The Economic Journal*, Vol 104, No 425, pp 918–30.

29 R. Lester and M. Piore (2006) *Innovation: The Missing Dimension*, Cambridge, MA: Harvard University Press.

30 S.G. Winter and R.R. Nelson (1982) *An Evolutionary Theory of Economic Change*, Cambridge, MA: Belknap Press.

31 A. Pacey (1990) T*echnology in World Civilisation*, Cambridge: MIT Press.

32 See, for example, B.Å. Lundvall (ed) (1992) *National Innovation Systems: Towards a Theory of Innovation and Interactive Learning*, London: Pinter.

33 N. Rosenberg (2009) *Studies on Science and the Innovation Process*, Palo Alto, CA: Stanford University Press.

34 See, for example, H. Chesbrough (2006) *Innovation Intermediaries, Enabling Open Innovation*, Boston, MA: Harvard Business School Press.

35 E. von Hippel (1998) *The Sources of Innovation*, New York: Oxford University Press.

36 See, for example, C. Freeman (2008) *Systems of Innovation*, New York: Edward Elgar.

37 For an excellent overview of the whole field of innovation studies, see J. Fagerberg, D.C. Mowery and R.R. Nelson (eds) (2005) *The Oxford Handbook of Innovation*, Oxford: Oxford University Press.

38 A.B. Markman and K.L. Wood (eds) (2009) *Tools for Innovation: The Science Behind the Practical Methods that Drive New Ideas*, Oxford: Oxford University Press.

39 I drew on some of this work to develop the framework called 'the universal language of innovation', which shows how accessible methods for creative innovation can be used by anyone, without the need for highly paid consultants. See DIY Toolkit, www.diytoolkit.org.

40 A. Smith ([1776] 1982) *The Wealth of Nations*, Harmondsworth: Penguin.

41 A. Smith ([1790] 2010) *The Theory of Moral Sentiments*, intro. A. Sen, ed. R.P. Hanley, Harmondsworth: Penguin.

42 I first set out a variant of this argument in G. Mulgan and C. Landry (1995) *The Other Invisible Hand: Remaking Charity for the 21st Century*, London: Demos.

43 T.K. McCraw (2007) *Prophet of Innovation*, Cambridge, MA: Harvard University Press.

44 J. Schumpeter ([1911] 1934) *The Theory of Economic Development*, Cambridge, MA: Harvard University Press, p 86.

45 Schumpeter ([1911] 1934).

46 I. Kirzner (1973) *Competition and Entrepreneurship*, Chicago: University of Chicago Press.

47 G.E. Shockley and P.M. Frank (2011) 'Schumpeter, Kirzner, and the field of social entrepreneurship', *Journal of Social Entrepreneurship*, Vol 2, No 1, pp 6–26.

48 I. Kirzner (1982) 'Uncertainty, discovery, and human action: A study of the entrepreneurial profile in the Misesian system', in I. Kirzner (ed) *Method, Process, and Austrian Economics*, Lexington, MA: D.C. Heath and Company, p 150.

49 L. von Mises ([1949] 1996) *Human Action: A Treatise on Economics*, San Francisco: Fox & Wilkes, pp 252–3.

50 R. Swedberg (2009) 'Schumpeter's full model of entrepreneurship: economic, non-economic and social entrepreneurship', in R. Ziegler (ed) *An Introduction to Social Entepreneurship: Voices, Preconditions, Contexts*, Cheltenham: Edward Elgar, pp 77–106.

51 W. Drayton (2006) 'Everyone a changemaker: social entrepreneurship's ultimate goal', *Innovations: Technology, Governance, Globalization*, Vol 1, No 1, pp 80–96.

52 L. Boltanski and L. Thévenot (2006) *On Justification: Economies of Worth*, Princeton, NJ: Princeton University Press; H.C. White (2002) *Markets from Networks: Socioeconomic Models of Production*, Princeton, NJ: Princeton University Press.

53 D. Stark (2009) *The Sense of Dissonance: Accounts of Worth in Economic Life*, Princeton, NJ: Princeton University Press.

54 See, for example, J. Defourny and M. Nyssens (2008) 'Social enterprise in Europe: recent trends and developments', *Social Enterprise Journal*, Vol 4, No 3, pp 202–28, and J. Defourny and M. Nyssens (2008) 'Conceptions of social enterprise in Europe and the United States: convergences and divergences', paper presented at the 8th ISTR International Conference and 2nd EMES-ISTR European Conference, Barcelona, 9–12 July.

55 C. Freeman and C. Perez (1988) 'Structural crisis of adjustments, business, cycles and investment behaviour', in G. Dosi, C. Freeman, R. Nelson, G. Silverberg and L. Soete (eds) *Technical Change and Economic Theory*, London: Pinter.

56 C. Perez (2009) *Technological Revolutions and Techno-Economic Paradigms*, Working Papers in Technology Governance and Economic Dynamics, No 20, Tallinn: Tallinn University of Technology.

57 Freeman and Perez (1988, p 60).

58 M. Castells (1996) *The Information Age: Economy, Society and Culture: The Rise of the Network Society*, Oxford: Blackwell; M. Castells (1997) *The Information Age: Economy, Society and Culture: The Power of Identity*, Oxford: Blackwell; M. Castells (1998) *The Information Age: Economy, Society and Culture: The End of the Millennium*, Oxford: Blackwell.

59 Y. Moulier-Boutang (2007) *Le Capitalisme Cognitif: La Nouvelle Grande Transformation*, Paris: Éditions Amsterdam.

60 E. Hobsbawm (1999) *Age of Extremes: The Short Twentieth Century 1914– 1991*, London: Abacus, p 87.

61 L. Menand (2001)*The Metaphysical Club: A Story of Ideas in America*, New York: Farrar, Straus and Giroux, pp xi–xii.

62 B. Latour (2008) *Le Public Fantôme*, Paris: Demopolis

63 D. Conniffe (1991) 'R.A. Fisher and the development of statistics: a view in his centenary year', *Journal of the Statistical and Social Inquiry Record of Ireland*, Vol 26, No 3, pp 55–108.

64 K. Popper (2002) *The Logic of Scientific Discovery*, New York: Routledge.

65 A.H. Cho (2006) 'Politics, values and social entrepreneurship: a critical appraisal', in J. Mair, J. Robinson and K. Hockerts (eds) *Social Entrepreneurship*, Basingstoke: Palgrave Macmillan, pp 35–56.

66 For example, OECD Better Life Index, http://www.oecdbetterlifeindex. org.

67 R. Ziegler (2010) 'Innovations in doing and being: capability innovations at the intersection of Schumpeterian political economy and human development', *Journal of Social Entrepreneurship*, Vol 1, No 2, pp 255–72.

68 M. Nussbaum and A. Sen (eds) (2010) *The Quality of Life*, Oxford: Clarendon Press, is one of the best compilations of thought on the theory. Also see N. Bacon, M. Brophy, N. Mguni, G. Mulgan and A. Shandro (2010) *The State of Happiness: Can Public Policy Shape People's Wellbeing and Resilience?* London: Young Foundation.

69 A. Damasio (2005) 'The neurobiological grounding of human values', in *Neurobiology of Human Values*, Berlin: Springer, pp 47–56.

70 Quoted in A. Green (2007) 'Marxism, education, and dialogue', in A. Green, G. Rikowski and H. Raduntz (eds) *Renewing Dialogues in Marxism and Education*, New York: Palgrave Macmillan, pp 11–31.

71 For example, see E. Ostrom and C. Hess (2007) *Understanding Knowledge as a Commons: From Theory to Practice*, Cambridge, MA: MIT Press.

72 F. Berkes, J. Colding and C. Folke (2003) *Navigating Social-Ecological Systems: Building Resilience for Complexity and Change*, Cambridge: Cambridge University Press, provides one of the best definitions of resilience: 'the capacity of an individual, organisation or system to absorb disturbances and reorganise itself while undergoing change in ways that retain or enhance its capacities to think and act'. This is also an intriguing lens for thinking about certain kinds of social innovation.

Chapter 8

1 This chapter contains content from a previously published blog post by the author: G. Mulgan (2019) 'Social science and intelligence design', Nesta, https://www.nesta.org.uk/blog/social-science-and-intelligence-design/

2 M. Eaton and C. Bertoncin (2018) *The State of Offices of Data Analytics (ODA) in the UK*, London: Nesta, https://www.nesta.org.uk/report/state-offices-data-analytics-uk/what-office-data-analytics.

3 G. Mulgan, M. Eaton and V. Straub (2018) 'Collective intelligence design and effective, ethical policing', Nesta, https://www.nesta.org.uk/blog/collective-intelligence-design-and-effective-ethical-policing.

4 'The uses and limits of Longitudinal Education Outcomes (LEO) data', Parliamentary briefing, Universities UK, https://www.universitiesuk. ac.uk/our-work-in-parliament/Documents/Universities%20UK%20 parliamentary%20briefing%20-%20uses%20and%20limits%20of%20 LEO%20data.pdf.

5 S. Thornton (2017) 'Police attempts to predict domestic murder and serious assaults: is early warning possible yet?', *Cambridge Journal of Evidence-Based Policing*, Vol 1, Nos 2–3, pp 64–80.

6 The Human Project, https://www.thehumanproject.org.

7 Social Science One, https://socialscience.one.

8 M.J. Salganik (2017) *Bit by Bit: Social Research in the Digital Age*, Princeton, NJ: Princeton University Press.

9 See, for example, https://waset.org/conference/2019/05/amsterdam/ ICCSS.

10 See, for example, Microsoft's essay collection, T. Hey, S. Tansley and K. Tolle (eds) (2009) *The Fourth Paradigm: Data-Intensive Scientific Discovery*, Redmond, WA: Microsoft Research.

11 G. Mulgan (2019) 'Social innovation – the last and next decade', Nesta, https://www.nesta.org.uk/blog/social-innovation-the-last-and-next-decade.

12 J. Junge, K. Schreiner and L. Pulford (2018) 'The role of philanthropy in using data to address complex challenges: a global scan', Social

Innovation Exchange, https://socialinnovationexchange.org/insights/role-philanthropy-using-data-address-complex-challenges-global-scan.

13 See Social Innovation Generation (no date) 'Social R&D', Social Innovation Generation, www.sigeneration.ca/social-rd; V. Rajasekaran (2016) 'Getting to moonshot: inspiring R&D practices in Canada's social impact sector', Social Innovation Exchange, https://socialinnovationexchange.org/insights/getting-moonshot-inspiring-rd-practices-canadas-social-impact-sector.

14 Nesta (no date) 'Digital R&D fund for the arts', Nesta, https://www.nesta.org.uk/project/digital-rd-fund-for-the-arts.

15 Innovation Growth Lab, https://www.innovationgrowthlab.org/; The Behavioural Insights Team, https://www.bi.team.

16 Nesta (no date) 'Experimentation', Nesta, https://www.nesta.org.uk/feature/innovation-methods/experiments-and-trials.

17 Alliance for Useful Evidence, https://www.alliance4usefulevidence.org.

18 Society of Evidence Based Policing, https://www.sebp.police.uk.

19 Education Endowment Foundation, https://educationendowmentfoundation.org.uk.

20 K. Popper (1945) *The Open Society and its Enemies*, Vol 2, London: Routledge, p 210.

21 See Cardiff University Social Science Research Park, https://www.cardiff.ac.uk/social-science-research-park.

22 Nesta itself contains several, including the Health Lab.

23 See G. Mulgan (2014) 'The radical's dilemma: an overview of the practice and prospects of social and public labs', Nesta, https://media.nesta.org.uk/documents/social_and_public_labs_-_and_the_radicals_dilemma.pdf.

24 R. Puttick (2014) *Innovation Teams and Labs: A Practice Guide*, London: Nest, https://www.nesta.org.uk/toolkit/innovation-teams-and-labs-a-practice-guide.

25 See Lab Notes, https://www.nesta.org.uk/project/lab-notes.

26 G. Mulgan (2016) 'Challenge-driven universities to solve global problems', Nesta, https://www.nesta.org.uk/feature/10-predictions-2016/challenge-driven-universities-to-solve-global-problems.

27 G. Mulgan (2018) 'Collective intelligence and achieving the Sustainable Development Goals', Nesta, https://www.nesta.org.uk/blog/collective-intelligence-and-achieving-sustainable-development-goals.

28 P. Miller and K. Bound (2013) *The Startup Factories*, London: Nesta, https://www.nesta.org.uk/report/the-startup-factories.

29 See Startup Europe Partnership 2.0, https://www.nesta.org.uk/project/startup-europe-partnership-20.

30 See, for example, Bethnal Green Ventures, https://bethnalgreenventures.com. See also P. Miller and J. Stacey (2014) *Good Incubation*, London: Nesta, https://www.nesta.org.uk/report/good-incubation.

31 G. Mulgan (2017) *Big Mind: How Collective Intelligence Can Change Our World*, Princeton, NJ: Princeton University Press.

32 Duncan Watts made a similar argument for social science to work more on solutions. See D. Watts (2018) 'How can social science become more solutions-oriented?', Kellogg Insight, https://insight.kellogg.northwestern.edu/article/how-can-social-science-become-more-solutions-oriented.

33 N. Christakis (2013) 'Let's shake up the social sciences', *New York Times*, https://www.nytimes.com/2013/07/21/opinion/sunday/lets-shake-up-the-social-sciences.html.

34 G. Akerlof and R.J. Schiller (2009) *Animal Spirits: How Human Psychology Drives the Economy and Why It Matters for Global Capitalism*, Princeton, NJ: Princeton University Press, p 1.

35 See eBird, https://ebird.org/home.

36 See SETI@home, https://setiathome.berkeley.edu.

37 S. Hecker, M. Haklay, A. Bowser, Z. Makuch and J. Vogel (eds) (2018) *Citizen Science: Innovation in Open Science, Society and Policy*, London: UCL Press.

38 Genetic Alliance, https://www.geneticalliance.org.uk.

39 G. Mulgan (2015) 'Mass futurism as an antidote to mass fatalism', Nesta, https://www.nesta.org.uk/blog/mass-futurism-as-an-antidote-to-mass-fatalism.

40 W.N. Dunn (ed) (1998) *The Experimenting Society: Essays in Honour of Donald T. Campbell*, Piscataway, NJ: Transaction Publishers, p 38.

41 Ureka, http://ureka.science; ResearchGate, https://www.researchgate.net; Academia, https://www.academia.edu; Iris, https://iris.ai.

42 BenchFly, www.benchfly.com; IN-PART, https://in-part.com; SciLine, https://www.sciline.org; Linknovate, www.linknovate.com; konfer, http://konfer.online; Pivot, www.scholaruniverse.com; Kolabtree, https://www.kolabtree.com; AcademicLabs, https://www.academiclabs.co; Ohio Innovation Exchange, https://www.ohioinnovationexchange.org.

43 Wonder, https://askwonder.com.

44 Thinklab, https://thinklab.com.

45 Real Scientists, http://realscientists.org.

46 The Conversation, http://theconversation.com/uk.

Chapter 9

1 C.W. Mills (1959) *The Sociological Imagination*, Oxford: Oxford University Press.

2 Charles Booth's London, https://booth.lse.ac.uk.

3 B.S. Rowntree (1902) *Poverty: A Study of Town Life*, London: Macmillan.

4 D. Hobbs (2013) *Lush Life: Constructing Organized Crime in the UK*, Oxford: Oxford University Press.

5 M. Young, K. Gavron and G. Dench (2006) *The New East End*, London: Profile Books.

6 P. Bourdieu (1993) *La Misère du Monde*, Paris: Editions Seuil.

7 S. Keller (2018) *Community: Pursuing the Dream, Living the Reality*, Princeton, NJ: Princeton University Press.

8 F. Abrams (2002) *Below the Breadline*, London: Profile Books.

9   For example, Rohinton Mistry: see 'Rohinton Mistry', https://www. theguardian.com/books/2011/mar/30/rohinton-mistry-profile; R. Mistry (1996) *A Fine Balance*, New York: Alfred Knopf.

10 K. Lewin (1951). *Field Theory in Social Science: Selected Theoretical Papers,* ed. D. Cartwright, New York: Harper & Row.

11 J. Banks (1989) 'From universal history to historical sociology', *The British Journal of Sociology*, Vol 40, No 4, pp 521–43.

12 A rare exception is Laurie Taylor's programme on BBC Radio 4, *Thinking Allowed*.

13 A. Briggs (2001) *Michael Young: Social Entrepreneur*, London: Palgrave Macmillan.

14 D. Robins (1992) *Tarnished Vision*, Oxford: Oxford University Press.

Chapter 10

1   M. Douglas (1966) *Purity and Danger*, London: Routledge.

2   M. Thompson and M. Verweij (2006) *Clumsy Solutions for a Complex World*, Basingstoke: Palgrave Macmillan.

3   A good overview of Douglas's work can be found in P. 6 and P. Richards (2017) *Mary Douglas: Understanding Social Thought and Conflict*, New York: Berghahn Books.

Chapter 11

1   M. Young and P. Wilmott (1957) *Family and Kinship in East London*, London: Routledge.

2   Some of this was captured in the subsequent report by G. Mulgan, B. Watts, D. Vale, M. Dale, R. Ali and W. Norman (2009) *Sinking and Swimming: Understanding Britain's Unmet Needs*, London: Young Foundation.

3   For example, M. Hewstone and R. Brown (1986) *Contact and Conflict in Intergroup Encounters*, Oxford: Blackwell.

4   S. Milgram (1972) 'The familiar stranger: an aspect of urban anonymity', in *The Division 8 Newsletter, Division of Personality and Social Psychology*. Washington, DC: American Psychological Association.

5   W. H. McNeill (1995) *Keeping Together in Time: Dance and Drill in Human History*, Cambridge, MA: Harvard University Press.

6   C. Taylor (1994) 'The politics of recognition', in A. Gutmann (ed) *Multiculturalism: Examining the Politics of Recognition*, Princeton, NJ: Princeton University Press, pp 25–73.

7   K. Appiah (2005) *The Ethics of Identity*, Princeton University Press.

8   This chapter also draws on the following: M. Brewer and M. Hewstone (eds) (2004) *Self and Social Identity*, Hoboken, NJ: Wiley-Blackwell; M. Douglas (1970) *Natural Symbols: Explorations in Cosmology*, London: Barrie & Rockliff/Cresset Press; S. Khagram and P. Levitt (eds) (2007) *The Transnational Studies Reader: Interdisciplinary Intersections and Innovations*, New York: Routledge; S. Milgram (2010) *The Individual in a Social World: Essays and Experiments*, London: Pinter and Martin; C. Tilly (2006) *Identities, Boundaries, and Social Ties*, London: Paradigm.

Chapter 12

1 This chapter contains content from an article by the author previously published in *Prospect* magazine: G. Mulgan (2005) 'Charles Tilly', *Prospect* (25 September), https://www.prospectmagazine.co.uk/magazine/charlestilly.

2 C. Tilly (1998), *Durable Inequality*, Berkeley, CA: University of California Press.

3 These and the other quotes in this chapter come from an interview I did with Charles Tilly shortly before his death.

4 When in government I commissioned a major review of this topic. S. Aldridge (2001) *Social Mobility*, London: Performance and Innovation Unit/Cabinet Office.

5 C. Tilly and S. Tarrow (2003) *The Politics of Collective Violence*, Cambridge: Cambridge University Press.

6 See R. Layard (2006) *Happiness: Lessons from a New Science*, London: Penguin.

7 P. Bearman, J. Moody and K. Stovel (2004) 'Chains of affection: the structure of adolescent romantic and sexual networks', *American Journal of Sociology*, Vol 110, No 1, pp 44–91.

8 C. Tilly (2004) *Social Movements, 1768–2004*, Boulder, CO: Paradigm Publishers.

9 H. Rheingold (2002) *Smart Mobs*, New York: Basic Books.

10 Charles Tilly (2004) *Social Movements*, Boulder: Paradigm Publishers.

11 Mulgan (2005).

12 J.P. Murmann (2003) *Knowledge and Competitive Advantage: The Coevolution of Firms, Technology and National Institutions*, Cambridge: Cambridge University Press.

13 R.E. Goodin, B. Headey, R. Muffels and H.-J. Dirven (1999) *The Real Worlds of Welfare Capitalism*, Cambridge: Cambridge University Press.

14 C. Tilly (2006) *Why?* Princeton, NJ: Princeton University Press.

Chapter 13

1 L. Wittgenstein, (1960) *On Certainty*, Oxford: Blackwell, §160.

2 A saying attributed to Ralph Waldo Emerson.

3 For an overview of RCTs in public policy see S. Oliver , A.M. Bagnall, J. Thomas, J. Shepherd, A. Sowden, I. White, J. Dinnes, R. Rees, J. Colquitt, K. Oliver and Z. Garrett (2008) *RCTs for Policy Interventions? A Review of Reviews and Meta-regression*, Birmingham: University of Birmingham.

4 A. Robertson (2018) 'OLPC's $100 laptop was going to change the world – then it all went wrong', *The Verge* (16 April), https://www.theverge.com/2018/4/16/17233946/olpcs-100-laptop-education-where-is-it-now.

5 T. Wilson (2011) *Redirect*, New York: Penguin.

6 The Head Start programme in the US was launched in 1965 to prepare children from low-income families prior to their entry into elementary

school. The programme was expanded in 1981 and subsequently revised in 2007.

7   See the work of Imre Lakatos commenting on Thomas Kuhn, described in: A. Mannan (2012) Investing criterion for theory-choice in science, *Philosophy and Progress*, Vols. LI–LII, January–June, July–December, p 64.

8   T. Eagleton (2013) *Ideology*, New York: Routledge.

9   https://www.southampton.ac.uk/wessex-institute/about/staff/jcw1v15. page.

10 A good summary is J. Breckon and J. Dodson (2016) *Using Evidence: What Works?*, London: Alliance for Useful Evidence.

11 T. Kuhn (1970) *The Structure of Scientific Revolutions* (2nd edn), Chicago: University of Chicago Press.

12 J. Agar (2013) *Science in the Twentieth Century and Beyond*, London: Polity.

13 D. Berwick, (2004) 'Some is not a number. Soon is not a time', 16th Annual Institute for Healthcare Improvement National Forum Keynote Address Excerpt, https://www.youtube.com/watch?v=VFZwclQIi9s.

14 What Works Cities, https://whatworkscities.bloomberg.org.

15 A. Goodman (2006) *The Story of David Olds and the Nurse Home Visiting Program*, Social Impact Exchange, http://www.socialimpactexchange.org/sites/www. socialimpactexchange.org/files/RWJ%20DavidOldsSpecialReport0606. pdf.

16 John Hattie (2008) *Visible Learning: A Synthesis of Over 800 Meta-Analyses Relating to Achievement*, New York: Routledge.

17 W. Isaacson (2011) *Steve Jobs*, New York: Simon and Schuster.

Chapter 14

1   I. Kant (1998 [1797]) *Groundwork for the Metaphysics of Morals* (trans. Mary Gregor), Cambridge: Cambridge University Press, pp 42–43.

2   Quoted in J. Graham (2019) 'Is social enterprise part of the elite charade of changing the world?', *Medium* (3 March), https://medium.com/here-and-now/is-social-enterprise-part-of-the-elite-charade-of-changing-the-world-2d141bb3ce6f.

3   'From seers to sen', http:// www.rrojasdatabank.info/widerconf/Nafziger. pdf.

4   J.H.T. Johnson and R.S. Kaplan (1987) *Relevance Lost: The Rise and Fall of Management Accounting*, Boston, MA: Harvard Business School Press.

5   'Oregon Benchmarks', Government Innovators Network, https://www. innovations.harvard.edu/oregon-benchmarks.

6   S. Cattan, G. Conti, C. Farquharson and R. Ginja (2019) *The Health Effects of Sure Start*, London: Institute for Fiscal Studies , https://www.ifs.org.uk/ publications/14139.

Chapter 15

1   A saying attributed to Cedric Price.

2 See the work of Stilgoe, Callon, Wilsdon, Lövbrand, Stirling, Rayner, Hajer, Wynne, von Schomberg, to mention just a few. For example, J. Stilgoe, R. Owen and P. Macnaghten (2013) 'Developing a framework for responsible innovation', *Research Policy*, Vol 42, No 9, pp 1568–80.

3 European Commission, 'Responsible research & innovation', https://ec.europa.eu/programmes/horizon2020/en/h2020-section/responsible-research-innovation.

4 R. Bhatia (2016) 'The inside story of Facebook's biggest setback', *The Guardian* (12 May), https://www.theguardian.com/technology/2016/may/12/facebook-free-basics-india-zuckerberg.

Chapter 16

1 M. Gabriel and S. Reynolds (2018) 'EU Commissioner: "We will put more money into social innovation"', Nesta, https://www.nesta.org.uk/blog/the-eu-will-put-more-money-into-social-innovation.

2 In 2006 the Young Foundation and CCCPE, officially the Communist Party's translation bureau but also a very fertile centre for thought, jointly organised an event in Beijing which led to the creation of SIX, the Social Innovation Exchange (https://socialinnovationexchange.org). The event brought together foundations, innovators, social entrepreneurs and corporates, along with senior figures from governments in China, the UK and elsewhere. It set out a rough roadmap towards making social innovation more mainstream which was later published as *Social Silicon Valleys* by the Young Foundation and the Skoll Centre for Social Entrepreneurship (https://youngfoundation.org/wp-content/uploads/2013/04/Social-Silicon-Valleys-March-2006.pdf).

3 DIY Toolkit, https://diytoolkit.org; IDEO, www.ideo.com.

4 Digital Social Innovation, https://digitalsocial.eu.

5 Global Social Entrepreneurship Network, http://www.gsen.global; Impact Hub, https://impacthub.net; makesense, https://entrepreneurs.makesense.org.

6 Solid, https://solid.mit.edu; Indie, https://ind.ie.

7 This is the DECODE programme (https://www.nesta.org.uk/project/decode), which has run pilots in Barcelona and Amsterdam and has developed the thinking and policy ideas for citizen control over personal data.

8 Next Generation Internet – Engineroom, https://www.nesta.org.uk/project/next-generation-internet-engineroom.

9 The premise of many of the discussions a decade ago was that too much of the convening around social entrepreneurship and innovation was celebratory and promotional. Not enough was informed by action, and the tough lessons of practice. That led to initiatives like SIX (see note 2), which aimed to be guided by practitioners and were oriented to learning as well as celebration. These initiatives also aimed to be more global in spirit than an earlier generation of mainly US-based initiatives, partly out of a recognition that no part of the world was leading.

Chapter 17

1 N. Wiener (1988 [1950]) *The Human Use of Human Beings: Cybernetics and Society*, Cambridge, MA: Da Capo Press.

2 This chapter contains content from a blog post by the author: G. Mulgan (2013) 'Three ways to think about the future', Nesta, https://www.nesta.org.uk/blog/three-ways-to-think-about-the-future.

3 R. Lenzner and S.S. Johnson (1997) 'Peter Drucker: Seeing things as they really are', Forbes (10 March), https://www.forbes.com/forbes/1997/0310/5905122a.html#70c962a624b9.

4 I describe many of these in G. Mulgan (2007) *The Art of Public Strategy*, Oxford: Oxford University Press.

5 A.O. Hirschman (1991) *The Rhetoric of Reaction*, Cambridge, MA: Belknap Press.

6 Charles Tilly (2002) *Stories, Identities and Political Change*, Lanham, MD: Rowman and Littlefield.

7 C. Spinosa, F. Flores and H. Dreyfus (1999) *Disclosing New Worlds: Entrepreneurship, Democratic Action, and the Cultivation of Solidarity*, Cambridge, MA: MIT Press.

8 G. Mulgan (2013) *The Locust and the Bee: Predators and Creators in Capitalism's Future*, Princeton, NJ: Princeton University Press.

9 E. Bellamy (1889) *Looking Backward, 2000–1887* (2nd edn), Boston: Houghton: Mifflin.

10 Quoted in R. Maharajah (2016) 'The future has arrived', *Medium* (24 May), https://medium.com/not-evenly-distributed/the-future-has-arrived-fed56cec3266.

11 G. Mulgan (2008) *The Art of Public Strategy*, Oxford: Oxford University Press.

12 See Future Generations, http://futuregenerations.wales/about-us/future-generations-act.

13 P. Tetlock (2017) *Expert Political Judgement* (new edn), Princeton, NJ: Princeton University Press.

14 E. Cabet (2003) *Travels in Icaria (Utopianism & Communitarianism)*, Syracuse: Syracuse University Press.

Chapter 18

1 C. Alexander (1978) *A Pattern Language*, New York: Oxford University Press.

2 S. Page (2018) *Model Thinker*, New York: Basic Books.

3 L. Valiant (2014) *Probably Approximately Correct*, New York: Basic Books.

4 G. Mulgan and V. Straub (2019) *The New Ecosystem of Trust*, London: Nesta.

5 Nesta has run a few big funds supporting this kind of work, including the Centre for Social Action innovation funds with the Cabinet Office. These promoted the idea that the best public services often combine expert professionalism with voluntary input from the public.

6 J. Rae, S. Westlake and L. Marston (2014) 'Innovation population', Nesta, https:// www.nesta.org.uk/report/innovation-population.

Index